WHO KILL

WHO KILLED KENNEDY?

The Definitive Account of
Fifty Years of Conspiracy

MATTHEW SMITH

With a foreword by Cyril H. Wecht, leading researcher and

America's foremost pathologist, author of Cause of Death

And with contributions from William Matson Law and Colin McSween

MAINSTREAM
PUBLISHING

EDINBURGH AND LONDON

First published in Great Britain in 2013 by
MAINSTREAM PUBLISHING company
(EDINBURGH) LTD
7 Albany Street
Edinburgh EH1 3UG

ISBN 9781780576572

A catalogue record for this book is available
from the British Library

Printed in Great Britain by
CPI Group (UK) Ltd, Croydon, CR0 4YY

1 3 5 7 9 10 8 6 4 2

The quest for the truth about the assassination of President John F. Kennedy has now been in progress for 50 years. This book is to mark the 50th anniversary of the assassination and to examine and record what we have learned from the results of all those who have contributed to the investigation into how and why and by whom the president was killed. It is to those seekers of truth that this book is dedicated.

* * *

In 1964, Thomas G. Buchanan's book *Who Killed Kennedy?* was published in England by Secker & Warburg. He was an American citizen working in France. His was one of the very first books to appear on the assassination of President Kennedy. I am taking the liberty of using the title for this book, which is to mark 50 years of research and investigation into the tragedy, of which he was a leader in the field.

President John F. Kennedy. (Courtesy John F. Kennedy Library)

'My fellow Americans,
ask not what your country
can do for you, ask what
you can do for your country.

My fellow citizens of the world,
ask . . . what together we can do
for the freedom of man.'

ACKNOWLEDGEMENTS

SINCE I BEGAN RESEARCHING THE EVENTS OF 22 November 1963 and the assassination of President John F. Kennedy a very, very long time ago, the number of people who have helped me has grown and grown. To all of them I am intensely grateful, and I must now add to that number those who have helped me in the preparation of this present book.

I am greatly indebted to Dr Cyril Wecht, who writes the foreword to this book. Very closely identified with and, obviously, with a particular interest in medical matters, he continues to press for new information and strives to facilitate the work of other researchers. He is one of the most knowledgeable persons I know on the subject of the assassination and especially autopsy data. He was a panel member for the House Assassinations Committee in their re-examination of the wounds Kennedy received. Dr Wecht, recognised as the leading pathologist in the United States, also provided me with data relating to the work of COPA (Coalition on Political Assassinations), of which he was a founding member.

I met William Matson Law, a fellow researcher, in Dallas quite a few years ago now and we have become good friends as well as close colleagues. He has contributed two chapters to this book on specialist subjects in which I could never match his competence. The word 'unique' springs to mind when I consider that in his writings on the autopsy carried out on the president's body he drew all of his data from the observations of those actually present when it happened, obtained in face-to-face interviews with those involved. His second contribution stems from interviews with FBI special agents James Sibert and Francis O'Neill, whose names are deeply engraved in any account of the autopsy. These interviews are indeed, again, unique. William Matson Law is the only researcher to be granted an interview with either of these agents in their retirement. I should add that most of the interviews mentioned above were either sound-recorded or filmed, and since as time takes its toll, most of their subjects are no longer with us, Law's records have become a treasure trove beyond price.

Advancing years add to the difficulty of flying out to the United States to conduct research, and William Law, for some time now, has been my eyes and ears over there. I am extremely grateful for his efforts.

Colin McSween and I also became friends when we met in Dallas, and I have followed his progress with great interest as he has made himself a leading expert on the events at Parkland Hospital, where surgeons and staff desperately tried to save the life of President Kennedy. He has also contributed a chapter from his vast knowledge of the proceedings there. Indeed, the work of William Matson Law and Colin McSween, carried out across the 50 years since the president was killed, represent remarkable improvements to our understanding of what occurred immediately afterwards. I thank them both for the incredible insight they bring to their areas of special expertise.

Debra Conway and Larry Hancock, the stalwarts behind the JFK Lancer operation in Dallas and the annual conference held in that city each November, have both contributed data on the work of that organisation, which has grown and grown rather than diminishing over the 50 years since the assassination. Much has been going on in Britain also, and Stuart Galloway of Dealey Plaza UK has given me an account of that organisation's work and its development.

Among those who have died in recent years Wayne January, to whom I am indebted for exclusive material relating to Red Bird airfield and the breakthrough on the murder team, will never be forgotten. I lost not only a valued source of information but a very good friend when he died. The late Mary Ferrell supported me and encouraged me from the beginning of the time I began writing on the assassination and has left us a wonderful legacy in data unrivalled in its depth and coverage. Harold Weisberg is another who, from the time I started writing, shared his knowledge and wisdom liberally. We also 'hit it off' from our meeting at his home in Maryland.

The assistance of the good people at the National Archives at Washington and Maryland, along with those in the JFK Library at Boston, cannot go unmentioned. They are incredible in anticipating what you need and prompt, indeed immediate, in fulfilling requests. Please accept my sincere gratitude for your contributions to my book. I am also indebted to Debra Conway (Lancer organisation) and Paul Schrade for contributing pictures, and to Mark Davies of the Sixth Floor Museum in Dallas for his help.

From this point I am, pleasurably, faced with a galaxy of the names of those who have assisted me in my research and encouraged me in my writing. Alas, they are too numerous to mention and an attempt would risk neglecting someone who might be hurt. I must, therefore, say an enormously big thank you to all of those I have met, talked to on the telephone or with whom I have corresponded. Thank you all.

I have not by any means forgotten my friends at Mainstream Publishing, Bill Campbell and Peter MacKenzie and their helpful and patient staff, notably Graeme Blaikie, when it comes to expressing gratitude. They have published all five of my books dealing with the assassination of President Kennedy, including this one. Could anyone have wished for a better publishing house or better people?

Finally, I could not have achieved anything without my mainstay and support, Margaret, my patient and understanding wife, my help at all times, my daughter Tracey, who is my ace reader/checker, and my family, also, who have been behind me all the way.

Matthew Smith
Sheffield, England

CONTENTS

ILLUSTRATIONS

FOREWORD

By Cyril H. Wecht MD, JD
Former President of the American
Academy of Forensic Sciences
Author of *Cause of Death*

AFTER 50 YEARS, WHY ARE SO MANY PEOPLE STILL interested in the assassination of John F. Kennedy? What is the basis for their continuing rejection of the Warren Commission Report? After five decades, would it not be reasonable to believe that enough investigation has taken place and to accept the official version of what happened on Friday, 22 November 1963 in Dallas, Texas?

The fact of the matter is that even two generations later, students in high schools and universities throughout the United States, as well as their middle-aged parents, remain fascinated by a discussion of the JFK assassination. It has been my experience that when a full presentation is made setting forth the findings of the Warren Commission, relating those conclusions to the indisputable scientific facts and extensive investigative information compiled by numerous Warren Commission Report critic-researchers since that fateful event 50 years ago, audiences overwhelmingly reject the Warren Commission Report's conclusions that Lee Harvey Oswald was a sole assassin and that nobody else was involved in any way.

It should be kept in mind that there is no statute of limitations on murder cases in the United States. Indeed, there have been several cases in recent years in which homicide charges have been filed three, four and five decades after the homicidal death of an individual.

Furthermore, exhuming a body for re-examination after a long period of time is not unheard of either. Recently, the body of Yasser Arafat was dug up for examination. An American president who died suddenly and unexpectedly in the nineteenth century was exhumed several years ago for an autopsy. It is not at all ghoulish to talk about exhuming a dead body when there is a question of murder and the need to determine who committed the act.

If the Warren Commission and government authorities who accepted that report in 1964, and all the government people who have continued to defend it since that time, genuinely believe that it is definitely valid, why do they still refuse to release all the documents, records and materials that are extant regarding this matter? Despite the recommendations of the Assassination Records Review Board, thousands of documents and other materials are still being withheld from bona fide investigators.

For those people who are among the minority that continue to accept the Warren Commission Report, it is important to make certain that they are aware of who performed this autopsy. Dr Humes and Dr Boswell, Bethesda Naval Hospital military pathologists, had never performed a gunshot-wound autopsy in their careers. Dr Pierre Finck, called in as an afterthought and arriving one hour later from the Armed Forces Institute of Pathology in Washington DC, had limited experience with gunshot-wound cases, dealing almost exclusively with military-type fatalities associated with the Vietnam War. When he attempted to dissect out the wound in the president's back and asked who was in charge, a gruff voice informed him, 'I am, Doctor, just proceed as ordered.' We came to learn years later that among the 33 people present in the autopsy suite that evening there were some generals and admirals.

The foremost forensic pathologists in the United States in 1963 were all deliberately excluded from involvement in this autopsy. They shared a common flaw, namely their civilian status. There would have been no guarantee that the top-level civilian experts with lifetime reputations would have been willing to compromise their professional stature by going along with what was obviously a limited, government-controlled undertaking.

In 1972, when I was given access to the JFK autopsy materials at the Smithsonian Institute, I discovered that the president's brain was missing. The brain had not been serially sectioned and examined on 7 December 1963 (two weeks after formalin fixation) by the pathologists. There does not exist any record or memorandum of any kind to indicate what happened to the brain, which was listed in a Memorandum of Transfer dated 26 April 1965 but which was no longer included in an inventory of the same materials done a year and a half later in October 1966. This is an example of the kinds of surreptitious, inexplicable, legally indefensible actions in which the US government has engaged in the past 50 years regarding the JFK assassination.

Hearkening back to the date of the assassination, there are so many things that defy explanation and are truly indefensible from a basic forensic scientific investigative standpoint. The president's limousine was not examined to determine the direction of the bullet hole in the windshield. Evidence from the car was not collected in meticulous fashion. A basic homicide investigation done by any metropolitan police force in the United States or Great Britain would have undertaken numerous tests and studies that were not performed in this very important political assassination.

When New Orleans Parish District Attorney Jim Garrison undertook his investigation of Clay Shaw, he immediately became the subject of a concerted, vicious ad hominem attack. All kinds of defamatory statements were made about him. Every one of his official moves requesting information and records from official agencies and organisations in other jurisdictions, including the federal government, were either rebuffed or simply ignored.

In 1977, the United States Congress established the House Select Committee on Assassinations (HSCA). The appointed executive director, highly respected and experienced Philadelphia attorney Richard Sprague, was soon removed from that post when he began to undertake an investigation just as he would have done with any other homicide case in the district attorney's office in Philadelphia. That was simply too much for governmental authorities to accept, and so Sprague was summarily removed.

And even though the HSCA ultimately concluded that there was evidence of other people involved and called for further investigation, nothing was ever done.

Every national poll that has been taken in the United States since the late 1960s regarding the JFK assassination has revealed that 75–85 per cent of people do not accept the Warren Commission Report's conclusion regarding Lee Harvey Oswald as a sole assassin. A similar number do not accept the so-called 'single-bullet theory', more descriptively referred to by me and other long-time Warren Commission Report critic-researchers as the 'magic-bullet theory'. This theory holds that one bullet produced seven wounds in President Kennedy and Governor John Connally and yet emerged with a weight loss of only 1–1.5 per cent, essentially pristine, after performing horizontal and vertical gyrations of a physically impossible nature. The single-bullet theory is the *sine qua non* of the Warren Commission Report's conclusion vis-à-vis a sole assassin. I and others have clearly demonstrated the unquestionable scientific absurdity of the single-bullet theory, hence proving that there were two shooters.

Many well-written books and articles about the JFK assassination have been published over the past 45 years. This excellent book, *Who Killed Kennedy? The Definitive Account of Fifty Years of Conspiracy*, by Matthew Smith, is a very complete, up-to-date review and analysis of the JFK assassination. Mr Smith has been a long-time critic-researcher of the Warren Commission and has devoted countless hours and extensive efforts to an objective study of this murder. In this book, Matthew Smith undertakes an examination of all the major aspects of the JFK assassination from the very outset to the present time. He has done a masterful job in organising a huge amount of material, and he has presented his thorough research in a manner that is clear, detailed and well organised.

Readers of *Who Killed Kennedy?*, whether they have had previous interest in and knowledge of the JFK assassination or not, will find this book revealing, fascinating and intellectually satisfying.

INTRODUCTION

THIS IS A DAUNTING TASK. HOW DO YOU encapsulate in a single volume the activities of the many and varied people across the world who have contributed, bit by bit, to the massive 50-year-long investigation into the assassination of President John F. Kennedy?

It would be an absolute impossibility to list and detail every aspect of activity, deliberation, successful and failed endeavour involved, and, since a degree of selection, priority and subjectivity is necessary, I must say at once that no slight is intended to anyone who may feel neglected in these pages. Another dimension to this study relates to the fact that there may be many unsung heroes who have contributed to the knowledge we have now, whose names have gone unrecorded and their work unacknowledged. I salute them. I must acknowledge that, if not to result in a weighty textbook tome, this exercise of necessity must embrace, to some measure, judgements on what to put in and what to leave out.

In an article I read somewhere, the question was asked, *What do we know now that we did not know at the outset?* The implication, if I recall it correctly, was that we should not feel, in any sense, complacent. In fact, I felt it was implying, in summary, *not that much!* If that had been true, it would have been both disheartening and bewildering, and I am able to refute the implication made in the strongest terms. The activity generated by those involved in the quest for the truth has been such as to be overwhelming in total. We know an enormous amount about the assassination now. We have also amassed an incredible amount of background detail and have obtained considerable insight into the motivation for, and planning of, the plot to kill President Kennedy.

Mind you, those researchers and investigators who have accomplished so much have not achieved it without the anti-conspiracy people doing their best to discredit their work, sometimes quite blatantly. The two most voluminous books ever written on the subject of the assassination, one by Gerald Posner (*Case Closed*, 1993), which ran to about 600 pages, and the other by Vincent Bugliosi (*Reclaiming History*, 2007), which occupied some 1,600 pages, attempt, in general terms, to put back the clock, dispense with the massive search for the truth and re-establish the veracity of the findings of the largely discredited – some would say totally discredited – investigation ordered by President Johnson and chaired by Earl Warren. While I deplore the way in which this kind of book presents its 'facts', I must defend the right of the authors to write them. However, in view of the newly released revelations regarding the opinions on the assassination of the late Robert F. Kennedy, emanating from his son Robert in an electrifying interview in Dallas earlier this year (see Chapter 5), I think they will have a harder time than ever turning the clock back.

Who killed Kennedy? In spite of all the opposition to our work, a massive undertaking of research and investigation spread across 50 years, we believe you will find the truth presented in these pages. I gave up on any idea of putting everything in chronological order, since to accomplish such a task would have involved writing a somewhat dull book, in addition to one of considerable size, which would have tempted few people. Instead, I have attempted some kind of order and a degree of brevity and have employed a style which past readers have found conducive to 'easy reading'. I am conscious that I drop into writing in the first person in places. These are where I was personally involved with the subject matter and it seemed rather natural to do so.

But in my first chapter I must outline the events of 22

November 1963, as a refresher to those who know and for the benefit of those not familiar with what happened when President Kennedy was shot and killed on a street in Dallas.

Matthew Smith

1

THE PRESIDENTIAL VISIT TO TEXAS

PRESIDENT KENNEDY HAD SOUND REASONS FOR visiting Texas. The state leaders of the Democrats were at each other's throats. Governor John Connally was at war with Senator Ralph Yarborough, and politically it was a festering sore which had to be dealt with. Kennedy had his eye on his re-election campaign, in which he was trying to consolidate the enormous advances he had made since his election to the presidency. His popularity had grown, and he had accomplished many important tasks in government. Above all, he had established himself as a man of peace and reconciliation. Even the country's enemies respected Kennedy, and, under Kennedy, the United States had begun to shine out as a beacon of peace.

1. President and Mrs Kennedy with Caroline and John Junior.
(Courtesy John F. Kennedy Library)

The president did not have an easy time achieving this. Since its involvement in the Second World War, the United States military had grown to become the greatest fighting force in the entire world, and from time to time the military flexed its muscles and would have been a ready contender for a fight, with whomever or for whatever reasons. The fact that President Kennedy kept them on a short rein did not endear him to those who would have liked to follow the lead of the CIA in the ill-fated Bay of Pigs invasion of Cuba, for instance, a plan Kennedy inherited when he was installed as president. And later, at the time of the nervous exhaustion experienced by the American people – and indeed the peoples of the entire world – in facing up to Khrushchev in the 'eyeball to eyeball' confrontation caused by the location of Russian missiles supplied to Cuba and assembled on the very doorstep of the United States, he ignored the advice of the generals who recommended that he bomb them out of existence. Furthermore, to add to the unhappiness of the Pentagon, there was the fact that the president showed his intention to withdraw from the tentative involvement of the US in the dispute between North and South Vietnam initiated by his predecessor, Dwight D. Eisenhower, before an escalation took place.

It is important to remember that in the United States there was a well-established close relationship with the military and what was known as the industrial complex, the steel industry, those who manufactured and supplied the wherewithal of war: the tanks, the planes, the guns of many descriptions and the ammunition. And then there was the oil industry which made it all work. President Kennedy may have achieved a great deal in a short time in endearing himself to the American people, but on the way he had also made many powerful enemies, opponents outside his government and some inside it. That the young president frustrated the desired activities of the military, clipped the wings of the steel men and looked to re-examine the generous depletion tax benefits for long enjoyed by the oil industry will suffice for a start. But topping the list of his enemies was the CIA, who blamed the president and his brother Robert, who was the attorney general, for not getting behind them in their Bay of Pigs debacle, regardless of the president having made it clear he would not take the nation to war on the coat-tails of such an action. The incursion was entirely planned by the CIA and based solely on the CIA's recruiting, training and arming of Cuban rebels anxious to overturn Castro.

2. CIA agent E. Howard Hunt.

Kennedy had declared his only support was for Cuban to face Cuban in the conflict. US personnel, he declared, were not to get involved at any price, an instruction completely disregarded by CIA agents who landed with the rebels on the beaches of Cuba. The CIA had been revealed to the president as so powerful and independent as to constitute another form of government which went its own way, sometimes contradicting the decisions of the legitimate government. In conversation on the subject with Senator Mike Mansfield, an angry Kennedy had declared his intention to 'tear it into a thousand pieces and scatter it to the winds'.

So here was the president attempting to sort out the political mess in Texas that his vice-president, Lyndon Johnson, a Texan himself, had been unable to resolve. Kennedy was warned by colleagues and friends to keep out of Dallas, a recognised hornet's nest of extreme right-wing activism. But then he was on record as saying he would never admit to any part of the United States being a no-go area for the president.

The tour he was on had taken him to San Antonio and then Houston. In both places, things had gone very satisfactorily and, if anything, his popularity had actually begun to grow even there. His entourage then went on to Fort Worth, where he would deliver an after-breakfast speech at the hotel he stayed in before going on to Dallas. Before breakfast that morning he appeared outside the hotel for a semi-informal address to the people on their way to work. It was raining, but that did not prevent a huge crowd from gathering to hear him. The weather was due to improve, becoming fine and sunny as the day progressed. Kennedy's speech after breakfast at the hotel was extremely successful and the mood for the trip to Dallas was as upbeat as was possible in the circumstances.

2

DALLAS

UPON ARRIVAL AT DALLAS'S LOVE FIELD, THE president met with a mixed reception. He politely ignored changes to the established protocol when meeting the notables lined up to shake his hand. There were many in the crowd which amassed behind them who displayed warmth and affection to him and his lovely wife: the liberal minority here was determined to put on its best show. Then there were others, from the majority, who did not welcome the president. The motorcade, which would drive him and those accompanying him to a luncheon appointment at the newly built Trade Mart, moved slowly off and the cheers from those lining the streets were encouraging. It was noticeable, however, how many people stared but did not cheer. Those lining the route were laced with a not insubstantial number of detractors, including some with banners: 'Help Kennedy Stamp Out Democracy' and 'Your A Traiter [*sic*]'.

First Mockingbird Lane then Lemmon Avenue, which led to Turtle Creek Boulevard, Cedar Spring Road, Harwood Street and then a right turn to Main Street. This brought the procession to a point at which it was but five minutes from its destination. When it reached the intersection of Main Street with Houston Street, instead of proceeding straight ahead, it took another right turn and followed a route which was a revision of the original one planned. A dog-leg left turn from Houston into Elm Street was necessitated and then he was in Dealey Plaza.

3. Full page 'advertisement' in the local Dallas paper on the day of Kennedy's visit. (Courtesy National Archives)

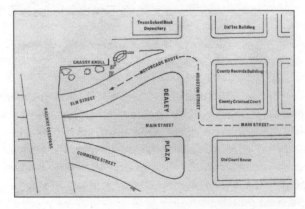

4. Sketch showing the route of the motorcade. (Matthew Smith Collection)

It was here at 12.30 p.m. that shots rang out. Kennedy clutched his throat following one shot, while Jackie looked on anxiously. A moment later he was visibly pushed forward by a shot from the rear. She screamed at the sight of blood, and then almost immediately his head snapped back as a final shot was fired. Governor Connally and his wife occupied the seats in front of the president, and Connally was also injured three times.

5. First hit. Kennedy clutches his neck. Taken from the Zapruder film.
(© Sixth Floor Museum, Dallas)

Secret Service agent Bill Greer, who was driving the modified Lincoln, which had raised seats for the president and his wife to enable people to see them more easily, revved up and sped away. Their destination, however, was no longer the Trade Mart, where luncheon awaited: they headed directly for Parkland Hospital. There a team of surgeons worked desperately to give the shattered president the best chance of survival possible, but it was to no avail. At approximately 1 p.m. he was pronounced dead and the shock waves quickly travelled around the world.

In Dealey Plaza, from the moment of the sounds of the sniper's bullets, the crowds were in disarray. Onlookers had thrown themselves to the ground. Some said three shots were fired, some four, some as many as six. It was impossible to be certain because the Plaza formed something of a natural echo chamber. The Texas School Book Depository occupied the corner of Elm Street and people pointed to that building in particular when trying to determine from where the shots had been fired. Others pointed to the Dal-Tex Building, which was immediately next to the School Book Depository on the adjacent corner, and others to the County Records Building across the way (see fig. 4). Some were convinced shots had come from the much nearer grassy knoll, some the overpass, and chaos reigned. The President of the United States had been slain on the streets of Dallas while on a friendly visit.

6. The aftermath in Dealey Plaza.

* * *

A few minutes after the shooting took place, the staff of the Texas School Book Depository had begun to disperse. Some had collected in front of the building to see the motorcade. After the shots had been fired, quite a few decided that there would be no more work done there that day. Lee Harvey Oswald, who worked at the depository filling book orders, appeared to have just finished his lunch in the lunchroom on the second floor. British readers should be reminded that the first floor in the US is the ground floor to them. Oswald, who worked on the sixth floor, was therefore not far from the exit to the street when a policeman dashed in moments after the shooting accompanied by the warehouse superintendent, Roy Truly. It was noticed that the elevator was located at a higher floor due to someone failing to close the gates. The officer asked if he (Oswald) was an employee and when Truly confirmed he was, the officer raced off elsewhere and Oswald drifted straight out of the building. This was literally but minutes after the noise of the shots had died away. Within approximately 15 minutes of the shooting, however, an APB (all-points bulletin) was broadcast giving the description of Lee Harvey Oswald and declaring that he was wanted for questioning in connection with the assassination of the president.

7. Lee Harvey Oswald (Courtesy National Archives)

* * *

Lee Harvey Oswald had first taken a bus to get to his lodgings, but the bus became hopelessly bogged down in traffic. He then tried for a taxi, although, when successful, noticed a little old lady who was also trying to get a taxi. He stood back, gave the cab to her and resumed his search. Succeeding again, he asked to be taken to the vicinity of North Beckley Avenue, where he lodged. He left the taxi a block or so from the rooming house where he lived and completed the journey on foot. On arrival he went to his room.

It was at this point that Earlene Roberts, his landlady, heard a car 'pip' its horn outside, as though giving a signal, and, peeping through the window, she saw it was a police car. Having changed his jacket, Oswald promptly left, making his way at first to a bus stop which, oddly, was for buses going in the opposite direction to where he was next seen, which was in Oak Cliff, about a mile away. There, he was identified as seen talking to a police officer, J.D. Tippit, who had stopped his car to speak to him. Seen to get out of his car and move in the direction of Oswald, the officer was shot several times and died instantly. Oswald then made his way to the Texas Theatre, a nearby cinema, where, it was reported, the girl at the box office phoned the police to tell them someone had entered the cinema without paying.*

Incredibly, this brought several police cars and numerous police officers to apprehend the offender. They identified him easily in a sparse audience and arrested him. At Dallas police headquarters he was charged with the shooting of Officer Tippit and that was later followed by the charge of shooting and killing the President of the United States.

---

* Asked if this was true some years later by a researcher, she burst into tears and left the room. A later attempt by the same researcher obtained the same result. Since a simple 'yes' if true would have been enough, there has to be serious doubt that this was the case.

8. Oswald's arrest.

Two days later, while in the process of being transferred to the county jail, Oswald was shot on police premises by one Jack Ruby, said to be grieving the death of his president. Oswald died at Parkland Hospital, the same hospital to which they had taken President Kennedy. Ruby, identified as a low-tier mafioso and owner of a local nightclub, was arrested and charged with the murder of Oswald. Briefly, Ruby was tried, found guilty and jailed for murder.

3

TENSE TIMES, LIES AND DECEIT

ON THE DAY KENNEDY WAS KILLED, NOT ONLY America but the entire world stood still on hearing the news that President Kennedy had been shot and killed in downtown Dallas.

There are few people who were living on that day and of an age to understand what was happening who do not remember exactly where they were when the news was announced, and probably who they were with, and from whom or from where they learned the disastrous tidings. To say that people were worried about what might follow would be a gross understatement. The main terror people suffered was that the event might be the forerunner of an atomic bomb attack. They pondered which enemy might be responsible for this atrocity. Communism was greatly feared and was clearly in the front of people's minds. This might have involved Soviet Russia or communist-dominated Cuba, both smarting from the victory of President Kennedy in the 'eyeball to eyeball' confrontation between him and the Russian president, Nikita Khrushchev, at the time of the Cuban missile crisis, the consequence of which was that Cuba was made to dismantle the offending missiles.

The incoming president, Lyndon Baines Johnson, was well aware of the fears people had and it was without delay that he ordered an inquiry into the murder of President Kennedy. He first contacted the FBI with instructions for them to carry out an investigation but soon changed his mind when members of the Senate proposed the establishment of an investigation and other important bodies voiced similar intentions. He spiked the guns of all of them by ordering the establishment of a Presidential Commission. He promptly contacted the man who would answer to the description of being the most highly respected person in the law profession in the United States, Chief Justice Earl Warren, and called upon him to chair the investigation. Earl Warren, however, declared himself unwilling to take this on and this led to a face-to-face confrontation with Johnson. After that meeting Warren was reported to have left distressed and in tears. This led to speculation that the new president had confronted him with the nightmare question of whether he was prepared to have the deaths of 41,000,000 Americans on his conscience, which might be the outcome of a worst-case scenario. It amounted to nothing but an arm-twisting exercise on Johnson's part and Warren left having reluctantly agreed to chair a commission of investigation, giving it his highest priority. It is more than interesting that Melvin Eisenberg, who became a commission staff lawyer and who reported on the meeting between Warren and Johnson, said afterwards that President Johnson had convinced Warren that this was an occasion when 'actual conditions had to override general principles'.

9. Castro and Khrushchev. (Courtesy National Archives) **10.** Earl Warren.

What might have been said by President Johnson about the young man who had been quickly arrested and eventually charged with the shooting of President Kennedy – the only man ever to be so charged – very soon after the assassination is not known. But it is wondered if Warren was primed that this was his way out, the way to defuse the tense situation, to find this man guilty of all that went on, especially as the young man had within two days been killed himself by another assassin in police headquarters en route for the county jail.

11. The Warren commissioners.

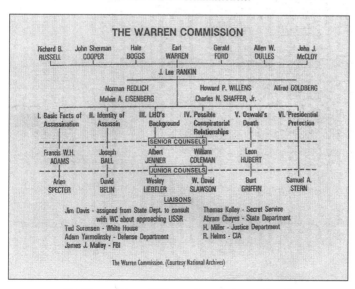

12. Composition of Warren Commission and staff.
(Courtesy National Archives)

Warren promptly gathered to himself a team whose various backgrounds, it was thought, brought a degree of respectability to the assembly: lawyers and others who were to contribute their know-how and other attributes. Their deliberations resulted in a twenty-six-volume, ten-million-word report, which was published ten months after the event, in the fall of 1964, by which time it had occupied, in dribs and drabs, the front pages of every newspaper in the United States with news of the interviews and investigations conducted, and had also commanded headlines in many countries abroad. Briefly, they stated unequivocally that the young man arrested on the day of the assassination, Lee Harvey Oswald, had alone and unaided shot and killed President Kennedy: no one else was involved and there was no one else to seek. The people of America could carry on without further concern, breathe normally and have no more worries about an aftermath to the assassination. The Warren Commission, no doubt, achieved relief of the post-assassination tension but, along with the government which had appointed it, came out extremely tarnished in how it achieved it. And it is doubtful that the American people ever again carried on as normal.

From the day the assassination took place, the obvious questions were asked around the world. What was the motive behind the president's murder? It was suspected from the outset that it was not the work of one solitary assassin. Who wanted him killed? Why did they want him killed and how could it possibly happen? What were the authorities doing about it? My task is to take you through the events which followed, through the eventual flow of questions and thence through the research and investigation into the assassination to where we are now. Perhaps then you will be able to judge how successful has been all the effort that has gone into penetrating what many, from the beginning, perceived as a conspiracy of enormous proportions to kill the President of the United States.

Investigation was made unbelievably difficult by the veil of secrecy dropped immediately the noise of the gunfire had ceased in Dealey Plaza, punctuated by the publication of officially sanctioned inaccuracies and incorrect data. Therefore the first task for those who challenged the Warren Report, those who became known as 'the critics', was to chip away at the wall of secrecy, which was clearly intended to render further investigation fruitless. This, then, became the first recognisable certainty for those dedicated to investigating: it was realised that at all costs it was intended that the people be prevented from finding out the truth.

Fifty years later the United States government still clings to the Warren Report as their official version of what happened the day the world stood still. Meanwhile, however, it has been shown to be flawed, inaccurate over and over again and, indeed, untruthful. Surveys conducted long ago showed that fewer and fewer people trusted the report, and worst of all, as a result of the overall handling of the investigation, together with the attitudes displayed, the people's trust in government had been shattered. Prior to the assassination, people in general trusted the government; they trusted what they said and what they did. No longer. As what might be called 'the people's investigation' developed – and it took a little while – they realised they had been duped, even lied to, by their politicians.

It is small wonder the people came to lose faith in their government. Had they known it at the time, they had every reason in the world not to trust the Warren commissioners to begin with. We have that veteran researcher Harold Weisberg to thank for winkling out a document which contained a well-kept secret in government. It was a memo which was circulated before the Warren commissioners had assembled, let alone had had time to consider anything about the assassination. It emanated from the deputy attorney general, Nicholas Katzenbach, who was in charge of the Department of Justice immediately after the assassination in the absence of Attorney General Robert Kennedy.

Weisberg had got on to this memo and its contents as only Weisberg could have done. He was a tenacious researcher and pursued documents via the Freedom of Information Act extremely frequently. (I know: I saw the array of filing cabinets in his cellar.) The memo he sought ran as follows:

It is important that all the facts surrounding President Kennedy's Assassination be made public in a way which will satisfy people in the United States that all the facts have been told and that a statement to this effect be made now.

1. The public must be satisfied that Oswald was the assassin; that he did not have confederates who are still at large; and that the evidence was such that he would have been convicted at a trial.
2. Speculation about Oswald's motivation ought to be cut off, and we should have some basis for rebutting thought that this was a Communist conspiracy or (as the Iron Curtain press is saying) a right wing conspiracy to blame it on the Communists. Unfortunately the facts on Oswald seem about too pat – too obvious (Marxist, Cuba, Russian wife, etc.). The Dallas police have put out statements on the communist conspiracy theory, and it was they who were in charge when he was shot and thus silenced.
3. The matter has been handled thus far with neither dignity nor conviction. Facts have been mixed with rumour and speculation. We can scarcely let the world see us totally in the image of the Dallas police when our President is murdered.

I think this objective may be satisfied by making public as soon as possible a complete and thorough FBI report on Oswald and the assassination. This may run into the difficulty of pointing to inconsistencies between this report and statements by the Dallas police officials. But the reputation of the Bureau is such that it may do the whole job.

The only other step would be the appointment of a Presidential Commission of unimpeachable personnel to review and examine the evidence and announce its conclusions. This has both advantages and disadvantages. I think it can await publication of the FBI report and public reaction to it here and abroad.

I think, however, that a statement that all the facts will be made public property in an orderly and responsible way should be made now. We need something to head off public speculation or Congressional hearings of the wrong sort.

Nicholas deB. Katzenbach
Deputy Attorney General

13. Nicholas deB. Katzenbach.

The memo, addressed to 'Mr Moyers', was dated 25 November 1963, **three days after the assassination**. It was recovered from a Department of Justice file, 129-11 Records Branch, stamped and dated 21 May 1965. The original was written by hand. It was derived from a file bearing the initials HPW (Howard P. Willens, a Warren Commission staff counsel). Other copies later materialised from other files.

Remarkably, an FBI memo from 'Jenkins', dated 24 November (1963), stated: 'Hoover says Oswald alone did it, **Bureau must "convince the public Oswald is the real assassin** [author's emphasis]".'*

Another memo emanating from J. Edgar Hoover, the director of the FBI, dated 26 November (1963), four days after the assassination, stated: 'wrap up investigation; seems to me we have the basic facts now'.

---

* The word 'real' used here raises interesting questions.

It should be noted that both of these memos were written before the Warren Commission had so much as assembled.

14. Captain Will Fritz.

Mary Ferrell, a leading researcher from the beginning and about whom we have more to say elsewhere, reported learning that Captain Will Fritz of the Dallas Police Department, lunching with a friend the day after the assassination, told how he had received a call direct from President Lyndon B. Johnson personally, instructing him, 'You've got your man. The investigation is over.'

4

THE WARREN REPORT

WE WILL NOT GET FAR WITHOUT AN EXAMINATION of certain of the contents of the Warren Report and especially instances where those contents were challenged by the critics. Those who wish to have a copy of the report in front of them are best advised to find out which libraries hold copies. Of those copies sold, few ever change hands and if they do they will fetch thousands of dollars. On the other hand, St. Martin's Press (New York) published a paperback reprint of the report itself, minus the volumes of hearings etc., and copies of this may still be found. Having had to travel from my home in Sheffield, England, 200 miles to consult the original at the British Library in London, I have found the paperback reprint quite adequate as far as it goes.

When the Warren Report was finally published, the early critics were appalled at the confusion and disorder they found in the document, which was quite a tome. Facts had been distorted and frequently ignored. Important witnesses had simply not been called, and where they were the records made of questioning were, in certain cases, quite dubious, with too many instances of questions asked 'off the record'. These were questions and answers which, apparently, were recorded nowhere and never published. Instances of questioning off the record occurred on 240 occasions.

The Warren Commission agreed to have the FBI do their legwork, which proved a distinct mistake. It appeared the FBI had a vested interest in protecting themselves at times and therefore could not be relied upon. This is not to mention a serious claim, which the commission was compelled to investigate, that Oswald himself was an FBI agent. This crisis, duly considered, resulted in one of their number, J. Lee Rankin, being dispatched to ask Mr Hoover if it was true. Hoover simply denied it and it was swept under the carpet. Rankin and Hoover were old friends.

The commission had included in their work a detailed examination of the murder of Officer J.D. Tippit, and this sparked off problems because it was a foregone conclusion that Lee Harvey Oswald would be identified as the killer. Officer Tippit was killed in the vicinity of the junction of 10th Street and Patton Avenue. The commission's chief witness in this matter was a Mrs Helen Markham, who claimed she had witnessed in its entirety the gunning down of the police officer. She recounted seeing the police car Tippit was driving cruising slowly alongside a man who was walking along the sidewalk. She recalled that the window was rolled down and a conversation then took place between the two. This was followed by Tippit stepping out of the car and, according to Mrs Markham, the man on the sidewalk firing at him. On the face of it an excellent witness, but, unfortunately for the commission, her evidence almost immediately began to fall apart at the seams.

15. Mrs Helen Markham.

First, Mrs Markham claimed she had spent some 20 minutes alone with the dying police officer. This was quite impossible in the light of other evidence which showed that the officer had died almost immediately. Consequent to whatever she saw, however, Mrs

Markham flew into a fit of hysterics which was to last for some hours. Taken to a police line-up a few hours after the time Tippit had been shot and while still suffering from her attack of hysteria, she selected a man who she claimed was the one she had seen shoot the officer. He proved to be a police officer himself and it was at her second attempt that she selected Lee Harvey Oswald. Her subsequent questioning by the commission, which appears verbatim in the report, indicated clearly how unreliable she was. She was being questioned by Joseph Ball about the line-up:

Ball: Now when you went into the room you looked these people over, these four men?

Mrs Markham: Yes, sir.

Ball: Did you recognise anyone in the line-up?

Mrs Markham: No, sir.

Ball: You did not? Did you see anybody – I have asked you that question before – did you recognise anybody from their face?

Mrs Markham: From their face, no.

Ball: Did you identify anybody in these four people?

Mrs Markham: I didn't know nobody . . . I had never seen none of them, none of these men.

Ball: No one of the four?

Mrs Markham: No one of them.

Ball: No one of all four?

Mrs Markham: No, sir.

Ball: Was there a number two man in there?

Mrs Markham: Number two is the one I picked . . . Number two was the man I saw shoot the policeman . . . I looked at him. When I saw this man I wasn't sure, but I had cold chills just ran all over me.

She had to be led and prompted to make her statement. Far from consolidating her identification, the questioning revealed clearly how shaky it was. One has to wonder how far this whole episode would have gone in a regular courtroom with a defence lawyer present. Nonetheless, she was the best the commission could do in respect of putting Lee Harvey Oswald in the frame. Her testimony, therefore, was accepted and honoured by the commission: they had their man.

Before she succumbed to a hysterical attack, during which Mrs Markham curiously placed her shoes on a police car, she had described the man she saw shooting Officer Tippit to one officer as being about 25 years old, about 5 ft 8 in. tall, with brown hair and wearing a white jacket. Following her attendance at the line-up, however, she was interviewed on the telephone by lawyer/researcher Mark Lane. This time she described the man she saw as being short, on the heavy side and with slightly bushy hair. At a later interview with the commission she denied talking to Lane, but he had recorded the conversation, which was replayed to the commission, following which she denied having said what was on the tape. This did not, however, change Mrs Markham's status with the commission.

In the case of Mrs Acquilla Clemons, another witness to the shooting, who was never called to give her evidence, she was advised by a Dallas police officer not to tell the commission what she had told them or else she might get killed. She had given descriptions of two men at the scene of the shooting, one tall and thin and wearing khaki trousers and a white shirt. The other, whom she named as the killer, she described as 'kind of a short guy' and 'kind of heavy'. Mrs Clemons was not the only witness to be intimidated.

16. Mrs Acquilla Clemons.

* * *

Though the Warren Commission cannot be defended for the manner in which it conducted its so-called case against Lee Harvey Oswald as the lone killer of the president, it is nevertheless true that the commission was not conducting its totally biased investigation in isolation. Indeed, it might be said that it was aided and abetted by agencies defaulting on the provision of available information that never reached them. Dallas Police Department was prominent in deciding what would reach the commission and what would not. And this is not to mention that their primary source for intelligence input, the FBI, was filtering out what it did not want them to know. Their treatment of a potentially important witness, Richard Randolph Carr, serves as an example of this.

17. Richard R. Carr.

Mr Carr was a steelworker employed on the building site of the new courthouse at Commerce and Houston, and therefore quite close to the scene of the assassination. Watching the motorcade from a vantage point on the seventh storey, he looked across at the Book Depository and saw at a sixth-floor window a man, heavily built, wearing a tan sportscoat, hat and horn-rimmed spectacles. He also saw a Rambler station wagon, reported elsewhere by Deputy Sheriff Roger Craig. He witnessed two men run from the Book Depository or from behind it and get into the Rambler, which sped off with one of its doors flying open.

18. Was this the Rambler car in Elm Street reported by Roger Craig?

Carr saw the man from the sixth-floor window again when he came down to ground level, presumably to find out what was going on. He rushed off towards Commerce Street, Carr said, 'in an extreme hurry and looking over his shoulder'. All relevant and possibly vital evidence, but Richard Randolph Carr was never called to give his evidence to the Warren Commission. He said later, 'The FBI came to my house – there was two of them [*sic*] – and they told me, "If you didn't see Lee Harvey Oswald in the School Book Depository with a rifle, you didn't witness it."' He replied, 'Well, the man I saw on television that they tell me is Lee Harvey Oswald was not in the window of the School Book Depository. That's not the man.' The FBI agent then told him,

'You'd better keep your mouth shut.' Said Carr, 'He did not ask me what I saw; he told me what I saw.'

S.M. Holland, a railway employee, got as far as giving evidence to the commission. He heard four shots fired, he said, and witnessed a puff of smoke about six feet above the grassy knoll area at the time the shots were fired, and other activity in this same area. This, he said, was when the presidential car was proceeding down Elm Street in Dealey Plaza. This, of course, was grossly unpopular with the Warren commissioners, who were anxious not to deviate from their 'single shooter' theory. Holland stuck to his story. This apparently even earned the disfavour of his employers, but nevertheless he persevered.

Holland, with other railway employees, watched from a spot on the railway overpass, from where they had a clear view. He told the commission that afterwards he, with others, raced to the place from which the smoke had emanated. In this area, used as a car park, they found footprints and cigarette butts in the vicinity and a muddy bumper on one of the cars, indicative, they suggested, of someone having stood there to see over the picket fence which surrounded the grassy knoll. This was corroborated by others who had joined Holland. They did not expect to find a shooter lingering a minute or two later when they arrived to investigate, but they found evidence which demanded further investigation.

19. S.M. Holland.

The commission lightly dismissed all this, and in their report changed his four shots to three, an acceptable number to them, and said simply that when he went to investigate he found no one there. Holland was incensed. He went with his lawyer to challenge this and correct his testimony. 'We red-pencilled that statement from beginning to end,' he said, 'but it made no difference.' The report contained the commissioners' original version. I do not apologise for repeating the comment Holland made on seeing this, which I recorded in the very first book I wrote on the subject of the Kennedy assassination. He said, acidly, 'When the time comes that an American can't tell the truth because the government doesn't, that's the time to give the country back to the Indians – if they'll take it!'

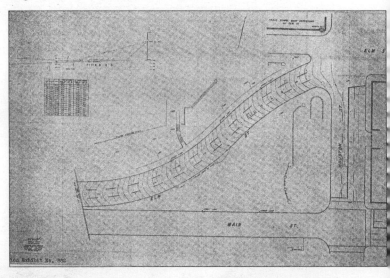

20. From the West/Breneman survey. (Courtesy National Archives)

The most blatant example of the commission changing evidence to suit its case came with the results of a special survey of Dealey Plaza which had been requested by the FBI for the Warren commissioners. Two prominent local surveyors, Robert West and Chester Breneman, carried out the survey of distances and elevations to instructions. Their completed, detailed work was submitted fully to the commissioners. When it was published in the Warren Report, they were astounded to see that alterations had been made to some of their figures.

FRAME NO.	STATION NO.	ELEV.	RIFLE IN WINDOW		TOP BRIDGE	HANDRAIL
			ANGLE TO HORIZON R-K-H	LINE OF SIGHT DIST. K-R	ANGLE TO HORIZON B-K-H	LINE OF SIGHT DIST. K-B
A		431.97	40° 10'	91.6	-0°27'	447.0
161	3+29.2	429.25	26° 58'	137.4	-0°07'	392.4
166	3+30.1	429.20	26° 52'	138.2	-0°07'	391.5
185	3+49.3	428.13	24° 14'	154.9	+0°03'	372.5
186	3+50.8	428.05	24° 03'	156.3	+0°03'	371.7
207	3+71.1	427.02	21° 50'	174.3	+0°12'	350.9
210	3+73.4	426.80	21° 34'	176.5	+0°22'	348.8
222	3+85.9	426.11	20° 23'	188.6	+0°24'	336.4
225	3+88.3	425.98	20° 11'	190.8	+0°26'	334.0
231	3+93.5	425.69	19° 47'	196.0	+0°28'	329.0
235	3+96.8	425.52	19° 26'	199.0	+0°30'	326.8
240	4+02.3	425.21	19° 01'	204.3	+0°34'	320.4
249	4+10.0	424.79	18° 32'	211.9	+0°40'	313.1
255	4+16.4	424.46	18° 03'	218.0	+0°44'	307.1
313	4+65.3	421.75	15° 21'	265.3	+1°28'	260.6

COMMISSION EXHIBIT 884

21. Survey data published in the Warren Report.

FRAME NO.	STATION NO.	ELEV.	RIFLE IN WINDOW		TOP BRIDGE	HANDRAIL
			ANGLE TO HORIZON R-K-H	LINE OF SIGHT DIST. K-R	ANGLE TO HORIZON B-K-H	LINE OF SIGHT DIST. K-B
A		431.97	40° 10'	91.6	-0°27'	447.0
168 / 161	3+29.2	429.25	26° 58'	137.4	-0°07'	392.4
171 / 166	3+30.1	429.20	26° 52'	138.2	-0°07'	391.5
185	3+49.3	428.13	24° 14'	154.9	+0°03'	372.5
186	3+50.8	428.05	24° 03'	156.3	+0°03'	371.7
207	3+71.1	427.02	21° 50'	174.3	+0°12'	350.9
208 / 210	3+73.4	426.80	21° 34'	176.5	+0°22'	348.8
222	3+85.9	426.11	20° 23'	188.6	+0°24'	336.4
225	3+88.3	425.98	20° 11'	190.8	+0°26'	334.0
231	3+93.5	425.69	19° 47'	196.0	+0°28'	329.0
235	3+96.8	425.52	19° 26'	199.0	+0°30'	326.8
240	4+02.3	425.21	19° 01'	204.3	+0°34'	320.4
249	4+10.0	424.79	18° 32'	211.9	+0°40'	313.1
255	4+16.4	424.46	18° 03'	218.0	+0°44'	307.1
313	4+65.3	421.75	15° 21'	265.3	+1°28'	260.6

22. Survey data as corrected by the surveyors.

Referring to frame numbers derived from the 8-mm movie shot by Abraham Zapruder at the time of the assassination, frame 168 became 161, 171 became 166 and frame 208 became 210. Just enough, the surveyors claimed, to allow the commission to argue that the second shot came from the same location as the first. This made a huge difference. The surveyors' work had convinced them shots had come from two directions, but this was totally unacceptable to the commission. A survey West and Breneman had carried out for *Life* magazine prior to their engagement by the FBI had resulted in the magazine's investigator becoming convinced the shots could not have been fired by the same person. Neither of the surveyors was called to give evidence to the commission.

But perhaps the most controversial of all the claims made by the Warren Commission were those which related to what became known as the single-bullet theory. The commission had a problem: they could account for three bullets being fired and no more. It would have been unacceptable to maintain that Lee Harvey Oswald, with his outdated Mannlicher-Carcano rifle, had discharged more than three rounds at the president in the time the shooting took place. Adding to their problem, one of the three shots had missed, struck the pavement and thrown up a fragment of concrete to injure a bystander, James Tague.

All of the shots had come from behind, the commission maintained, from the rifle of Lee Harvey Oswald located on the sixth floor of the Book Depository building. One shot having missed left only two shots in the Warren assessment to account for all of the injuries sustained by the president, including the fatal head shot. Then there were the wounds sustained by Governor John Connally, who was sitting in front of the president in the Lincoln, to be accounted for.

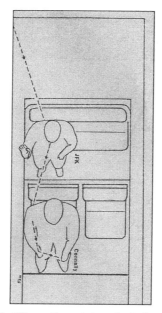

23. According to the Warren Commission, the bullet would have had to have performed something like this. (Matthew Smith Collection)

24. Parkland Hospital's Dr Malcolm Perry.

A complication came also from Dr Malcolm Perry in a written statement he promptly issued. Dr Perry was one of the team of doctors at Parkland Hospital, where the president had been taken after the shooting, and in his statement he referred to a front entry wound to the throat. This they had enlarged to pass down a tube, substituting the wound the bullet had made for a tracheotomy, he explained, necessary in the attempt to save his life. He was prevailed upon to change this wound to an exit wound, achieved by claiming the press had misquoted his statement, omitting the word 'possible' with regard to the wound being one of entry. This fudge enabled the commission to claim the bullet had exited from Kennedy's throat into Connally's back, exited again via his chest, struck his right wrist and embedded itself in his left thigh. Leaving one shot for the fatal head wound, all of the wounds were then accounted for.

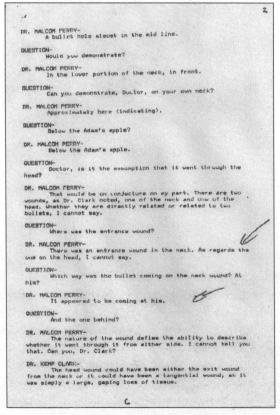

25. Excerpt of interview with Dr Malcolm Perry.

It is small wonder that the critics immediately denounced this inventive theory, prompting the bullet which had reputedly achieved all this henceforth to be tagged 'the magic bullet'. A photograph of the missile, commission exhibit 399, showed it to be, remarkably, in relatively pristine condition, arousing further disbelief. It was said to have rolled off a stretcher at Parkland Hospital. How it got there, no one knows, but a claim that it came from a stretcher which had been occupied by Governor Connally was denied by hospital staff.

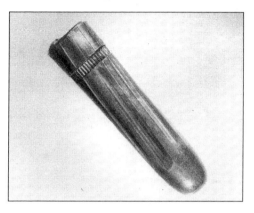

26. Commission Exhibit 399, the 'magic bullet'. Could it have caused all the wounds to JFK and Connally and looked so pristine afterwards? (Courtesy National Archives)

* * *

More about the Warren Report and its contents cannot fail to appear elsewhere in this book, but an interesting sequence of events ran alongside the Warren proceedings. Jack Ruby – strongly suspected of having been sent by those who had assassinated the president to kill Lee Harvey Oswald, silencing him – told Earl Warren that he had things to say regarding the assassination but couldn't say them in Dallas. He asked to be taken to Washington, where he would tell all. Warren refused.

In November 1965, well after Warren's refusal to hear Ruby's evidence elsewhere, celebrity reporter and television personality Dorothy Kilgallen was permitted to interview Jack Ruby. The interview was to take place in a room behind the area occupied by the judge and therefore not expected to be bugged, as might be thought with his cell. She returned to her New York home afterwards and announced to her friend Mrs Earl T. Smith that she was going to break the assassination mystery 'wide open'. Dorothy Kilgallen was found dead a few days later – an overdose, they said. Two days later Mrs Earl T. Smith was also found dead. While the cause of death was not determined, she was said to have taken her own life.

27. Dorothy Kilgallen.

This virtually confirms that the room in which the interview had taken place was, in fact, bugged and that Ruby's every word – anywhere he spoke – was being listened to. The entire episode has to raise the question of the wisdom of Earl Warren when he denied Ruby the opportunity of speaking up. It would appear Jack Ruby spoke up to Dorothy Kilgallen with dire consequences, denying him what proved to be his very last chance of being able to tell what he knew.

28. Jack Ruby.

Pertinent to this, Jack Ruby was scheduled for an appeal hearing at which his lawyers expected him to be acquitted. He was visited in jail by a 'doctor' who remains unidentified to this day. No one had heard of him and he wasn't listed in the appropriate references. He gave Ruby an injection and it was after that that Ruby, on examination, was found to have cancer. Jack immediately recalled the injection he had had and asserted he had been injected by the phoney doctor with whatever had caused the cancer. He died before his new hearing was held.

5

ROBERT F. KENNEDY JR
AND WHAT HIS FATHER SAID

29. Robert F. Kennedy, brother of the president.
(Courtesy John F. Kennedy Library)

WHEN ROBERT F. KENNEDY WAS ON THE CAMPAIGN trail in 1968, five years after his brother's death, by all accounts he was winding up to a colossal win in the primaries. Speaking in California, where he himself would be murdered, he reached a point where he knew he had to make a comment on the events of five years before, when his brother was assassinated. He did. It was a very carefully structured statement which seemed at first hearing to say neither one thing nor another. He said, 'You wanted to ask me something about the archives. I'm sure, as I've said before, the archives will be open.'

The crowd cheered and applauded. He was speaking at what is now the Cal State Northridge campus and he had 1,200 students in his audience. The speech was recorded and is available on a radio tape. He continued, as though not to let the response to his statement get out of control:

Can I just say, and I have answered this question before, but there is no one who would be more interested in all of these matters for ugh . . . the ah, ah, the death of President Kennedy than I would. I have seen all the matters in the archives. If I became President of the United States, I would not, I would not, reopen the, ugh, Warren Commission Report. I think I, uh, stand by the Warren Commission Report. I've seen everything in the archives, the archives will be available at the appropriate time.

The crowd again broke into loud cheers. Some assassination researchers took it that he meant he would not be in favour of a new investigation. His listeners on the day, largely students, did not hear it that way. They heard him say the archives would be opened and that meant another investigation, and that was why they cheered. And to them it clearly meant that it would happen when he became president. The Warren references are perplexing, but perhaps the most significant point is that he made it clear he would not be reconvening the Warren Commission.

At the time of writing this book, the news has broken that Robert Kennedy Jr is presently writing a book on the assassination of President Kennedy. Some researchers, it appears, have commenced to twitch and have not been welcoming of the news. This writer, and probably the vast majority of those who make up the mainstream of established researchers, does not agree with them. I think that Robert Kennedy Jr is to be highly commended in becoming the first of the close Kennedy family to comment on the subject, and indeed to be getting into print with what he has to say. I have already heard of a number of researchers who are offering him any help he requires.

30. Robert Kennedy Jr. (Courtesy Paul Schrade)

A lawyer and well-known environmentalist, Robert Kennedy Jr appeared with his sister, Rory, a documentary filmmaker, at a round-table discussion in January, marking the commencement of the 50th anniversary year of the assassination of his uncle. The choice of Dallas for this appearance was significant. He was making a statement in this also. There was no doubt that he was aware he was breaking a family taboo. The big news coming out of the discussion related to a statement in which he publicly announced his opposition to the Warren Report. Another revelation, which links to what we have said above, came in the news he broke that his father, Robert F. Kennedy, had dismissed the Warren Report as a 'shoddy piece of craftsmanship'. At the time of its release he publicly supported it, but Robert Kennedy Jr made it clear that privately his father suspected a conspiracy. This did not come as a surprise, but it had never been made public before.

Robert Jr began his anecdotes by telling of his father's response to seeing a picture of New Orleans DA Jim Garrison on a news-stand in 1966, when the case was being heard, brought by Garrison, accusing New Orleans businessman Clay Shaw, who had CIA connections, of complicity in the murder of JFK. Robert Jr said that his father sought information from an aide. He asked if there was anything to Garrison's theories and received the reply that Garrison was onto something, but 'the specifics of Garrison's investigation went on the wrong track, but he thought there was a link . . .'

Robert Kennedy Jr also stated, 'The evidence at this point, I think, is very, very convincing that it was not a lone gunman.' The discussion was held in front of a live audience at the Winspear Opera House. Robert and Rory were guests of the PBS talk show host Charlie Rose. Another nugget of information that came out of the hour-and-a-half interview was that, unimpressed by the Warren Report, Robert Kennedy Sr, as attorney general, had had Justice Department investigators look into allegations which had come to him of Lee Harvey Oswald receiving aid from the Mafia, the CIA or other organisations. Robert Jr said, 'My father thought somebody was involved.' At that point, interviewer Charlie Rose came in with, 'Organised crime, Cubans?' to which Robert Jr responded, 'Or rogue CIA.'

Charlie Rose wondered whether the aggressive campaign his father had conducted against the Mafia had any connection with the president's murder, and whether he had felt any kind of guilt, to which Robert replied that his father had spoken of it and had had investigators do research into the assassination, in which they had discovered that the phone records of Oswald and of Jack Ruby were 'like an inventory' of Mafia leaders his department had been investigating.*

Robert Jr also said that his aunt Jacqueline Kennedy had spent much of the five years following the assassination abroad because she feared for her children's safety.

---

* Jack Ruby was heavily involved in gun-running, and Oswald was known to have been present on one occasion when negotiations were going on. It is even a thought that the knowledge Oswald obtained at that meeting would have given Ruby a motive for killing him all by itself. Oswald was not known for dealings with the Mafia, though in his line of work (espionage) it was not impossible.

31. Jacqueline Kennedy. (Courtesy John F. Kennedy Library)

The programme at the Winspear Opera House was organised by the AT&T Performing Arts Center and was the first of a series of programmes to be devoted to commemorating the legacy of President Kennedy scheduled to be held throughout the year. They were not intended for broadcasting. The event focused chiefly on the lighter side of living in the Kennedy family and produced some amusing anecdotes. Rory said that she and her siblings grew up in a culture where it was important to give back. It can be certain, however, that the comments made by Robert Kennedy Jr relating to his father and the assassination of President Kennedy were not unplanned.

6

THE CASE AGAINST
LEE HARVEY OSWALD

WHEN IT COMES TO EVIDENCE, AN ESSENTIAL starter question to be answered is what drew the official investigators to the School Book Depository and to Lee Harvey Oswald in particular? The answer is complex, as might be expected, but it starts at the point of the shooting at the president. Fingers were indeed pointed in the direction of the upper floors of the building at which Lee Harvey Oswald worked but not by any means exclusively. Some pointed to the adjacent Dal-Tex Building and others to the buildings at the other side of the road. Some pointed to the grassy knoll, an area in front of the Book Depository, to the right of the motorcade as it proceeded down Elm Street. Others were looking at the overpass, directly in front of the motorcade. Some said three shots were fired, some four and some as many as six.

Linked to the preference for the School Book Depository building being the source of the shots was the incredible speed with which the police department issued an APB describing Oswald and declaring him wanted for questioning in connection with the assassination. When asked why Oswald had become a suspect so quickly, Police Chief Jesse Curry replied along the lines that the entire staff of the School Book Depository had been assembled and because Oswald was missing the APB was put out to locate him.

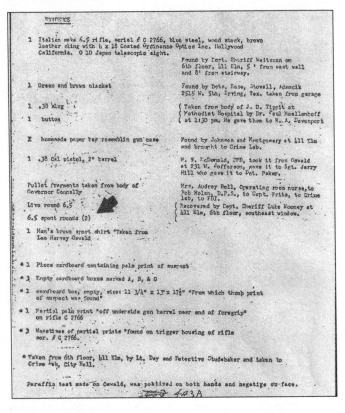

EVIDENCE

1 Italian make 6.5 rifle, serial # C 2766, blue steel, wood stock, brown leather sling with 4 x 18 Coated Ordinance Optics Inc. Hollywood California. O 10 Japan telescopic sight.

Found by Dept. Sheriff Weitzman on 6th floor, 411 Elm, 5' from west wall and 8' from stairway.

1 Green and brown blanket

Found by Dets. Rose, Stovall, Adamcik 2515 W. 5th, Irving, Tex. taken from garage

1 .38 slug
1 button

(Taken from body of J. D. Tippit at
(Methodist Hospital by Dr. Paul Moellenhoff
(at 1130 pm, He gave them to R.A. Davenport

X homemade paper bag resemblin gun case

Found by Johnson and Montgomery at 411 Elm and brought to Crime Lab.

1 .38 cal pistol, 2" barrel

M. N. McDonald, DPD, took it from Oswald at 231 W. Jefferson, gave it to Sgt. Jerry Hill who gave it to Det. Paker.

Bullet fragments taken from body of Governor Connally

Mrs. Audrey Bell, Operating room nurse, to Bob Nolan, D.P.S., to Capt. Fritz, to Crime lab, to FBI.

Live round 6.5
6.5 spent rounds (2)

(Recovered by Dept. Sheriff Luke Mooney at
(411 Elm, 6th floor, southeast window.

1 Man's brown sport shirt "Taken from Lee Harvey Oswald

* 1 Piece cardboard containing palm print of suspect

* 1 Empty cardboard boxes marked A, B, & C

* 1 cardboard box, empty, sizes 11 3/4" x 13" x 17½" "From which thumb print of suspect was found"

* 1 Partial palm print "off underside gun barrel near end of foregrip" on rifle C 2766

* 3 Negatives of partial prints "found on trigger housing of rifle nor. # C 2766.

* Taken from 6th floor, 411 Elm, by Lt. Day and Detective Studebaker and taken to Crime Lab, City Hall.

Paraffin test made on Oswald, was positive on both hands and negative on face.

403A

32. Original Oswald evidence sheet. (See next page.)

This was totally unrealistic in view of other members of the staff having drifted off after the shooting in the belief that there would be no more work that day. Furthermore, the idea of assembling the entire staff, even had they all been thereabouts, and making a check allowing them to put out the APB, roughly within 15 minutes of the shooting and Oswald having strolled out of the building without challenge, was unbelievable. Far more believable was that Chief Curry had been given Oswald's details in advance and primed to put them out in an APB, which he did a little prematurely.

EVIDENCE

1 Italian make 6.5 rifle, serial # C 2766, blue steel, wood stock, brown
leather sling with 4 x 18 Coated Ordinance Optics Inc. Hollywood
California. O 10 Japan telescopic sight.
Carcano carbine

Found by Dept. Sheriff Weitzman on
6th floor, 411 Elm, 5 ' from west wall
and 8' from stairway.

1 Green and brown blanket

Found by Detr. Rose, Stovall, Adamcik
2515 W. 5th, Irving, Tex. taken from garage

1 .38 slug

{ Taken from body of J. D. Tippit at
Methodist Hospital by Dr. Paul Moellenhoff
at 1:30 pm. He gave them to R. A. Davenport

1 button

X homemade paper bag resemblin gun case

Found by Johnson and Montgomery at 411 Elm
and brought to Crime Lab.

1 .38 cal pistol, 2" barrel, S&W, Rev.
sandblast finish, brown wooden handles
ser.# 510210. Rel. to FBI Agent 11-22-63
and again 11-26-63

M. N. McDonald, DPD, took it from Oswald
at 733 W. Jefferson, gave it to Sgt. Jerry
Hill who gave it to Det. Baker.

Bullet fragments taken from body of
Governor Connally

Mrs. Audrey Bell, Operating room nurse, to
Bob Nolan, D.P.S., to Capt. Fritz, to Crime
Lab, to FBI.

Live round 6.5

{ Recovered by Dept. Sheriff Luke Mooney at
411 Elm, 6th floor, southeast window.

6.5 spent rounds (3)

Found by Dep. Sheriff Mooney. Picked up by
Det. R. M. Sims. See pages L-130 and P-262.

1 Man's brown sport shirt "Taken from
Lee Harvey Oswald"

* 1 Piece cardboard containing palm print of suspect

* 3 Empty cardboard boxes marked A, B, & C

* 1 cardboard box, empty, size: 11 3/4" x 13" x 17½" "From which thumb print
of suspect was found"

* 1 Partial palm print "off underside gun barrel near end of foregrip"
on rifle C 2766

* 3 Negatives of partial prints "found on trigger housing of rifle
ser. # C 2766.

* Taken from 6th floor, 411 Elm, by Lt. Day and Detective Studebaker and taken to
Crime Lab, City Hall.

130

33. The Warren Commission version: two bullets become three, the number
of rounds the commission claimed Oswald had fired.

34. Police Chief Jesse Curry.

A search of the sixth floor, where Oswald had been working, resulted in a rifle being found, plus a number of spent cartridges. Four police officers were involved in the discovery of the rifle. Deputy Sheriff Eugene Boone was there first; then Luke Mooney, another sheriff's deputy, moved some boxes of books. Deputy Constable Seymour Weitzman was called to witness the discovery. Another deputy sheriff, Roger Craig, was near to hand, saw the rifle and heard the conversation which ensued. The gun was unanimously identified as a 7.65 Mauser of German manufacture. The rifle was also seen by Captain Will Fritz, who, it was claimed, agreed with the identification of the weapon. In accordance with procedures, therefore, affidavits were duly drawn up by Weitzman and Boone, who, in their statements, noted the colour of the sling and gave a detailed description of the rifle and its scope. The news travelled and District Attorney Henry M. Wade gave the details of the weapon in a television statement.

35. The rifle they called the 'Oswald rifle'.

The rifle picked up by Lieutenant J.C. Day to be taken to police headquarters, however, proved to be an Italian carbine, a 6.5 Mannlicher-Carcano, serial number C2766. Day was pictured carrying the rifle and it was logged in as the murder weapon. This rifle, it was claimed, belonged to Lee Harvey Oswald. Questioned by the Warren Commission, both Boone and Weitzman were pressed to reconsider their claim that it had been a Mauser they had found. It was quite true that at a superficial glance the Mauser resembled the Mannlicher-Carcano. Regardless that the Mannlicher-Carcano had the legend 'Made in Italy' clearly stated on the butt and the German rifle had 'Mauser' stamped on the barrel, the two men changed their testimony and said they were in error. But one of those present, Roger Craig, who had not signed an affidavit, would not budge. He stuck to the identification of the Mauser and became very unpopular with his superiors.

36. Lt J.C. Day carries away the 'Oswald rifle'.

Roger Craig had other evidence to give, also. He was a key witness to a sighting of a man who dashed from the back door of the Book Depository, ran down the slope to Elm Street and was immediately picked up by someone in a white Nash station wagon. (In some documents, the station wagon was referred to as green.) He identified the driver as either black or a dark-skinned Latin. Craig came face to face with Lee Harvey Oswald when he was being questioned by Captain Will Fritz in his office at police headquarters and immediately identified him as the man he had seen running to the car. On the face of it this might well have been a man resembling Oswald attempting to create a diversion at the point where the police were hunting Oswald, as at that point Craig was not to know the real Oswald's movements after leaving his place of work. Others who had seen the fleeing man agreed with Craig's identification, but since the evidence involved a second person – whoever it was who picked him up in a station wagon – this would indicate that a conspiracy was responsible for the assassination and was therefore ignored by the Warren Commission. In the case of it all having been a diversion, the implication of a conspiracy would be even stronger.

Attempts were then made to discredit Craig. Captain Will Fritz claimed Craig had never been present in his office while he was interviewing Lee Harvey Oswald, so that he could not have identified him as the man he had seen. Unfortunately for Fritz, when Police Chief Jesse Curry later published a book, the critics promptly identified a photograph he had included of Fritz's office in which Roger Craig was clearly shown to be present.

37. Photograph of Captain Fritz's office showing Craig present.

Craig, named Officer of the Year by the Dallas Traffic Commission, was promoted four times. After refusing to withdraw his submissions of evidence related to the assassination, however, he was never again to be promoted or receive any commendation. Craig was another who was amazed to find that his testimony to the Warren Commission had been changed. He identified 14 instances where alterations had been made. It was then that all his troubles began. He was ordered not to discuss his evidence with anyone, and when he disobeyed he was fired.

38. Roger Craig.

Following his dismissal, he spoke of feeling he was being followed. He was fired at, though the identity of the shooter was never discovered. But, since his head was grazed, he was reckoned to have had a lucky escape. After this, threats began to arrive and he was run off the road on a mountain pass, causing a back injury from which he was to suffer for the rest of his life. He reported that his car was bombed and, as a consequence of the pressures all this brought, his marriage broke up. His problems did not abate: he was shot and wounded by another gunman whose identity was never discovered. Death brought an end to 39-year-old Craig's suffering. He was found alone in a pool of blood in his father's house. He was listed as a suicide.

Recounting the story of Roger Craig in a previous book brought me under fire from Vincent Bugliosi in his book *Reclaiming History*. He dismissed the story most scathingly.

* * *

The case of the solitary eyewitness is interesting. The only eyewitness claiming to identify Lee Harvey Oswald on the sixth floor at the window they said the shots came from, was a man named Howard L. Brennan. Brennan had been sitting on a low wall opposite the

Book Depository (see fig. 39) and claimed he saw Oswald shooting from the sixth-floor window. On close examination, however, Brennan's evidence raised a number of questions which were difficult to resolve. He said Oswald was firing from a standing position, for instance. Since the windowsill was very low, anyone standing would have been showing his knees and would have had to stoop to fire a rifle. Also, every one of the many photographs taken of the sixth-floor window at that time shows that the upper part of the window was closed, making it quite impossible for anyone to shoot standing up. The Warren Commission were anxious to accept Brennan's identification of Oswald, however, and proposed that, with the windowsill being quite low, Oswald was probably either sitting or in a kneeling position to fire the shots. In changing their witness's statement, however, they created another problem. In his description, Brennan had testified to the height and weight of the man he saw, which would have been quite impossible if he had been in a sitting or kneeling position. The commission obliged yet again by saying he 'could have seen enough of the body . . . to estimate his height'. His estimation of the man's weight was, presumably, just taken for granted.

39. Howard Brennan sits where he was sitting when the shots were fired.
(Courtesy National Archives)

The validity of this shaky identification was further eroded when, later on the day of his 'sighting', Brennan was unable to positively identify Lee Harvey Oswald in a police line-up, in spite of having seen his picture on television in the meanwhile. In a later discussion with FBI personnel, he stated 'he was sure the person firing the rifle was Oswald,' though about three weeks after this he 'appeared to revert to his earlier inability to make a positive identification'. Notwithstanding, four months after this he gave further evidence in which he had changed his mind once more: 'Howard L. Brennan made a positive identification of Oswald as being the person at the window.' Needless to say, his evidence would have been worthless in a court of law.

Interestingly, in an interview with KRLD-TV two days after President Kennedy was assassinated, Police Chief Jesse Curry was asked, 'Chief Curry, do you have an eyewitness who saw someone shoot the president?' Chief Curry answered, 'No, sir, we do not.'

* * *

The rifle which belonged to Lee Harvey Oswald, an Italian Mannlicher-Carcano carbine said to have been designed around 1890, could hardly be thought a weapon of choice for a marksman. It was slow and considerably outdated in comparison with other rifles available. Oswald had bought it by post from a dealer in Chicago, which raised questions from the critics as soon as it was known. Why buy a rifle, unseen, from a Chicago dealer when there were gun stores galore in Dallas, shops where he could have been more selective and which carried the advantage, if it was required, of him remaining anonymous, with no documentation raised? The Chicago dealer was, for instance, immediately able to confirm Oswald's purchase with paper evidence.

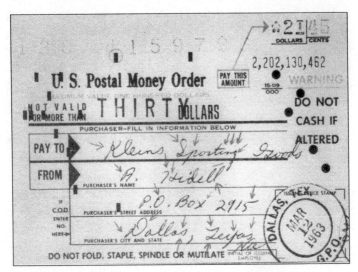

40. The Klein's paperwork showing the sale of the Mannlicher-Carcano to
Hidell – not Oswald, it is noted. Did Oswald's CIA handler order the rifle
to be delivered to Oswald's PO Box? And how come the Post Office
accepted a package for a person not registered for that box?

The answer to this question relates to the greater question of
whether Oswald was, as believed by many researchers, a CIA agent.
If he was – if he was ordered to buy the weapon and told exactly
how to buy it and where he should buy it from – he would not
have questioned making the purchase. Similarly, it should be asked
why, unless he did, in fact, plan to attempt to shoot the president
with this somewhat doubtful weapon, should he take it to work
that day? In the murky twilight of what had already been unearthed
by the early critics, even by this early point, it seemed quite as
likely that he had been instructed to take it – assuming, of course,
that he himself ever did take it to the Book Depository.

It was, naturally, tested for fingerprints. Nothing was found
except a palm print, which was later challenged for authenticity.
It was ghoulishly speculated that, no prints having been found at
all, the authorities had sought to obtain a palm print from the
body of the dead Oswald. In this, the critics had little to go on

and perhaps were over-zealous in their suspicions for, in fact, it mattered little. There was no denying that this was the rifle Oswald had bought and there was no reason why his palm print should not be on the weapon. It proved nothing. Neither did the few empty cartridge cases found near the sixth-floor window. The real question related to whether or not he had used the rifle to shoot and kill the president.

Evidence to support Oswald having shot the president with his Mannlicher-Carcano was not readily available from the wounds he sustained. But then neither, for that matter, was evidence to support that he had not. It was, however, generally accepted that Oswald was at the centre of what had taken place. His, they asserted, was the key role: he was the one and only shooter. It is important to bear in mind that from the beginning it was not questioned that Lee Harvey Oswald had killed the president: Warren had said so! But it would have alarmed the Warren commissioners, no doubt, had they known how soon the question of a second sniper would be raised and debated, remembering that even one additional participant on any level would indicate that a conspiracy had taken place. It would have alarmed them even further had they known that evidence of a conspiracy would soon be obtained and the investigation would take a whole new course.

* * *

The Warren Commission bolstered its condemnation of Lee Harvey Oswald by asserting that he had murdered Officer Tippit while 'on the run'. The so-called proof of this was extremely flimsy and it is hard to imagine that in a court of law he would not have been acquitted because of lack of evidence alone. A separate chapter on this subject spells out the details (Chapter 12). Similarly, he was declared to have attempted to murder General Walker, against the most convincing evidence that this was not the case. The casing of the bullet fired at General Walker was available and it patently was not from Oswald's rifle. Even the general did not believe Oswald was the culprit. A chapter on this will also be found in this book (Chapter 13).

The Warren case against Lee Harvey Oswald was under serious pressure, even before the report was written. Indeed, some would have said even at that early point that it was crumbling, with doubt befogging so many instances of what the commissioners were claiming as evidence. They could only surmise that he was on the sixth floor of the Book Depository building when the shots were fired, against conflicting evidence: his presence outside the second-floor lunchroom, confirmed by a police officer, for instance. Most of all, the idea of him firing the elderly Mannlicher-Carcano rifle so rapidly as to be the only shooter involved, and being so spectacularly accurate, bordered on the unbelievable. In fact, it appeared that what could be termed the straightforward, clear, hard evidence to support Oswald's guilt had proven to be non-existent. It is noted also that the one and only eyewitness to Oswald firing a rifle from the sixth-floor window of the School Book Depository was Howard L. Brennan, a most uncertain and quite unreliable witness. Not only that, but the one and only eyewitness to Lee Harvey Oswald shooting Officer Tippit was Mrs Helen Markham, who admitted suffering from hysteria. In giving her testimony to the Warren Commission, she had to be led by her questioner. As was said earlier, it appeared that had Oswald been tried in an open court, a lawyer would not have been hard pressed to dismantle the case against him. Was this in the minds of the conspirators, and was Jack Ruby therefore dispatched to kill him before he could make himself heard?

7

LEE HARVEY OSWALD

Whichever way the assassination of President Kennedy was viewed, Lee Harvey Oswald played the central role in every consideration. The case against Oswald was handed to the Warren Commission by Dallas Police Department. He was the only person charged with the murder of the president. To any lawman, this was an open invitation to simply develop the case as presented to him, and Earl Warren took the hint. It has to be remembered that, by all accounts, his prime objective was to defuse a tense political situation. To have the case for a crazy lone assassin immediately available was the answer to his most difficult problems. It should also be remembered that it is highly unlikely that Warren did not see the infamous memo from Deputy Attorney General Nicholas Katzenbach (see Chapter 3). A debate on the ends justifying the means did not seem to have any place in their deliberations; it appears that the risk of hotheads in high places making up their own minds and taking the US into a conflict which may have escalated into an all-out nuclear war became the only consideration and that justifications therefore became unnecessary.

It was some time after the Warren Commission had produced its voluminous report, and long after the tensions had abated, that the critics began to land blows on Warren which eventually led his ten-million-word report to begin to lose whatever impact it had had. Lee Harvey Oswald figured largely in this period also, because the attack fatal to the Warren findings related to the impossibility of his being able to act alone and unaided. Probably the very first part of the attack was provoked by the Report's assertions that one of the bullets which had hit the president exited and hit Governor Connally, exiting again to hit him once more in the wrist and finally to cause yet another wound in his left groin.

The critics argued for another sniper and the growing belief was that he was shooting from the grassy knoll. Those who had access to early illicit copies of the Zapruder film could not believe the fatal head wound to the president was caused by a shot from behind, from the sixth-floor window of the School Book Depository. Those with access to the film were not many, however, and the American people as a whole were prevented from seeing the movie for 12 years.

From an early stage, however, the spotlight was turned on Lee Harvey Oswald as a person. Who was he? What was he? Where had he come from? What was his background? As answers were sought and his background probed, a great deal of important and indeed illuminating material began to be assembled.

* * *

The background produced by Edward Jay Epstein (*Legend: The Secret World of Lee Harvey Oswald*) showed a deprived child from a somewhat splintered family. His schooling was spasmodic and lacked continuity. He was moved from city to city and school to school, which only added fuel to the fire. Epstein's work was the first attempt to make a serious assessment of who Oswald was and where he had come from.

41. Lee Harvey Oswald with a friend in happier times.
(Courtesy National Archives)

Yet in other studies, Oswald was in fact seen to be a bright child with the capacity to rise above the deprivation he had suffered. As he grew in maturity, he was strongly opposed to continuing in education and, under the influence of others, receptive of ideas which were new to him. One of these strands was communism, a not unusual interest in a teenager of his time. Balancing this, it might be said, was a desire to join the US Marines. As soon as he was eligible, he enlisted and found in the armed forces the opportunities he had lacked elsewhere.

* * *

After his basic training at San Diego, he went to Camp Pendleton, about 20 miles north of San Diego, where he completed his combat training. It was at Keesler Air Force Base at Biloxi, Mississippi, that he opted to study radar and became greatly skilled in that area. Now an aviation electronics operator with the military occupation specialty code of 6741, he was shipped out to Japan, to the US base at Atsugi. It was here that life, it seems, began to change for him, and this period presents a great deal of opportunity for various researchers to piece together an interesting account of his progress. What follows is an amalgam of the work of various researchers.

Women did not appear to interest him and he preferred staying at base to roaming the bars of the district. Those around him found this odd and ragged him for it, whereupon he joined the poker school, enjoyed a drink and spent some time with the local girls. His fellows found him easy to get along with and a well-informed individual with whom it was comfortable to get into conversation. Those around him rated him a 'good egg', good-natured and likeable.

This did not prevent him from getting into trouble from time to time. Having shot himself in the foot – believed to be an attempt to dodge a mission in the Philippines and keep himself at Atsugi – he was found to have used a 'personal' small-calibre gun. One interpretation later placed on this was that, unknown to his fellows at the camp, he had been keeping secretive company with a group of communist acquaintances on visits to Tokyo. To them, it was likely to appear that he had gone to great lengths to stay at Atsugi to continue his relationship with them. The incident constituting the first black mark on his record suggested that it was meant to convey to his communist friends that he was no pushover: he was his own man and, in support of this, he had procured his pistol, which was distinctly not for his masters' purposes. Other incidents in which he was later involved earned him more black marks and added to what was perceived as a 'background'. The shot in the foot – if in fact there ever was one – did not keep him from the mission planned for his unit. After being disciplined, he was dispatched with the others. Interestingly, his Marines record showed that the injury was 'incurred in line of duty and not related to misconduct'. These and other events appeared to indicate that Oswald was being prepared for participation in something very special.

42. Lee Harvey Oswald. (Courtesy National Archives)

While away on this mission, he was involved in a mysterious event while on sentry duty. This was followed by him being returned to Japan for 'medical treatment', which in turn was followed by reassignment to Iwakuni, a US base 400 miles southwest of Tokyo. During his time there, he began learning to speak Russian; this is not an easy language to acquire, but by all accounts he did well at his studies. While this and other overt displays of interest in all things Russian bothered his new comrades – one drew the attention of an officer to what was going on – his superiors were clearly not concerned. He had acquitted himself well in his radar work and become highly thought of by his colleagues and their superiors; it was – much later – claimed by one of those he worked with that Oswald then had the highest possible clearance in relation to handling top-secret data.

It was at around the time of his transfer to Iwakuni that he is thought to have made an application for early release from the Marines on the grounds of his mother's hardship. The authorities could have discovered with the minimum of difficulty that his mother was not at that time suffering any troubles which would merit his early release. He was, however, sent back home to Santa Ana, California, where, significantly, he resumed his Russian language studies due to a Marine Corps examination revealing a lack of competence and the need of further study. Other examination results were interesting too. They showed that in a range of subjects he had reached a level about equal to a high-school diploma. No less than J. Lee Rankin, chief counsel for the Warren Commission, unearthed details of a course Oswald had been studying upon his return to California. It was at the Monterey School of the Army and he had taken a course in . . . the Russian language. Not a word or a hint of this was revealed by the commission. In fact, it came to light only in a release of top-secret documents in response to a Freedom of Information application in 1974. Small wonder Oswald became something of an expert in the language.

Oswald let it be known that after leaving the Marines he planned to travel to Switzerland to further improve his education. His 'mother's hardship' early release being granted, he obtained a passport extremely quickly and left for Europe.

* * *

43. Letter from Oswald to the Moscow embassy.
(Courtesy National Archives)

Oswald was next heard of travelling via France and England to Helsinki in Finland and thence to Moscow. In Moscow, he visited the US embassy and noisily declared that he was renouncing his American citizenship, whereupon he sought permission to become a Russian citizen and stay there. The Russians, who had been subject to a number of such defections by young men from the USA, were sceptical and decidedly unwilling to take him. His arguments were to no avail, but when he cut a wrist, necessitating hospital treatment, they reluctantly dispatched him a long way away, to Minsk, where he worked – with privileges – at a local factory. During his time in the Soviet Union, Oswald married a Russian girl, Marina, and they had a child.

44. Marina Oswald, photographed in Russia.

After about two years he suddenly had another change of heart and asked the US embassy for aid to return to America. With remarkable ease, this was provided for him, his wife and their child, and in due course they arrived back with no attention paid to them by US officials, other than one who was part of an organisation facilitating journeys from the port to home. No FBI, no CIA, no police officers. When Oswald became involved in the assassination of President Kennedy, his background was supposed to seal his fate: a man known to have communist connections, who had defected to Russia and returned to kill the president.

It was to the researchers' credit that – rather than remaining dazzled by the obvious implications of this 'lone-nut killer', as Oswald was painted by the Warren commissioners – they began to dig beyond the obvious to find a talented young man who may have been quite different from the portrayal of him in the report. They saw that it was far more likely he had been sent to Russia as part of the CIA infiltration programme. For clues to his being recruited into the CIA they had not far to look when they carefully, blow by blow, examined his career in the Marines. Certain of those with access to CIA records – such as they might be – claimed to find confirmation of his enlistment as an agent. Add to this evidence which was given to the Warren commissioners at the very beginning of their deliberations that he also had an identity with the FBI, and hints from correspondence between the US and embassy officials in Moscow that he might have been an agent of Naval Intelligence, and a picture of an out-and-out all-American spy emerges.

8

JACK RUBY

UNDERSTANDING THE ROLE OF JACK RUBY IS something against which quite a few researchers have pitted their wits. He certainly played a major role in proceedings immediately following the assassination of the president. What did he achieve? He removed Lee Harvey Oswald completely from any active role he might have played in the investigation and prevented him from contributing to our understanding of the events. Essentially, he made sure that the man who became the chief and only suspect never got into a court room to testify and defend himself.

45. Jack Ruby.

His stated reasons for killing Oswald? He was grieving for President Kennedy and anxious that Jacqueline Kennedy not be put through the torment of participating in a court case in which Lee Harvey Oswald was prosecuted. These were words which, on the face of it, were calculated to evoke sympathy from the millions who witnessed the brutal shooting on television. Not surprisingly, however, this cut no ice with those who found it hard to accept that a hard-boiled mafioso had been swayed by such sentiments. Ruby later admitted that the story had been the idea of his lawyer.

* * *

Ruby's background began to be poked into by researchers, though distinctly not the Warren Commission, and a very unsavoury picture was revealed. Born in 1911 as Jacob Rubenstein to an impoverished Jewish family, as a boy, attracted by the glamorous life he attached to Chicago mobsters, he ran errands for Al Capone, and as a young man became an official of the Scrap Iron and Junk Handlers Union. The union was suspected by the authorities of being a front for organised crime, and its books were at one point seized by the state of Illinois. In 1939, the founder of the union, Leon Cooke, a reputable lawyer, was shot dead. Fellow union official John Martin was believed to have been the murderer and Jacob Rubenstein complicit in the act. For this he is thought to have served a little over a year in jail. The Chicago Mob acquired the Scrap Iron and Junk Handlers Union and it was absorbed into the Teamsters union. It was declared to be a link between Mafia boss Jimmy Hoffa and the underworld by a Senate investigation.

Rubenstein changed his name to Jack Ruby after the Second World War and became part of a contingent numbering 25 dispatched by the Chicago Mafia to take over the slot machine, pinball and jukebox businesses in the surrounding states. He wound up running a nightclub, the Carousel Club, in Dallas, and by then his orbit had extended to drugs, prostitution and gambling.

There was more than a strong possibility here – if not a probability – that an interested party had sent Ruby to dispose of Oswald before he could reveal the truth. This, of course, would suggest the involvement of conspirators, and the Warren

Commission was always anxious to deal decisively with any suggestion of a conspiracy, which it was dedicated to oppose. When the commissioners were obliged to deal with the role of Jack Ruby, they were required to make a detailed investigation into his background, which they did not do. Instead, they sent their investigators to Chicago to find people to vouch for Ruby. This led to a Commission statement asserting, 'There is no evidence that he ever participated in organised criminal activity.' And, as a result of the questions asked by investigators, they declared, 'Virtually all Ruby's Chicago friends stated he had no close connection with organized crime . . . [and] several known Chicago criminals have denied any such liaison.' Incredibly, the commission accepted these friends' word for it and Ruby was found 'white as white can be'.

Since Jack Ruby was well known to members of the police department who frequented his club, the commission found it desirable to correct the 'misapprehension' that Ruby 'cultivated' members of the Dallas force. They said they 'found no evidence of any suspicious relationship between Ruby and any police officer'. This was another area in which the commission was clearly seen to be in serious error. An example of why they should not have been so blinkered when investigating Jack Ruby was given in an interview that the Warren Commission itself conducted with one of Ruby's girls, Nancy Perrin Rich, who was described as a bartender. She was questioned on this point by counsel and the transcript read:

Counsel: Are you saying that Jack Ruby told you that when any member of the police department came in, there was a standing order that you could serve them hard liquor?
Rich: That is correct . . .
Counsel: Did they pay?
Rich: Oh, no. Of course not.
Counsel: Was that an order, too, from Mr Ruby?
Rich: That was.

Nancy Rich added, 'I don't think there is a cop in Dallas that doesn't know Jack Ruby.'

The Warren Commission did not include her testimony in its report. All of which gives us another example of how selective the Commission was in accepting evidence, and, in the long run, how, at all costs, they were not going to allow their boat to be rocked by any suggestion of conspiracy.

Nancy Rich's testimony was confirmed by another hostess at the Carousel, and there was ample evidence forthcoming from elsewhere of Ruby's relationship with members of the police department. Ruby's generosity did not go unreciprocated. He received favours from the police department in return. Police records did not reveal that Ruby had been arrested for carrying a concealed weapon, permitting dancing after hours in the Carousel Club and offences related to liquor and traffic, not to mention violence towards others.

46. Ruby outside his Carousel Club. (Courtesy National Archives)

The findings of the Warren Commission regarding Jack Ruby stretched credulity to the limit and well beyond. They were, literally, unbelievable. And their anxiety to separate him from any conspiracy to kill the president indicated strongly that, in fact, that was the case.

* * *

Mystery surrounds Jack Ruby's willingness to kill Oswald. He was in and out of police headquarters for one reason or another from soon after the time Oswald was arrested, which indicated clear premeditation to eventually kill Oswald. It also strongly supported the idea that he was carrying out the instructions of another. Ruby was no kind of philanthropist. If he was under directions from someone else, it would appear he had been put on the spot and had no alternative but to shoot Oswald. The alternative, that he was offered the prospect of massive gains in return for putting his own life on the line and risking the electric chair, represented a gamble that Ruby just might have been crazy enough to take on, and, on that subject, it was reported that Ruby's finances took a huge turn for the better at that time. He was heavily in debt but visited the bank later in the day the president was killed, apparently withdrew about $7,000 and had about half that amount still in his pocket when he was arrested after shooting Lee Harvey Oswald.

About 30 years ago a story surfaced of a lawyer sent by his boss, a very highly placed Dallas citizen, to police headquarters on the day following the assassination to make an assessment of how tight the security was around Lee Harvey Oswald. He returned reporting that it was extremely lax and saying that when he had entered the elevator he had found himself sharing it with Lee Harvey Oswald, handcuffed to a police officer. This was, many years later, confirmed by the lawyer himself, John W. Currington. His boss was oil billionaire H.L. Hunt, who was said to be delighted with the news. The rest of the story was that that night he sent for Jack Ruby, although that remains unconfirmed. Ruby must have caused much heartburn to the conspirators, who eventually found themselves utterly dependent on a local hoodlum for the success of their removal of the man they saw as their 'troublesome president'. Ruby could have blown it all to save his own skin and he was not the type to trust with anything resembling a secret.

To add another dimension to events, in the brief time between Oswald's arrest and his transfer to the county jail, at which point Ruby leapt forward and shot him, a number of interesting phone calls had taken place. Some had carried threats to Oswald's life and ought to have resulted in an extreme tightening of security around Oswald. From Ruby's frequent visits to police headquarters, he would have been aware that, as others had observed, security for Oswald appeared not to be a top priority. There was speculation, therefore, that it was Ruby making those calls, by that time anxious to wriggle out of shooting Oswald, on the grounds that it would have become difficult if not impossible with the introduction of the right kind of security. The calls were, perhaps significantly, first made to the sheriff's office and the FBI, where Ruby's voice would likely not be so readily recognised, rather than to police headquarters, where many knew him. Even the Warren Commission noted the calls, made on Sunday, 24 November, in the early hours of the morning:

> Between 2.30 and 3.00 am, the local office of the FBI and the sheriff's office received calls from an unidentified man who warned that a committee had decided 'to kill the man who killed the President,' . . . The police department and ultimately Chief Curry were informed of both threats.

47. This appeared in a local newspaper **the day after** the calls were made.

There was more to it than was recounted by the Warren Commission, however. On the morning of 24 November a caller, presumably to the police department this time, asked who was on duty and when he was told it was Police Lieutenant Billy R. Grammer asked to speak to him. Refusing to give his name, the caller replied, 'I can't tell you that, but you know me,' and then, remarkably, detailed the plans to transfer Oswald, including the deployment of a decoy vehicle. 'You're going to have to make some other plans or we're going to kill Oswald right there in the basement.' All was duly reported, including a report intended for Chief Curry's desk. Later, as soon as he was wakened and told about the killing of Oswald, Grammer retrospectively recognised the voice on the phone as that of Jack Ruby. As we have said, it is realistic to speculate that Ruby's objective was to establish that it had become impossible to carry out his mission, about which he had had second thoughts. This call was made regardless of the risk of his voice being recognised, suggesting that he had grown even more anxious to make it impossible for him to carry out the task he had been set. The calls being ignored, Oswald was, in fact, murdered exactly as threatened in the basement of police headquarters while being transferred to the county jail.

48. Jack Ruby shoots Lee Harvey Oswald. (© Bob Jackson)

Of all researchers, few if any would disagree that Ruby's objective was to silence Oswald on behalf of the conspirators. Considering for a moment that it may have been in the conspirators' plan to eliminate the possibility of Oswald 'making his escape', taking the long view it may well have been the case that in quickly slipping away from the Book Depository building, Oswald, without realising it, had jumped the gun, literally. Could this possibly account for the premature APB marking him as wanted for questioning? Another opportunity to eliminate him arose when he was confronted by Officer Tippit. Though previously I never considered Tippit as being more than innocently drawn into the conspiracy, it may have been he knew just enough of what was happening for his purposes and those of the conspirators.

But then perhaps Oswald, a great deal brighter than he is usually given credit for, had by this time realised he was in a set-up and got out of the way of the situation faster than whoever was representing the conspirators could cope with. Finally, his arrest in the Texas Theatre, which represented another opportunity to remove him, may have answered more questions than at first realised. It has become known that CIA agents 'in trouble' went to the nearest movie house and waited for a contact or their handler to fish them out. That was precisely what Oswald did. It raises the question of how the police knew he was a CIA agent, however. The conspirators knew, but did they confide in the police department?

Another instance of Oswald's agent training showing came when he was approached by police officers bearing weapons in the theatre. He cried out, 'I am not resisting arrest,' for all in the theatre to hear and, in view of that action, it would have been extremely difficult for any kind of execution to have taken place. If Oswald was not supposed to survive to be placed in custody, this must have placed the entire conspiracy in jeopardy.

49. Crowds quickly form to witness the arrested Oswald being led out.
(Courtesy National Archives)

I still favour the theory that Oswald was meant to begin what he believed was his new mission to go back to Russia via Cuba for his CIA masters. This would have been the final part of the conspiracy achieved: for him to take off in a small aircraft, regardless of whether he made it to Cuba or not. Mind you, whatever was the case: as already stated, I would hazard a guess that from the moment of his arrest there were those anxiously nursing ulcers and being treated for nervous conditions at the prospect of having to rely on Jack Ruby to rescue the conspiracy.

* * *

50. Captain Will Fritz.

Given all the claims by Captain Will Fritz that he interviewed Oswald for a period said to total 12 hours without making notes, without a stenographer present and without a tape recorder running, it would bear speculation that Oswald spent a great deal of that time assuring Fritz that he was an agent of the CIA and attempting to obtain his support in contacting the Agency. This would link to a story which came out of police headquarters at the time about Oswald asking to make a phone call. When he gave his number to the switchboard, he was told that it was unobtainable. Another operator salvaged the scrap of paper with the telephone number written on it from the waste bin and, on checking it, found it was a Raleigh, South Carolina number. Raleigh was the location of an important CIA centre from which 'defectors' to Russia were run. Oswald never got his call to Raleigh. In any case, in his circumstances it is unlikely they would have owned him. That would have constituted standard practice for the CIA.

Returning to the conspirators' need to remove him, we are back to Jack Ruby. The big question is who sent him to do this? Whom did he represent when he shot and killed Lee Harvey Oswald in cold blood? Some fingers pointed to the CIA, some to members of the Establishment and in particular, perhaps, the oilmen. On reflection, another group with a vested interest emerges: certain members of the Dallas Police Department. Here I am not suggesting the department was involved per se, but, as I have indicated above, there are quite a few mysterious aspects relating to the assassination in general and the slaying of Lee Harvey Oswald in particular which would be explained by individuals being knowledgeable about the assassination and indeed party to it. And, all considered, it would seem that Ruby was compelled by someone able to pressure him – with knowledge and clout – and that must rate as a very strong indicator.

During my many years as a researcher, I have become acquainted with a number of cases being made for the blame to rest with one or other of the 'axe-to-grind' parties said to be so strongly anti-Kennedy as to wish to be rid of him: this, indeed, would include some regarded as being willing and able to actually dispose of him. This is a subject I do not neglect in upcoming chapters. But first more input on Oswald is required.

9

OSWALD AND THE CIA

THE WHOLE ISSUE OF CIA INVOLVEMENT IN THE assassination is further complicated at the point where we are faced with the almost certainty – complete certainty, most researchers would assert – that Lee Harvey Oswald was recruited into their ranks while serving in the Marines in Japan. The indications of this are more than outstanding and the claimed head-on evidence appears indisputable. I should make it clear that the following is derived from the work of a whole variety of researchers working for quite a number of years following the assassination, and, of course, my own investigations. In acknowledging this, I point out that this invaluable data did not necessarily appear in the order I show it. I have the benefit of being able to give it some kind of chronology.

To the other evidence must be added the testimony of third parties. Fletcher Prouty, for instance: Colonel L. Fletcher Prouty, who was chief of special operations for the joint chiefs of staff, made it clear that he was convinced Oswald had been recruited as a CIA agent. During the time of the Kennedy administration, he had been focal point officer between the CIA and the Pentagon. He was knowledgeable when it came to CIA recruitment at the Japanese Atsugi base, where Lee Harvey Oswald was stationed. He could, therefore, hardly be doubted when, in unvarnished terms, he declared, 'Lee Oswald was not an ordinary Marine. He was a Marine on cover assignment.'

51. Colonel L. Fletcher Prouty claimed Oswald was recruited by the CIA.

Indications of Oswald's connection with the CIA began to be obvious not only during his time at Atsugi but certainly at Iwakuni, and we observe there were strong indications of it very early in his Marine service, when he was stationed at Keesler Air Force Base at Biloxi, Mississippi. From Keesler he paid frequent weekend visits to New Orleans, a 100-mile journey. Retrospectively, these were easy to link to the time he spent there after his return from Russia, not to mention his particular undertakings in New Orleans and the people with whom he associated. What is more, around the time of his first visits to New Orleans the CIA were recruiting suitable young men as 'defectors' to the Soviet Union, where they would carry out espionage assignments.

At Keesler, as we have seen, Oswald became an aviation electronics operator. He was equipped to handle secret and sensitive information from this point. It is thought that his mysterious trips to New Orleans, which he strictly never discussed with anyone else, may have been to have his aptitude for secret assignments assessed.

This would all connect with what we know of his time in Japan, particularly at Iwakuni, where he became interested in all things

Russian and settled down to learn the language very seriously. We have already commented that while his fellows were puzzled by all this and brought it to the attention of their superiors, they displayed a distinct lack of concern.

While in Japan, Oswald had made an early application for repatriation on the grounds of his mother's hardship. At that point it was quite unrealistic for this to be considered, let alone granted. It was important that he had applied and was turned down, however, to illustrate to his fellows that he was not being given special treatment. It made it easier, and less obvious, to grant the request when it was repeated some time later.

There were other indications of his having been recruited by the CIA scattered throughout his Marine service. Many of these seemed in some ways trivial or of no consequence. One example, however, came when his request for release was granted. On packing his bags, he is known to have included a number of photographs he had taken at Atsugi, which apart from being a Marine base was also a base for the CIA. Furthermore it was one of the locations from which the 'spy in the sky' flights were made across Russia; the Soviets found these almost impossible to deal with because of the incredible height at which they flew. When Oswald was seeking permission to stay in Russia, he revealed he had secret information for them. Given the fact that not one of the 'spy in the sky' aircraft was ever touched previously, it seems pronouncedly odd that while Oswald was there one was shot down. The pilot, Gary Powers, survived and was later repatriated to the US, but the Russians made enormous capital out of their achievement. It was wondered whether Oswald had been given details of how they could achieve shooting down this elusive plane by his CIA mentors as a particular gift to present to Russia to support his position there. Coincidentally, it was said at the time that the plane's period of usefulness was coming to an end because of the development of satellite surveillance.

52. Gary Powers, spy plane pilot. He thought Oswald had passed details to the Russians. (Courtesy National Archives)

53. US dark secret: spy planes flew at incredibly high altitudes. (Courtesy National Archives)

Oswald was to spend the better part of two years in Russia. From Moscow he was relocated to Minsk. There he was given handsomely paid work at a radio and electronics factory and a desirable apartment to live in. It is thought that he obtained a wealth of useful information for his CIA masters while in Russia, and when he – or his masters – decided enough was enough, he quickly made the necessary applications to be returned to the United States and they swiftly facilitated his return.

When Oswald arrived in Moscow, he had made a noisy demand (the louder the better for the KGB listening bugs) of Richard E. Snyder, the senior consul at the US embassy, that his US citizenship should be revoked, since he intended becoming a citizen of the USSR. Was it by luck or with prior instruction that Snyder had never processed this request? It made it much easier for Oswald to press for repatriation. With the minimum of fuss and the greatest of alacrity, his request was granted and he sailed home with Marina and their baby daughter.

When he arrived back in the United States, was he surrounded by police? Was he questioned by FBI agents? CIA agents, perhaps? Even besieged by reporters? The answer to all of these, very markedly, is no. There was no one there to meet him or question him at any level. No one except a lone representative of a charitable organisation prepared to help with the cost of travel for him and his family across the country to his home. His entire reception, therefore, was Spas T. Raiken of Traveler's Aid of New York. There may have been a very simple explanation for the apparent lack of interest in a returning defector. It is strongly believed he had been debriefed on the ship on his journey home. The absence of reporters would be easily explained if announcements were simply not released and therefore not available to be picked up for the press agency wires.

What then would be the future of a CIA agent quietly returned from the USSR? What happened next is very revealing to those with eyes to see and ears to hear.

10

A CLOSER LOOK AT OSWALD

LEE HARVEY OSWALD CERTAINLY DID NOT ADVERTISE his connections with the CIA. Nor did he reveal his link to the FBI and possibly Naval Intelligence, in both of which he is thought to have served at the same time as the CIA.

When he returned home from Russia he became close friends with George de Mohrenschildt and his wife, Jeanne. De Mohrenschildt was, by rights, a White Russian count and was entitled to the title of baron, often given to him. He was also a man with a shadowy background, notably suspected of being in the employ of the CIA and of having been involved in the training of recruits destined for the Bay of Pigs invasion. His past, long before this, had made him a suspicious character anyway. He was believed to have served the Nazis in the Second World War on the one hand, and had more recently had connections with oil billionaires H.L. Hunt and Clint Murchison on the other. Much taken with Oswald's command of the Russian language, he introduced him to Russian immigrants in the locality. It seems indicated that, if not Oswald's appointed CIA handler, he was nevertheless following out CIA instructions to keep Oswald 'in his care'.

It seemed almost inevitable that Oswald would eventually take up residence in New Orleans. He became all things Cuban when in New Orleans. In other words, he was being – in CIA parlance – 'sheep-dipped' for a new assignment. With hindsight, of course, we may ask what kind of assignment they had in mind. Those with whom he associated had long FBI and CIA connections. It was at this point that he formed a new chapter of the Fair Play for Cuba Committee. It attracted but one member: himself, under the name of A.J. Hidell, but it gave him an excuse for handing out leaflets for that organisation on the streets of New Orleans. Some of the literature he handed out gave his home address, but not all. Some bore his Post Office box address; this was strictly illegal, since he was using a pseudonym instead of his own name, which was registered to that box. Perhaps, however, this was an indication of the influence of those with whom he was then working. Other FPCC literature gave an address in Camp Street. The Camp Street address, number 544, was also that of the office of Guy Banister Associates, which was surprising since Guy Banister was likely Oswald's CIA handler in New Orleans and the location of Banister's office was extremely interesting.

54. Baron de Mohrenschildt.

55. Oswald handing out leaflets. (Courtesy National Archives)

The office was located in a corner building. Around the corner from 544 Camp the street name became Lafayette and the address of the first building was 531. It would be surprising if an entrance from that Lafayette Street address did not lead to Banister's office, since it was simply another side of the same building. A little further down Lafayette Street was the William B. Reily Coffee Co., where Oswald found work. Reily was strongly anti-Castro and the anti-Castro Cuban Revolutionary Council had offices at 554 Camp Street. Another close neighbour was the Office of Naval Intelligence, just a bit further down Lafayette Street. Another little subterfuge on the part of the FBI was unearthed when they reported to the Warren Commission on Oswald's Fair Play for Cuba connections. He operated his 'one-man band' from an office one floor above Banister's, with the Camp Street address, but rather than reveal that link the FBI provided the Lafayette Street address. Oswald's connection with Banister was to be a dark secret.

When Oswald formed his Fair Play for Cuba chapter in some literature he used his home address and in others the Camp Street address, where it appeared he had an arrangement with Banister. Later, just to confuse matters, he made contact with the anti-Castro organisation and offered his help to them. With hindsight, the suggestion must be that this was clear evidence that Oswald's handler – Guy Banister, by all indications – was preparing him for a new CIA assignment which necessitated connections with organisations related to Cuba. The question is, was it a genuine assignment or was it all a cover for setting him up as the patsy for the murder of President Kennedy?

Before he returned to live in Dallas, Oswald made a mysterious trip to Mexico City, where, it seemed, he was seeking a visa to go to Cuba, from where he was to travel once again to Soviet Russia. The confusion which occurred in Mexico is well documented, though the facts supposedly confirmed in the documentation are wide open to doubt. Suffice to say that though Oswald was said to have produced all his credentials, perhaps including 'infiltrating' the anti-Castro movement, as well as his forming of a new chapter of the Fair Play for Cuba Committee, his application was refused.

Whether it ever was Oswald actually making the application or – as seems far more likely – a CIA agent substitute, he could not have it. But, of course, this would have to be the case if he was scheduled for Dallas and his role in the assassination. Interestingly, with regard to a necessary call at the Russian embassy in Mexico City, the staff recounted that 'Oswald' spoke to them in 'halting' Russian. Oswald's Russian, as was confirmed by de Mohrenschildt, was almost flawless. All this does throw light on what the CIA was out to achieve, as we shall see.

56. 'Hands off Cuba' leaflets handed out by Oswald.
Note the addresses appended.

Back home, Oswald's marriage to Marina was not an easy affair. They rowed and disagreed, but while in most marriages a resolution in agreeing to differ was reached, in this case it appeared to result in Marina moving in with her daughter to the home of Ruth Paine, though that might have been part of Oswald's preparations for his planned absence from home. Ruth Paine's father had links with de Mohrenschildt and Ruth herself was eager to improve her

Russian, her stated reason for welcoming Marina and her children. The apparent de Mohrenschildt circle now seemed closed. But whose side was de Mohrenschildt on? Regardless of being CIA, was he representing the CIA proper or those in the CIA who had formed a group to eradicate the president? Had he rowed in with those plotting to kill Kennedy, using Oswald as the patsy, or was he being duped also?

* * *

It may be of some importance that when Lee Harvey Oswald and family returned home from Russia they first went to live in Fort Worth and were persuaded to move to Dallas by George de Mohrenschildt. To try to make sense out of the de Mohrenschildt connection, however, it is required that we jump a little forward to the time of the House Assassinations Committee in the '70s. At that time it became known that he had written an unpublished book, entitled *I Am a Patsy! I Am a Patsy!*, in which, while not implicating himself in the assassination, he had named names of FBI and CIA agents who, up to this point, were distinctly to be protected, not to be implicated under any circumstances.

De Mohrenschildt also claimed he was secretly drugged. Jeanne, his wife, asserted that in the 1970s a doctor whom he was seeing for bronchitis gave her husband therapy for two or three hours at a time and also injections. De Mohrenschildt was eventually committed to a mental institution and on the day he agreed to be questioned by the House Committee he was found dead of a gunshot wound to his mouth. Declared a suicide, his wife challenged this. The question revolving around this is does his death in any way support the theory that he was part of a CIA plan to kill President Kennedy? Was he prepared to come clean? It might have meant that the material he had acquired of the kind he had put in his book he was now prepared to make public. Did he really decide neither to speak out nor to publish? Was it the case that those who, by that time, were controlling the 'fallout' had decided he must not speak?

One way or another, it would seem likely that de Mohrenschildt had become another statistic in the count of those who were disposed of by the conspirators to keep their secrets. And we know there were many.

* * *

Lee Harvey Oswald was certainly not a layabout and neither did he look for handouts. He seemed always to be in employment. From October 1962 to April 1963 he worked at Jaggars-Chiles-Stovall, a photographic establishment which carried out work for the US Defense Department. Upon his move to New Orleans he obtained a job there with the Reily Coffee Co., for which he worked in the summer months of 1963.

57. Earlene Roberts' boarding house, where Oswald had a room.
(© JoAnne Connaughton)

Oswald, who had brought his wife and family to live in New Orleans, now had to return to Dallas. When he separated from his wife he went to live in 'digs'. He took a room in Earlene Roberts' boarding house on North Beckley. It was from here that he travelled daily to work at the Texas School Book Depository, usually by way of lifts in the car of a fellow employee, since he himself was not a driver. Earlene Roberts recalled observing a very interesting occurrence which took place on the day of the assassination. Oswald had returned home in his shirtsleeves about half an hour after the time of the assassination. After donning a jacket, he dashed off again just a few moments later, zipping it up as he went. Immediately prior to this, Mrs Roberts had observed that a police car – she gave the number – had pulled up outside her house and the driver had pipped his horn twice, upon which Oswald left quickly. She saw him next, briefly, at the nearby bus stop, but he soon disappeared. Had he had been signalled to proceed elsewhere?

58. Was this the police car Mrs Roberts saw? (Courtesy National Archives)

The police department said the car bearing the number Mrs Roberts quoted could not have been the one she saw, since it was deployed in the Dealey Plaza area. Earlene Roberts suggested other numbers it might have been, but the police department insisted there were no police cars in the vicinity of her house. Mrs Roberts soon fell victim to a heart attack and died before she might have contributed more about Oswald in general and the police car incident in particular.

After leaving his digs, Oswald was next said to be in the Oak

Cliff district, near to where Police Officer J.D. Tippit was killed. By all accounts, it was at this point that everything in the plan to kill the president went completely awry. To explain this, it is necessary for me to render an outline of what I believe, as a consequence of my many years researching the assassination, talking to other researchers and reading what they have written. This forms Chapter 34.

Meanwhile, our examination of who and what Lee Harvey Oswald was continues with him under the name of Alek Hidell.

11

ALEK JAMES HIDELL

LEE HARVEY OSWALD ADOPTED A PSEUDONYM. IT was Alek James Hidell, which he added to his New Orleans Post Office box and other things. Interesting suggestions have been made about why he chose this particular name – possibly after a friend in the Marines – but that is not as important as why he felt he needed a pseudonym in the first place.

It is noted that all agents working under cover had their mail delivered to a Post Office box. This appears to have been standard procedure. The name Alek Hidell did not surface on the day Lee Harvey Oswald was arrested. Sergeant Gerald Lynn Hill, a Dallas police officer, was present at the arrest of Oswald at the Texas Theatre. It was while he was at the scene of the murder of Officer Tippit that Hill was said to have heard that an identity card bearing the name of Alek Hidell had been found in a billfold said to have been picked up nearby.

59. Marines identity card for A.J. Hidell. (Courtesy National Archives)

It has been established that Oswald used the pseudonym Alek Hidell during the time he spent in Russia. That is hardly surprising, since with a Western name such as his he would have been unnecessarily conspicuous. It is also known that he used the name when he placed an order with a Chicago mail-order store for the purchase of a Mannlicher-Carcano rifle and again when he bought a handgun. Interestingly, with this latter order he included a holster and ammunition, but before posting it he deleted all but the handgun. For those accepting that Oswald was a CIA agent, this lends support. It was likely he ordered the weapons on the instructions of his masters, and it is realistic to speculate that, though he thought the holster and ammunition necessary, he did not have the authority to include them in his purchase. In fact, however, he possessed both at a later stage. He received these purchases in his postal box, PO Box 2915 Dallas. Strict Post Office regulations stated that the mail delivered to any box had to be addressed to the person whose name was registered for it. In the case of Oswald, his was the only name registered for 2915, which raises the question of how the rifle and handgun were claimed to have been delivered to that box, though there is no doubt that was the delivery address attached to the orders. Post Office Inspector Harry D. Holmes, who was revealed also to be in the pay of the FBI, was quoted in an interview with the *New York Times* as declaring that 'no person other than Oswald was authorized to receive mail'. This was shortly after the time of the assassination, but when Holmes appeared before the Warren Commission the following year, he said he could neither confirm nor deny that the name 'Hidell' had been added to the list of those permitted to receive mail. He said that the documents which would have clarified whether this was the case had by then, according to regulations, been destroyed. It appears Mr Holmes did not know his regulations, which stated that such files should be retained for two years after the box was closed. Had it been established that Oswald was the only name registered for his box, a whole new investigation would have been triggered. Agents regularly used Post Office boxes for receiving mail and Oswald knew the regulations. When he opened a Post Office box in New Orleans, 'Hidell' was clearly entered as a recipient.

The name Hidell was used again by Lee Harvey Oswald while he was in New Orleans, where, having made contact with the national headquarters of that organisation, he formed the New Orleans chapter of the Fair Play for Cuba Committee. This was during the period in which it was believed he was being 'sheep-dipped' in preparation for a new assignment either in Cuba or again in Russia. We are not sure which, but he purported to be applying for a visa to enter Cuba and then to proceed to Russia. This episode is dealt with in more detail in a later chapter. The Fair Play for Cuba Committee, as we have seen, enlisted but one supporter, Alek Hidell, and is believed to have been formed solely to provide Oswald with credentials for entry into Cuba. If this was so, it was underlined by his offer to assist the opposition, the anti-Castro movement in New Orleans, for when he was found on the streets of the city distributing pamphlets for Fair Play for Cuba by a leader of the rebel organisation, he was embroiled in a fight and arrested. This, no doubt, was exactly what he wanted, for it attracted much attention locally, including that of the newshounds at the New Orleans television station, which featured him talking about himself and passers-by describing the incident, providing a big plus in his application to enter Cuba.

60. Oswald leafleting again, but the opposition was watching.
(Courtesy National Archives)

The entire proceedings in New Orleans appear to have been under the direction of CIA agents in that city and it seems clear that their intention was not to prepare him for a new mission to either Cuba or Russia: he was being prepared for his role as a patsy in the conspiracy to kill the president. The agents showed their hand when they deliberately fouled up his visa application in Mexico City, where he had travelled especially to seek the entry document, and about which we have more to reveal in a later chapter. Their plans were for him to be back in Dallas and working in the Book Depository building at the time the assassination was carried out.

It is on the day of the assassination that we hear again of Alek Hidell. Several Military Intelligence personnel were in Dallas that day and when Lieutenant Colonel Robert Jones, operations officer for the 112th Military Intelligence Group, wanted information on events, they obliged with what they knew. They told him that Alek Hidell had been arrested by the Dallas Police Department. On checking their files, they found one under the name of A.J. Hidell. The events relating to Alek Hidell that day produced mysteries all round. For one thing, Military Intelligence did not volunteer that they had such a file, which indicated the name as being an alias for Lee Harvey Oswald and had apparently been kept updated. The file and its contents remained secret, and its existence did not come to light until the time of the House Assassinations Committee in the '70s. By that time, it was reported, it had been routinely destroyed.

Then questions arise about how an identity card was stated as found on Oswald's person on the day of the assassination. It was said that after his arrest he was searched and a Navy Selective Service card showing Oswald's photograph and bearing the name of Alek James Hidell was found among his possessions by the Dallas Police Department. But then the arresting officer, Officer Bentley, said that Oswald did not reply when asked his name. He told how he had to go through his belongings to establish his identity, but no mention was made of uncertainty as to whether he was Oswald or Hidell, which would have been the case had two identity cards been on his person. In fact, the Hidell identity was never mentioned on the day of his arrest: it was first spoken of the next day. This introduces questions relating to how the military personnel quoted Hidell as having been arrested the day before, and whether the Hidell identity card was in fact planted among Oswald's possessions in order to establish Oswald quickly as the purchaser of the 'assassin's rifle'. It will be recalled that the Mannlicher-Carcano was 'found' by an officer on the sixth floor of the School Book Depository building soon after the president had been assassinated. It was promptly identified as having been purchased by Oswald and the paperwork confirming the purchase from Klein's of Chicago obtained almost as if by magic. It suggests that the whole thing was part of the conspiracy and that Oswald was the designated patsy from long before the assassination took place. It also suggests that officers at Dallas Police Department were either party to the conspiracy or had been roped into it, 'evidence' having been provided beforehand. That, of course, would also explain how the APB seeking Oswald came to be transmitted roughly 15 minutes after the shooting of the president had ceased.

I have not overlooked that 'Oswald's wallet', in which the Hidell identity card was said to have been discovered, was found at the spot where Officer Tippit was killed. (See next chapter.) This, from the outset, also looked decidedly fishy and suggested Oswald was being set up as the patsy in this killing too.

12

WHO KILLED TIPPIT?

61. Officer J.D. Tippit.

WE HAVE ALREADY HEARD AN ACCOUNT OF HOW Officer J.D. Tippit approached Lee Harvey Oswald and the story adopted by the Warren Commission that he turned and shot him dead before fleeing the scene. There were vital clues, like the cartridge cases found at the scene, which could not have come from Oswald's gun; there is a great deal of confusion in the accounts rendered by eyewitnesses and those who observed possible and probable participants in the killing. It is most certainly not the clear-cut story adopted by the Warren Commission.

62. Tippit's car. (Courtesy National Archives)

63. In front of Tippit's car, blood can be seen on the ground.
(Courtesy National Archives)

The bullets recovered from Tippit's body plus the cartridge cases
picked up at the scene of the shooting ought to have given conclusive
proof, if not of who killed the officer then of whether or not it was

Oswald. The confusion in the police department could easily merit a chapter of its own. There was apparently jiggery-pokery galore over the bullets fired. Instances of this abound. The Warren Commission declared that four bullets had killed Tippit. A Dallas police captain addressing the American Society of Newspaper Editors said that the officer had been shot three times. And when a submission was made by Dallas Police Department to Cortlandt Cunningham, the FBI firearms expert, it consisted of one bullet. Cunningham, testifying to the Warren Commission, told them they said the one bullet was the only one they had or was recovered. Sent back to the Dallas Police Department on the matter, he later testified that they had 'found in their files that they actually had three other bullets'. The remaining bullets were not dug out of the police files until March 1964, four months after the murder took place. Congressman Boggs asked his fellow commissioners the highly pertinent question 'What proof do you have, though, that these are the bullets?' A particularly good question since the identification marks 'JMP', placed on the shell cases by Officer J.M. Poe when they were picked up, could not be found later. No answer was ever given to Congressman Boggs and no one ever challenged the Dallas Police Department about its apparent misleading of the FBI over vital evidence.

64. Congressman Hale Boggs asked a very awkward question. He confessed to misgivings about the Warren findings. He died in a plane crash.

It is interesting that the Dallas Police later went elsewhere, to Illinois, to find a ballistics expert, who eventually declared he had found that one bullet had 'sufficient individual characteristics' to 'lead him' to the conclusion that it was 'fired from the same weapon that fired the [test] projectiles', which was presumably Oswald's gun. Tenuous to say the least, but it was the nearest Dallas Police ever came to establishing a link between the bullets and Oswald's gun. It is also interesting to consider why the shell cases were at the scene of the crime in the first place. Oswald's revolver did not eject empty cases. They had to be emptied out, and when he was arrested his gun was fully loaded, whereas witness Domingo Benavides saw the cases being thrown to the ground by the killer. It might be said that there was not a better way for the killer to leave his calling card behind, but a claim was made that another 'find' at the scene was the wallet containing Oswald's identification! Hard to believe?

* * *

At one time, if I had been asked whether Tippit was part of the conspiracy my answer would have been a simple no, but I confess that more recent evidence now tends to persuade me to say that he at least knew something. I doubt that he was told the whole story. I have never believed that Officer Tippit was part of the overall conspiracy to kill the president, and I still do not believe this was the case. I see evidence, however, which would indicate that he was given a limited brief and knew what was going on. Hitherto, I had believed that he was a completely innocent party involved by another police officer.

The other officer was a man named Roscoe White. A man answering to the description of Roscoe White was seen at the scene of the Tippit shooting. Who was Roscoe White? As briefly as it may be stated, he had been employed as a CIA agent before joining the ranks of the Dallas police force a few months prior to the time of the assassination. It is quite possible that he was placed there as part of the conspirators' plan. He, no doubt, had many friends and contacts among serving agents and whatever the case he would be a likely candidate for recruitment to the assassination plan. If I am right, he was asked to find someone among his new friends in the police department willing to participate in giving a ride to a young CIA agent who had to get to Red Bird airfield to catch a plane and who, without help, would likely get tangled up in traffic en route.

65. Roscoe White, a CIA man who had recently joined Dallas Police Department.

White died in an industrial accident in 1971, but a further indication of his involvement in the assassination came in the form of his widow's claim that he had left a diary which revealed he had been one of the snipers shooting at the president **and that he had killed Officer Tippit**. The diary, if it existed, is suspect. It was said to have been taken by FBI agents who never returned it. The description of it has to raise doubts about its authenticity, however. It was written, or written in part, in a fibre-tip pen, a variety of pen which had not reached popularity at the time Roscoe might have been using it. A mention of Watergate in the diary also raises doubts, since the term was not coined until two years after White's death. I spoke to the Reverend Jack Shaw, a minister to whom, claimed his widow, Geneva, he had made a full confession on his deathbed. The Reverend Shaw confirmed that he had confessed to killings carried out for the CIA in the US and in foreign countries, but, he said, there was no mention of killing President Kennedy or Tippit.

It is interesting that Roscoe's son Ricky claimed that his father had been killed by the CIA. An insurance assessor, David Perry, told me he found no evidence of foul play, though this, of course, carries no guarantees of innocence on the part of the Agency. And it would likely have suited the conspirators to get rid of a key facilitator, especially one who had bungled the job. Then the question arises, did Geneva White and her son pick the idea of stories about Roscoe's assassination involvement 'out of the blue'? Possible, and it would have been very profitable, too, had it achieved any degree of authenticity. I know that Oliver Stone, who was in Dallas making his famed movie *JFK* at the time, was offered the story for half a million dollars by a representative of the Whites. Not surprisingly, he declined.

But why invent a story of Roscoe's involvement in the killing of both JFK and Tippit? To many of the people in what was known as 'the hate capital of Dixie', had he killed the president he would have become a folk hero. But as the killer of Officer Tippit, a cop-killer, he would have become the scum of the earth. The Roscoe family was likely to have been more aware of this than I. On the other hand, if the Whites knew that Roscoe was part of the conspiracy to kill President Kennedy, they might just have been anxious to make some money from the knowledge. We must return to known events, however, and I must say why I can accept that Roscoe White was the likely killer of J.D. Tippit.

* * *

Tippit had been sitting in his car with, probably, a hefty degree of uncertainty about what he was involved in. He had no doubt been listening to broadcasts which informed him of events in

Dealey Plaza and here he was, stuck out in the sticks, alone, when everyone else was downtown. Perhaps he had not been informed that the young CIA man he was to ferry to Red Bird airfield would be the chief suspect in the assassination of the president, and here he was about to be ensnared in all he had been listening to. He knew about events elsewhere from his radio, though, and very soon he was listening to an APB released by the police department in which Oswald was described as wanted for questioning in relation to the murder of the president. A classic piece of mistiming on the part of the conspirators, it would seem. Tippit, however, whose sole job was to get Oswald to Red Bird airfield as soon as possible, no doubt began to wonder at this point how deep was his commitment to all this, especially as the description of Oswald fitted the young CIA man he was designated to pick up.

Getting out of his car and confronting Oswald, he was merely carrying out his duty. It was probably at that moment, however, that Lee Harvey Oswald realised what was happening. Why did Tippit not simply open the car door and invite him in? Oswald no doubt reasoned that the officer would have to have some reason for approaching him to ask questions.

Mrs Helen Markham, testifying very uncertainly to the Warren Commission, gave a fair description of Oswald as the killer of Tippit, as we have recounted in detail elsewhere. Others rendered descriptions of the killer not consistent with the clothing Oswald had been wearing and describing a man with dark hair. At a later date, incidentally, Mrs Markham gave another account of her witness experience to an FBI agent whose name was Odum; this time she said that the man she saw was white, about 18, black hair, red complexion, wearing tan shoes, a tan jacket and dark trousers. Whoever she was describing this time, it certainly was not Lee Harvey Oswald. Unbelievably, later still, she gave a telephone interview to author/lawyer Mark Lane, writing *Rush to Judgment*, a posthumous defence for Oswald which had been requested by his mother. This time, Mrs Markham described Tippit's killer as short, on the heavy side and with slightly bushy hair. To illustrate how unreliable she was as a witness, however, in further testimony to the Warren Commission she denied ever speaking to Mark Lane and even when he played her a taped recording of his interview with her, she claimed the voice she was hearing was not hers.

66. Officer Tippit was slain close to this junction. (© JoAnne Connaughton)

To those carrying out a detailed study of the murder of Officer Tippit, a review of statements by those claiming to have seen the killing or have seen an individual fleeing the scene supports that there were a number of witnesses who saw different people. A complete list will not be found in the Warren Report, since the commissioners were both selective and devious enough to feature those supporting the line they wished to take: that Lee Harvey Oswald killed Tippit. The Mrs Markham testimony, even by itself, is ample evidence of that. It is extremely interesting, however, that in at least three reports describing Tippit's killer his hair is said to have been 'black wavy' or black bushy', and he is said to have been 'kind of short and on the heavy side' in at least two. It was certainly not Oswald being described. Roscoe White, on the other hand, who was thin on top, wore a bushy black wig.

I see Roscoe White being there to monitor the pick-up he had arranged. He was concealed until he saw that things were going wrong. He realised Oswald would not get his ride to Red Bird airfield, the special task White was to manage, which would give him much pain from those who had given him the job to do. More than that, he saw a loose-cannon cop who might tell all he knew and cause mayhem to the conspiracy. Tippit knew too much and he was killed to keep him silent. By this time, Lee Harvey Oswald had gone to follow out the procedure adopted by agents who found themselves in trouble. He went to the nearest cinema, the Texas Theatre, to await contact from his handler. Instead, he was very soon in the hands of the police, believed by some to have been waiting for him in their car around the corner from the cinema. If that is true, it suggests all kinds of treachery. Further skulduggery is evidenced if we consider the claim by an eyewitness that he saw a man being brought out of the back door of the cinema and bundled into a police car. This man was later astonished to see newspaper photographs showing Oswald being brought out of the front entrance of the cinema. But then stories abound of a 'second Oswald' being involved in the Tippit affair. Exactly how and why, we are not sure, but author John Armstrong made a valuable contribution to our knowledge of this subject.

Mark it: whatever went on in Oak Cliff that day, this was the point where the conspirators' plan went terribly wrong.

13

THE RIDDLE OF GENERAL WALKER

IT MAY FAIRLY BE SAID THAT GENERAL WALKER appeared to invite trouble. An avid right-winger, he was recalled from active duty and fired by President Kennedy for circulating blatantly right-wing and anti-Kennedy literature among his troops. Lee Harvey Oswald attempted to kill General Walker, the Warren Commission claimed.

It appears that the Warren Commission had one intention and one intention only in including the events surrounding General Walker in their considerations. They wanted to blacken the character of Lee Harvey Oswald and make him more acceptable as the stony-hearted villain who went on to murder the president. In their anxiety to achieve this, they claimed that he had attempted to take the life of Major General Edwin Anderson Walker in a shooting incident at his home, and they introduced evidence of sorts to prove their case. Corroboration for this was very hard to find. It is true that Marina, Oswald's wife, agreed that he had admitted the shooting, but at that time Marina would have agreed with anything, her position as a Russian national was so insecure. Frankly, this was not in any way to be relied upon.

When it came to actual evidence, things became difficult. The bullet from the shooter's rifle was found by the police department, recorded as a 30.06 missile and reported by the media as such. The Warren Commission, however, ignored this and now said it was a 6.5 missile, shot from the same gun which had killed the president. How they got away with gross distortion of evidence and determination to find everything they could to pin on Oswald is hard to believe. Even General Walker protested that it was not a 6.5 missile that had been fired at him, but all to no avail. This is a clear instance of obvious inconsistencies being ignored, and inconsistencies, it would appear, created by the commission itself.

Reasons why someone might want to take a potshot at General Walker were not difficult to find. He was an abrasive character. When President Kennedy was engaged in his desegregation programme at the University of Mississippi in 1962, who was there to oppose it but General Walker! Walker relied on his aides for protection, which brings us back to the shooting. On the night of 8 April 1963 Robert Alan Surrey, an aide, observed two men acting suspiciously. They were looking in the windows of the general's house. Surrey saw them getting away in a Ford sedan and decided to follow them, but he lost them in traffic. Another aide saw a 1957 Chevrolet drive slowly round the house in a suspicious manner, so there was no doubt the general was informed of his house being under surveillance.

67. General Walker: extremely right wing.

It was on Wednesday, 10 April that the shot from a rifle came. The bullet narrowly missed Walker, who finished up covered in plaster dust but nothing worse. A young neighbour, Kirk Coleman, aged 14, heard the shot and dashed to see what was happening. He saw two men racing towards parked cars; one drove off in a Ford and the other in another car. It is to be noted that there was no mention of a third man being present and Oswald could not drive a car. No one was described dashing off to catch a bus.

When General Walker tried to talk to Kirk Coleman he found that the boy had been forbidden to talk to officials. He had been silenced. It should be said, in fairness, that though General Walker attempted to acquaint the Warren Commission of all this, no attempts were made to investigate. One uncontroversial fact remained, however. A picture of Walker's backyard showed up. Purported to be a picture taken on the night when Walker was shot at, it showed a car, a 1957 Chevrolet, with the rear number plate in view. This photograph was said by FBI agents to have been found in Oswald's possessions, though when it was shown to Marina this was something she could not corroborate. She saw the photo again at a later point, when giving evidence to the Warren Commission; she pointed out a significant black scar which had not been there before. The black scar, seemingly caused by a pencil or some such having been thrust through the print, conveniently obliterated the number plate. The implication of this was, clearly, that the obliteration had taken place when it was in the hands of the police, to whom the FBI had given it.

But then who was going to give any credence to what Marina said? Admittedly she lied, contradicted previous statements and was evasive in her answers. As we said previously, she was a Russian national, extremely unpopular in the US during the Cold War, and fearful about her future. If she had been sent back to Russia, she would have had a difficult time when the USSR was resolute in showing a clean pair of hands in relation to the death of President Kennedy. But in fact she was right about the photograph being mutilated while in police hands. Chief Jesse Curry, in a book he wrote on the assassination, showed a picture of items he claimed were found in Oswald's possession. *Among the items shown there was the photograph of the rear of General Walker's house, with the parked 1957 Chevrolet showing and no black scar obliterating the number plate.* Unfortunately, in the print of the print the number was not readable.

This chapter is important for several reasons. It illustrates the determination of the Warren Commission to blacken Oswald's character at all costs, underlined by the fact that when General Walker protested that the bullet recovered from his house was a 30.06 and not a 6.5 he was ignored. It also shows two things about Oswald's wife, Marina. First, her testimony was often unreliable, but there was very good reason for her anxiety to please those in authority and her reluctance and uncertainty over many of her answers. But then the picture of the car in General Walker's backyard proved that this was not always the case.

68. The bullet fired at General Walker. The Warren Commission changed its description to pin the shooting on Oswald.

The details included in this chapter, it should be said, derive from various sources. It is obvious that some of the research was carried out during the time the Warren Commission was still at work and the rest soon afterwards. It demonstrates a zeal for accuracy and a sense of fair play for Oswald. At that time, researchers generally did not doubt that Oswald played a role in shooting the president, though they were seeking evidence of a conspiracy. But they were not prepared to see distortions of evidence entered into the Warren account, apparently for the sole purpose of blackening Oswald's character, without a challenge.

14

INVESTIGATION: THE
DEVELOPING MOVEMENT

THE PROBLEMS EXPERIENCED BY THE FIRST CRITICS were compounded, to a great degree, by the attitude adopted by the media at large. There was little point approaching the news industry as represented by the press, television and radio, which looked upon those who found shortcomings and inaccuracies in the Warren Report with disdain. These were judged to be persons disloyal to the government and to America, and encouraging them was strictly taboo. What they might write was classed along with the scandal-mongering 'yellow press' and what they might say was to be ignored. Any publisher tempted to put their words into print was not long in realising that this risked the good name of the company by appearing to go along with the ideas of those who challenged the Warren findings.

For those who found it impossible to get a book deal, the alternative was to self-publish, which was often taken as an indication that established houses did not think their writings worth putting out. Harold Weisberg, that giant among the first critics, became a pioneer in self-publication of his work, defeating those opposed to allowing a voice to those who believed they had not been given the truth. He was turned down by US publishers and spurned by British houses, but his self-published books found their way slowly but surely into the hands of a public which had begun to think there was something worth looking into in what these persistent people were claiming. His books, when later taken up by publishers, sold like hot cakes; people were spellbound by the work he had done and the discoveries he had made.

Even when the Warren Report was published, ten months after the assassination, the early investigators were further handicapped by the fact that it had no index. This meant that, for students wishing to derive material from it for use in new investigations and studies, it was extremely difficult to use. The report and its hearings and findings totalled 26 volumes and 10,000,000 words. Sylvia Meagher came to the rescue here, writing a 'Subject Index to the Report and Hearings and Exhibits', which opened up the report to anyone who wanted to use it for serious study. This incredible undertaking was considered by some to be the most awesome accomplishment of the investigation. Sylvia Meagher would also write *Accessories After the Fact*, published in 1967, a greatly respected contribution to what, by then, was becoming a recognisable movement to discover the truth behind the assassination. With the Warren material unlocked, the floodgates began to open, and the volume of new output on the subject of the assassination resulted in this becoming an acceptable area into which publishers were prepared – perhaps compelled – to move.

One of the first in with a book, even before the report was finished, was Thomas G. Buchanan. Putting pen to paper in an outspoken book which was published in 1964, he had no knowledge of the workings of the Warren Commission or the content of its report other than what had been released to the newspapers. He called his book *Who Killed Kennedy?*, and it is from Buchanan's book, with acknowledgement, that I deemed it appropriate to borrow the title I give to this one. It seems fitting to account for 50 years of investigation with a title which has been associated with the movement from the start. It is also appropriate, incidentally, since Buchanan's book was published in Britain, by Secker & Warburg.

Another pioneer critic was Penn Jones Jr, who ran a small newspaper in Texas. He wrote and self-published a book, *Forgive My Grief*, followed by three other volumes and a newsletter. What he wrote was widely read, far beyond the borders of Texas.

Harold Weisberg's first book, *Whitewash*, was a head-on attack on the Warren Report. It appeared in February of 1965, a few months after the Warren Report itself was published. At that time it was regarded as unthinkable that government agencies were concealing the truth. The very idea of challenging the government on this subject was strictly taboo. It brought no involvement of the media and publishers did not want to know. Unable to find a publisher in the United States or in London, Weisberg published the work himself. This book was followed by *Whitewash II*, which targeted the FBI and Secret Service, *Photographic Whitewash*, *Oswald in New Orleans* (*Whitewash III*), *Whitewash IV* and *Post Mortem*.

Weisberg, originally a farmer, was an investigative reporter, Senate investigator and editor, OSS analyst and legal investigator. Through legal battles with the government and persistence in taking advantage of the Freedom of Information laws, he amassed for himself documents which supported his arguments over and over again. I was greatly privileged to meet him and spend time with him. We became friends and I was extremely flattered that he made his immense file of documents available to me.

Gerald Posner's *Case Closed* was published in 1993, to mark the 30-year anniversary of the assassination, and was described as 'the antidote to the conspiracy theorists'. Weisberg wrote his answer to Posner in a book called *Case Open*, which was published the following year (Carroll & Graf). This was to be his last. In it, he drew attention to what he referred to as Posner's 'omissions, distortions and falsifications'.

One man I never met, and would have been honoured to, was Jim Garrison, District Attorney of New Orleans, who conducted the only case raised in a courtroom with a charge of complicity in the murder of President Kennedy. The case and the outcome are discussed in Chapter 32. Garrison wrote *On the Trail of the Assassins* and *Heritage of Stone*.

Others among the early critics were Germany's Joachim Joesten, whose work was widely published and appeared in the English language, Léo Sauvage, Robert Sam Anson, Josiah Thompson, Jim Bishop and Robert Groden. These are only a few in an incredibly long list. Each made his own contribution, adding something to our knowledge and understanding of what happened in Dealey Plaza on the fateful day of the murder of President Kennedy. It is true that the theories at times conflicted, which did not detract from the integrity of the authors or the wealth of vital data which, on analysis, came out of their work. One area which, in my opinion, suffered badly during the period when literally hundreds of books were written about the assassination was the subject of Lee Harvey Oswald's role. The received wisdom seldom went unchallenged. It had been 'established': he was the shooter from the sixth floor of the Texas School Book Depository; even if there was a conspiracy to kill the president, he played a major role. This was broadly accepted as fact. No doubt this was, in some measure, a case of one author leaning on another's deliberations.

During the time of the Warren Commission's work it became obvious that no one else was being sought in connection with the assassination and that the task of the commission was largely that of building a case against Lee Harvey Oswald. No defence for Oswald was provided by the Warren Commission. It was a one-sided 'court case' with, it would appear, only one possible verdict. One who apparently gathered this fairly early on was Oswald's mother, Marguerite, who sought lawyer Mark Lane to establish some kind of defence for him. Though this might not affect the outcome of the commission, it might at least reach the ears of the many out there who had only the commission and its edicts to inform them. Mark Lane published his findings in a book, *Rush to Judgment*, in 1966. By then all Marguerite's fears had been realised when the Warren Report condemned her son to an ignominy of rare proportions.

Lane's book was extremely creditworthy, even though it itself attracted critics. It served a very useful purpose, highlighting how the Warren Commission had taken advantage of the fact that their 'guilty party' was dead and could not answer their accusations. Many have voiced the opinion that had Oswald survived to go into a courtroom he would have been acquitted, the so-called evidence being unconvincing and readily challengeable.

The real name of the author James Hepburn, who wrote *Farewell*

America, was Hervé Lamarr. In my opinion, he is one of the unsung heroes of assassination research. It appears he had access to Secret Service Chief James Rowley or someone close enough to quote him. In his book, he claimed that Rowley knew there had been three, even four shooters in Dealey Plaza, and that he had known this within hours of the assassination. Another claim was that Rowley had reported to Robert Kennedy that a powerful organisation was behind the murder of his brother, the president. It is unsurprising that Hepburn could not find a publisher for his book in the United States. He seems to have had a finger on the pulse and to have been gifted with an incredible amount of remarkable insight. His book was eventually published in Canada and Belgium.

15

EARLY WRITERS AND
DEVELOPING SPECIALISMS

WE HAVE ALREADY BEGUN TO IDENTIFY RESEARCHERS
who, from an early stage, established themselves in one or other
of the many emerging special areas which begged investigation.
When the complexity of what they had identified as a conspiracy
of huge proportions was accepted, it became necessary to rationalise
and tackle manageable portions of the picture which was rapidly
emerging. This is not to mention that such an approach brought
in those with special talents in the various areas, which included
many professionals and academics. Britain's Bertrand Russell and
Canada's Peter Dale Scott, for instance, in their respective periods,
were two outstanding academics who contributed to the
investigation into the death of President Kennedy, and Peter Dale
Scott has added to his initial contribution in no small measure
through the years.

It should not be thought that there was any kind of overall
planning in the selection of specialist areas for investigation.
Individuals identified what they felt they were best equipped to
look into. As time progressed and organisations were developed
to allow researchers the opportunity to share what they had to
offer, there was still no attempt to regiment those involved in
research or investigation.

Some made outstanding contributions through their skills in
photography and their understanding of their profession. Jack
White was a relentless hunter of photographic material and his
keen, practised eye identified features of them that would otherwise
have gone unnoticed. Robert Groden excelled with his enhancement

skills and his ability to analyse the work of others. His powers of analysis provided a highly valued and effective tool where attempts had been made to doctor prints. Though largely successful, if my memory serves me right, he was not entirely satisfied with his matching of all the sounds of the shots heard in the audio evidence to the Zapruder footage, but time was limited. Perhaps it was the perfectionist in him showing itself, for a great deal was achieved by him when he worked with acoustics experts Aschkenasy and Weiss in the basement of the building used for the meetings of the House Select Committee on Assassinations. What became baffling was the number of shots heard on the sound recording. They exceeded the shots known to have struck the president and far exceeded those put forward in the Warren Report. (See Chapter 16 for more on the HSCA.)

Gary Mack must amply feature when photographic investigation is being considered. Probably his biggest achievement in this area was his enhancements of a Polaroid picture, the subject of which has famously become known as 'the badge man'. The picture was taken by Mary Moorman, who became Mrs Mary Kramer. She was standing roughly opposite the steps which led away across the rise from the road to access the grassy knoll area. Obviously pointing her camera at the president in the passing motorcade, she took a photograph which showed the semblance of a figure standing at the corner of the palisade which fenced in the crown of the knoll and ran alongside the pathway at the top of the steps. This was incredibly important because it was believed that a shot had been fired from exactly that spot. The 'badge man' tag was attached because it appeared that the man was wearing a badge of some sort.

That picture, which Mary Moorman kindly permitted me to use, came instantly to mind when Joachim Marcus and I examined the first results of a study which we had combined to carry out, and which was to take us four years to complete. Joachim, located at Herdecke in Germany, was a computer programmer whose background featured considerable surveying experience. Because of an incredible three-dimensional benefit he could derive from a new technique he had developed, he decided he wanted to reproduce and rerun the assassination all over again, stopping whenever and wherever he chose to identify locations and obtain measurements. For this, he needed considerable photographic and other data.

My part in the study was to provide the essential data Joachim required, including photographs galore. Joachim's demands were more than challenging. In some respects, his requirements equated to no less than near perfection. For instance, after having a friend of mine stride about the knoll taking measurements he needed, which I sent to him, the figures were discarded as unsuitable and he insisted we obtain the services of an established firm of surveyors. Landmark Surveys of Dallas were duly engaged and it was their highly skilled work which underpinned all we achieved. It was essential to the success of the study that the measurements Joachim used were absolutely spot-on correct: no doubts.

The work, which became known as the Smith-Vidit study (Vidit being Joachim's company's name), established some important findings. One related to the shot which was first claimed to be to the president's throat, a front-entry wound. That this was the case was firmly established in the study. The trajectory of the bullet to the throat was accurately traced . . . exactly from the spot occupied by the badge man. Assuming the bullet had exited the president's upper back, the trajectory was followed and coincided with a bullet mark in the road which had previously been identified by R.B. Cutler in a map he produced. It is amazing how one unrelated study supports another. The trajectory of the bullet to the throat took it to the middle of the road behind and to the side of the president's car. Cutler is another who deserves praise for a great deal of what might be termed foundational work.

To return to Mary's grainy Polaroid picture, Gary Mack was the stalwart who doggedly derived every bit of reliable information possible from it. He is due the highest credit for his achievements in this respect, though his work did not end there.

We are long overdue for lauding the accomplishments of that distinguished researcher and archivist Mary Ferrell, who, literally from day one, was observing, analysing and collecting data relative to the events in Dealey Plaza. This became a preoccupation which dominated the rest of her life. I would find it quite a task to estimate the number of new or established authors who sought her help or advice in their respective endeavours. I most certainly am honoured to be able to say that I was one of them.

A lawyer's secretary, she had made her mark in work of that description before the tragic events of 22 November 1963. She had a brilliant mind and soaked up data in an incredible fashion. She was always willing to share what she had with others and never lost the common touch. She rates as one of the most outstanding of all the researchers, with perhaps her greatest achievements being found in the work of others. An exception to this would be her amazing archive, which was translated onto CD format and, upon her death, became available to all. The Mary Ferrell Foundation now supports the furtherance of her work. (See Chapter 17.)

It is essential to tell of Mary Ferrell's work at this juncture because she and Gary Mack collaborated in making the staggering discovery of a complete sound recording of the proceedings in Dealey Plaza at the time of the assassination. She had been aware that police vehicles were in regular contact with headquarters during all their undertakings. Their transmissions were recorded on Dictabelts and thereafter stored away. When it was discovered that motorcycle officer H.B. McLain had reported that his microphone had become stuck in the open position, that particular Dictabelt was identified and submitted for examination. Unfortunately, at the time, the recordings were said to yield no intelligible information rated to be of value.

But as the years passed and new techniques in acoustics were developed and honed, Mary Ferrell and Gary Mack wondered if the old Dictabelt recordings, if they still existed, would realise anything useful if re-examined using new, advanced means of analysis. Their first task was to establish whether McLain's Dictabelt had survived. In their enquiries, they learned nothing, at any rate, that convinced them that it was not buried somewhere or other. They finally discovered that the Dictabelt in question had lain in a file at police headquarters for six years before being passed to the director of the Dallas Police Intelligence Division, Paul McCaghren, from whom they obtained it. It was sent to the firm of BBN (Bolt, Beranek and Newman) for analysis. The results, which I describe in more detail later, were eventually presented to the House Select Committee on Assassinations in their new investigation.

Edward Jay Epstein became known as a prominent writer following the publication of the Warren Report. His 1966 book *Inquest* provoked a great deal of criticism for certain inaccuracies, which could hardly be said to help the cause, but another book, *Legend: The Secret World of Lee Harvey Oswald*, published in 1978, earned him a great deal of praise for his work relating to the life and background of Lee Harvey Oswald. This is not to say that it was totally comprehensive, and there were those who disagreed with some of his assessments. However it was a scholarly piece of work and extremely helpful.

Jacqueline Kennedy suggested to William Manchester that he write a book on the assassination. There was no intention that she should endorse it, but she believed he could bring a lot to the recounting of events. His book *The Death of a President* appeared in 1967 and was both scholarly and meticulous. Not a book critical of the Warren Commission, it notably provided an enormous amount of detail and background, and it looked at the events surrounding the assassination in greater depth than most previous accounts. This is not to say he got everything right, an example of which was his odd assessment of Lee Harvey Oswald's rifle capabilities. He readily accepted Oswald as a superlative marksman and made no challenge to the Warren Report's findings. This was not borne out by those who knew Oswald and had knowledge of his prowess – or lack of it – with a rifle. This was an instance where Manchester revealed a distinct bias. In total, however, his work reflected great credit upon him and constituted an exceptionally important contribution to our knowledge.

Pulitzer Prize-winner Sylvan Fox wrote a book entitled *The Unanswered Questions About President Kennedy's Assassination*, which was first published in 1965, when it was advertised that it 'Shatters the Warren Commission Cover-Up [and] includes the latest revelations on the CIA and the Cuban Connection.' Like most books of the time, it had a limited knowledge of the whole picture; each, nonetheless, in its own way, made a valuable contribution.

Professor Richard Popkin authored an important little book entitled *The Second Oswald*, which appeared in 1966. This was an enormously useful book to those researchers anxious to identify and segregate the series of red herrings spread around immediately prior to the assassination. A number of books followed in the '60s, including Josiah Thompson's revealing *Six Seconds in Dallas* in 1967. In 1968, a fascinating volume by Jim Bishop, *The Day Kennedy was Shot*, was released. It became another must for those following the progress being revealed in the diggings of individual researchers.

* * *

As the '60s became the '70s, the work of the researchers and individual investigators could be perceived as relentless. Joining those dedicated seekers already obtaining results, distinguished authors, journalists, specialists from across the board, academics and respected professionals were throwing their weight into examining every aspect of what had occurred in Elm Street in Dealey Plaza. Among a galaxy of new books appearing from this time forward, *Bloody Treason* by Noel Twyman merits honourable mention, along with two books by Donald Gibson, *Battling Wall Street* and *The Kennedy Assassination Cover-Up*.

Rather than dark clouds descending, as early as the '70s, the work of the researchers was proving to be dark clouds lifting, as more and more data tumbled out to challenge the findings of the Warren Commission and those who were content to 'let sleeping dogs lie'. The '70s saw the two important investigations which we have previously mentioned take place: the first was a much-needed investigation into the activities of the CIA and the FBI, the Church Committee, named after its chairman, Frank Church. The second was a new investigation into the assassination of President Kennedy, which was linked to a parallel investigation into the murder of Martin Luther King in Memphis on 4 April 1968. This was the House Select Committee on Assassinations.

16

NEW INVESTIGATIONS:
CHURCH AND HOUSE

BECAUSE THE HOUSE SELECT COMMITTEE ON Assassinations followed soon after the Church investigation during the '70s, it should not be thought that the two were directly connected. There was no doubt, however, that the thinking of many senators related the one to the other. Among researchers, those anxious for a new inquiry into the murder of President Kennedy were fascinated by what the Church Committee revealed as a result of its investigation. In regard to other blatant criminal activities, the case of civil-rights activist Fred Hampton was reinvestigated. They found that Hampton's bodyguard was an FBI agent provocateur who supplied the Bureau with a detailed plan of Hampton's apartment, marking the man's bed with an X. In the raid which followed, Hampton's bedroom became a prominent target.

Criminal break-ins, thefts and disinformation campaigns designed to provoke attacks on individuals were also identified. One of the nastiest tactics by both the CIA and the FBI was anonymous letters sent to persuade employers to fire individuals whose politics 'qualified' them as targets. Unbelievably, similar letters were sent to spouses with the aim of breaking up marriages.

One particular activity exposed would no doubt be of great interest to those later investigating the Martin Luther King murder. It was revealed that the FBI had made Martin Luther King a target. They mailed him a tape recording made from secret microphones hidden in hotel rooms he had used. The suggestion was that they would release the tape to the public unless King committed suicide. He didn't, but someone shot and killed him.

Very much a dirty-work-at-the-crossroads business: the Church Committee exposed the seamy side of both the CIA and the FBI, which many people suspected had existed for a long time. To those unaware of such activities, however, it no doubt came as a nasty shock. It was a painful boil on the American world of secrets which desperately needed to be lanced.

In spite of exposing the ties the CIA had with the Mafia and criticising the Warren Report, the Church investigation failed to obtain the reaction these matters warranted. To add to much creditable work and all its important findings, however, the Church Report was also instrumental in contributing pressure to the demands for a new investigation into the assassination of President John F. Kennedy. This pressure was added to that of Senator Thomas N. Downing, who began campaigning for a new investigation in 1976, a campaign with which researcher Robert Groden was associated. It was interesting that a *Detroit News* poll taken that year revealed that 87 per cent of the population did not believe that Lee Harvey Oswald had killed the president alone and unaided. A later poll showed an increase in those who could not accept the Warren Report findings.

* * *

The House Select Committee on Assassinations might have been thought to have a level playing field before it as it began its work. Regretfully, this was not to be the case. Chairman Henry González replaced Thomas Downing on his retirement, but the first and perhaps most important and far-reaching of the committee's problems began with the appointment of its chief counsel. Richard A. Sprague was, it was believed, the best possible man to delve into the mire of the assassination. Researcher Gaeton Fonzi was to commend Sprague as 'tough, tenacious and independent', commenting, 'The Kennedy assassination would finally get . . . a no-holds-barred, honest investigation.' González might at first have agreed with this, but he found it hard to withstand the pressure of the CIA, who wanted Sprague fired. First it was González who quit and Sprague followed. Before going, Sprague said that his preoccupations were such while he was chief counsel that the actual investigative work he was involved in was so small as to border on too little to calculate.

Sprague's departure, frankly, was the undoing of the new investigation. Talking to Gaeton Fonzi, Sprague told him that he had demanded complete information on the CIA's operations in Mexico, that area of sensitive activity which to the time of writing this book has never totally and authoritatively been explained. Sprague was seeking full access to all CIA employees who might have anything to do with the photographs, tape recordings and transcripts. The Agency arched its back at this, but Sprague pressed on. Eventually the Agency agreed to Sprague having complete access to the information he sought provided he signed a CIA Secrecy Agreement. Sprague could not possibly sign such an agreement. Fonzi quotes him: 'How can I possibly sign [a secrecy] agreement with an agency I'm supposed to be investigating?' Sprague may, officially, have been said to resign. In fact, he was hounded out by those opposing an honest investigation, notably the CIA. Thereafter, the show was believed by many to be controlled by the CIA. It was of limited value, but, for all that, what emerged was certainly worth having.

This has presented me with the opportunity of drawing attention to the work of Gaeton Fonzi, who was far more than simply a researcher. He was once described as 'the investigator's investigator', and that goes at least part way to acknowledging the sterling work he has contributed to the overall investigation into the killing of President Kennedy. Fonzi was engaged in 1975 by Senator Richard Schweiker, who headed a Senate subcommittee of the Senate Select Committee on Intelligence. Impressed by what Fonzi had had published, he wanted an investigator into CIA activities in Florida. Fonzi's work for Schweiker was impressive and led to his being asked to join the House Select Committee on Assassinations as an investigator.

His book *The Last Investigation* (1993, rev. 2008) was largely based on his experiences as a Congress investigator and afforded us unparalleled insight into the House Committee's work, achievements and the lack of them. What might be described as infighting, which reflected the fact that some senators were distinctly opposed to having an investigation at all, resulted in a situation where, when they were finally 'ready to go', so to speak, there were roughly only six months left for actual investigation before it was time to wrap up and produce a report to conclude affairs. It was hardly satisfactory and hardly likely to shower credit on the Senate. It is true that in the short time available the members of the committee threw up some interesting subjects for further study. Perhaps the jewel in the crown of the HSCA investigation was the acoustics evidence.

To start with, however, the basic credit for this input belonged to Mary Ferrell and Gary Mack. The blue Dictabelt recordings had been placed in the hands of BBN, to whom they had been sent for analysis. Since, as a general overall trend, the House Committee investigation leaned heavily towards propping up the Warren Report, it was small wonder that the initial submission of the acoustics material by BBN was 'placed on one side' until later, after more sophisticated tests had been made. The data and material were put in the capable hands of Dr Ernest Aschkenasy and Professor Mark Weiss at Queens College, City University of New York.

Perhaps chief counsel Professor G. Robert Blakey hoped that the two different analysts would fault BBN's work. Following new tests carried out in Dealey Plaza, however, they produced computerised graphics to compare with the Dictabelt recordings and confirmed that, of six shots identified, one was from the grassy knoll and two from behind the motorcade. The shot from the grassy knoll was traced in this study to the spot occupied by the so-called badge man in Mary Moorman's Polaroid picture. These findings were startling and totally contradicted the Warren findings. In regard to the whole submission being put aside until later, when the latest point of 'later' came along they had to face the hard reality that there was new evidence here which was set to blow the findings of the Warren Commission out of the water.

Regardless of what the new evidence was and the implications of it, the Committee, however reluctantly, was obliged to receive it all, which, for one thing, established that there was, as had been suspected by researchers all along, a second sniper on the grassy knoll. This did not rule out the presence of other members of an assassination team, but the establishment of a second sniper inevitably represented that a conspiracy had taken place to kill the president. In their report, with remarkable downplaying of this electrifying evidence, the HAC only got as far as **opining** that there had '**probably**' been a conspiracy, and it underlined that Lee Harvey Oswald had still been the principal assassin. This was unbelievable sleight of hand on the part of the Committee, but it was allowed to get away with it. The researchers had no doubts in their minds that it had finally been established beyond question that there had been a conspiracy to murder the president, as they had asserted all along.

The medical evidence was 're-examined' by the House Committee, which appointed a nine-man panel of distinguished medicos including leading pathologist Cyril Wecht. It appears that the panel attempted to make sense, as they saw it, of the wounds the president had received by, for instance, reducing the fatal head wound which blew away part of his skull to a mere bullet hole. Dr Wecht would have none of this and made it plain he would not append his name to such gross inaccuracy. This resulted in the findings of the panel in the Committee's report, when published, showing frequently eight in favour of what was asserted and one against. In each case, the dissenter was Cyril Wecht, who would not sacrifice his integrity by participating in the publication of what he saw as unreliable findings or, in fact, deceptions. In the case of the single bullet hole (in the rear of the head, to reassert the Warren position), frankly, as soon as the House Assassinations Committee's pictures relating to their re-examination were published, even I saw at once that there was a deception being promoted and denounced it, and I am no pathologist.

69. Dr Cyril Wecht.

One wonders how they got along with an impaired facility for photographic comparison. There is evidence that at the time of the Bethesda autopsy a variety of photographic items simply disappeared. Lack of organisation extended even to the very camera listed as the one used at the autopsy, which could not be verified as the actual one used for comparison purposes.

It is hard to find a great deal to applaud in the published results of the House Assassinations Committee. They officially exonerated Russia and Cuba from involvement in the assassination, which was highly desirable but which had been assumed by the mid-'70s anyway. They followed this, however, by a declaration that the Secret Service, the FBI and the CIA were also all absolved. If the acoustics evidence was a giant step forward, that was a giant step backwards. Richard Sprague, at the outset, knew it was the CIA and the FBI that the Committee had to investigate. The official exoneration of these bodies demonstrated who was in control.

What was not generally known during the time of the House Assassinations Committee was that whereas Richard Sprague was dedicated to openness in the work of the investigation, his eventual successor, Robert Blakey, was quite the opposite. His way was secrecy, muzzling of staff and rigid control of and access to the findings of the investigation. Blakey was 'accommodating' to the CIA and the FBI and, therefore, the investigation in total was placed into the hands of the very agencies which, as Sprague had insisted, should have been the subject of investigation. The 'establishment' of their innocence rang hollow, therefore. The situation had turned full circle.

But it was an incredible triumph for Mary Ferrell, Gary Mack and the teams who analysed the contents of the Dictabelts, BBN and Aschkenasy and Weiss. The results supported that bullets had been fired from two directions, from behind and from the grassy knoll area. They identified the direction of the shots in test shots carried out by their team, who recorded the sounds for specific examination. Remarkably, a shot was identified as likely emanating from the position occupied by 'the badge man', captured on the Polaroid picture taken by Mary Moorman. These results were devastating to the House Assassination Committee, which, from the time Professor Blakey was appointed chairman, appeared dedicated to re-establishing the Warren position. The Warren position was sunk without trace, as this evidence confirmed that a second sniper was involved and, therefore, a conspiracy to murder President Kennedy had existed. That there was a team of snipers and their aides involved in a highly professional operation became evident later.

Of all the organisations which should have been applauding the acoustics revelations, the government agencies should have led the field. This was not so; in fact, they were the only bodies to challenge the findings of the experts. First in the queue was the FBI, which sought to discredit the evidence as 'invalid'. Chairman Blakey, to his credit, acidly responded that their response was a 'sophomoric analysis . . . superficial, shoddy and shot full of holes'. This was quickly followed by another challenge: the National Science Foundation had been requested to undertake a new analysis of the Dictabelt evidence. Their challenge came at the behest of the Justice Department, no less.

On their behalf, a National Academy of Sciences panel took

this on and promptly dismantled the evidence presented to the House Assassinations Committee. They said that the existence of the sniper on the knoll had not been proven in the recordings and nor had the presence of a second gunman. This expensive piece of work – it cost $23,360, which at the time represented a lot of taxpayers' money – was immediately attacked by Gary Mack. Amazingly, he did not have far to look for the cause of their misleading and quite incorrect 'new' results. He pointed out that the study had assumed that the recordings had the benefit of automatic gain control, which, at that time, Dallas Police did not have. Furthermore, Dallas Police were credited with operating an AM system, whereas they used an FM system. The expensive findings were, therefore, quickly discredited, but the challenge to the submitted evidence confirmed how determined the government was to keep the truth covered up.

Those few still uncertain about the value of the Dictabelt recordings had to wait until 2001 for further reassurance. The journal of the US Forensic Science Society published the findings of Donald B. Thomas, who reanalysed the Dictabelt recordings and examined the data used by the National Academy of Sciences panel for the Justice Department. In a nutshell, he confirmed that the data they had used was inaccurate and therefore their results were invalid. Thomas made the appropriate adjustments to the data and his results supported that the submissions to the House Assassinations Committee in the first place were correct. Another milestone contribution from the Thomas findings may be found in Chapter 31.

* * *

If the acoustics evidence was the jewel in the crown of the report from the House Assassinations Committee, they had a second jewel in the offing. The potential was there with the revelation by former CIA man James Wilcott to the Committee that Lee Harvey Oswald had been 'recruited from the military for the express purpose of becoming a double agent on assignment to the USSR'.

Wilcott was a finance officer and told the Committee he had, without realising it at the time, handled funds for the Oswald mission under a 'cryptonym' – a code designation. He also told them that the mission had failed.

The press picked this up at the time, but it did not hit the headlines as it should have done. Perhaps this was evidence of the degree of control the CIA had over the House Committee. A quote from journalists Jack Anderson and Les Whitten, two who recognised the influence of the CIA on the House Assassinations Committee, is extremely pertinent to this situation. It also reveals that they were aware of the control it had exercised over the Warren investigation and pulls no punches when rendering an opinion on what a dangerous entity it had become:

> The CIA's strategy, according to [quoted] sources, is to stymie the House Assassinations probe. Too close scrutiny of the tragedy might embarrass the CIA, which withheld crucial facts from the Warren Commission. It was a mistake, we believe, for the CIA to operate at the KGB level.

Importantly, before it closed, the House Committee on Assassinations made a recommendation that the investigation into the death of President Kennedy be reopened. The recommendation was sent to the Justice Department, where, it appears, it still is without response from that day to this.

Like the Warren Commission before them, the House Assassinations Committee, almost certainly deliberately, ignored what may have been vital leads. For instance, the lawyer for the president's first personal physician, in a letter to the Committee, offered to present evidence to them that individuals other than Lee Harvey Oswald were involved in the murder of the president. No indication has been found that there was ever a response to the letter, and the evidence was lost.

* * *

So much for the only contribution from the US government towards the reinvestigation of who really killed President Kennedy and why they wanted him dead. From the beginning, researchers, investigators and authors have worked completely independently without help from any official body. They have never been directed to carry out work in general or in their specialisms. They have never been regimented into looking into this or that, as some form of organisation might have directed. They have, however, met up with one another to discuss their findings, compare notes and make available to colleagues and like-minded people what they have learned. These meetings blossomed into regular gatherings, which in the course of time have attracted so many who want to be kept up to par with developments, share ideas and be given the means of participating in discussion. The following chapters illustrate how the quest for the truth about the assassination of President John F. Kennedy has been broadened, deepened and indeed greatly enriched through such organisations.

17

JFK LANCER

THERE IS NO DOUBT THAT MUCH CREDIT SHOULD be given to an organisation which started its work very early in the proceeding. It provided for the essential gathering of researchers and for the exchange of information between them under the name of the ASK (Assassination Symposium on John F. Kennedy) conference, which was held each year to commemorate the anniversary of the assassination of President Kennedy. Participants listened to reports and the results of research findings and had the opportunity to discuss them in an open forum as well as privately. Mary Ferrell, as her health permitted, was prominent in this connection and continued to assist as she was able. Another well-known researcher who was active in Dallas from the start was J. Gary Shaw, who, with Larry Harris, wrote the illuminating *Cover-Up*, published in 1976 and revised for a 1992 edition.

In 1995, Debra Conway and Thomas A. Jones founded JFK Lancer with the principal aim of making research materials concerning the assassination easily accessible to everyone. The organisation has established its position in regard to the basics of the assassination and seeks as its prime concern accuracy and truth. JFK Lancer publishes material in print and on CD. It produced the *Kennedy Assassination Chronicles*, a magazine featuring research news, new document releases and articles from respected researchers, in print form for several years and later in PDF format for the web. Much credit goes to leading researcher George Michael Evika for his work on the establishment of the *Chronicles* and the organisation of the conferences.

The annual conferences, which are well attended, have continued under the title of 'November in Dallas', and a high-profile historical research gathering is scheduled for 2013, to mark the 50th anniversary of the assassination, designated also to feature educational presentations on newer research into forensics, ballistics and crime-scene evidence in general. Lancer makes conference presentations available on DVD.

Very much computer and technology orientated, JFK Lancer also makes documents and articles available for individuals to obtain to pursue computer research themselves. It now offers website design and maintenance for its authors. The organisation has also been established as a publishing house. It acts as both publisher and bookseller of JFK-related items, and distributes via its website, Amazon and through publishing distribution channels. The intention is for the organisation to continue as a fundamental research asset.

Active, both inside and outside of JFK Lancer, is Larry Hancock, who contributed *Someone Would Have Talked*, published in 2006 and updated in 2010. He draws attention to the sterling work Debra Conway carries out, providing content to major research websites. Lancer also works with the media in general, assisting reporters, film-makers and video groups, as well as television news outlets.

Lancer's work in education does not go unnoticed. It works with high-school and college teachers and student groups and presents awards of money, book and CD collections annually to both students and teachers. The Mary Ferrell Awards are administered by the organisation, in which her endeavours are perpetuated. Lancer has come a long way from its early beginnings and promotes that the case of the assassination of President Kennedy is still open and that research should be ongoing.

18

THE COALITION ON
POLITICAL ASSASSINATIONS

OTHERWISE KNOWN AS COPA, THIS IS A NATIONAL organisation of medical, forensic scientific and legal experts, along with various academicians, authors, researchers and other individuals who are seriously interested in investigating major political assassinations in the United States and abroad.

The Coalition on Political Assassinations was formed in the mid-1980s. The initial meeting took place in Washington DC, with representatives from the AARC (Assassination Archives and Research Center), the Committee for Open Archives and the CTKA (Citizens for Truth in the Kennedy Assassination). At that meeting, Dr Cyril H. Wecht was elected as president and John Judge was chosen to be the executive director. The organisation was to be housed in Washington DC.

Beginning in the late 1980s, annual meetings were conducted in Dallas on and around 22 November of each year, commemorating the date of President John F. Kennedy's assassination. Other meetings were held in Washington DC, in Memphis, Tennessee (pertaining to the assassination of Dr Martin Luther King), and in Los Angeles (pertaining to the assassination of Senator Robert F. Kennedy).

At the annual COPA meetings in Dallas, which usually took place over a three-day period, various presentations were made by Warren Commission Report critic-researchers. These meetings were attended by several hundred people in the early years.

COPA played a major role in bringing about the creation of the JFK Assassination Records Act, which led to the establishment of the Assassination Records Review Board (ARRB). COPA also promoted the Martin Luther King Records Act, which called for a grand jury investigation into the deaths of President Kennedy and Dr King.

The tradition established by one of the early Warren Committee Report critic-researchers, Penn Jones, designated as a 'Moment of Silence', has been maintained by COPA. This has taken place annually at Dealey Plaza in Dallas, Texas, on 22 November each year.

In recent years, some of the participating groups have withdrawn as active participants in COPA. However, COPA continues as a national organisation, actively calling for the release of all documents pertaining to the JFK assassination, as well as other politically related assassinations.

So much for the history of COPA. It is not hard to discover how active it presently is and to sample its activities. For the 50th anniversary of the assassination of President Kennedy, for instance, a major programme is scheduled for 22–24 November 2013 in Dallas, with the traditional Moment of Silence conducted on Friday, 22 November, and this will be detailed soon afterwards on the Internet.

A peek at recent postings on their website illustrates much of the above and demonstrates how really active COPA is. The anniversary conference of 2012 featured a galaxy of the leading researchers and commentators on the assassination, including Peter Dale Scott and Robert Groden, and by making what was said readily available to everyone without restriction they are quietly providing an outstanding contribution.

Taking last year's conference alone, the material emanating is pertinent, exciting and reveals how much work on the assassination goes on relentlessly. Additionally, the selection of printed and other matter closely related to assassination research reveals careful monitoring of what happens at COPA and elsewhere. The hyperlinked version of the keynote speech at COPA, facilitated by Dave Ratcliffe, features Jim Douglass, who authored the greatly acclaimed *JFK and the Unspeakable*, with Paul Schrade prominently involved in this recording. Another example is detail of the link to the live radio coverage record of President Kennedy's visit to Dallas on that fateful day. Those interested in the evolvement of the research into the assassination are invited to take advantage of what COPA offers via the net.

19

THE BRITISH ORGANISATIONS

THE ORGANISATION 'FAIR PLAY FOR OSWALD' CAME into being in the '70s. It was located in Liverpool and, though its membership was not great, it attracted interested parties from the length and breadth of Britain, from places as far flung as Scotland in the north and London in the south. Few who were present will forget the well-attended conference they held in a huge Liverpool hotel. Two of the speakers were from the US, Dr Charles Crenshaw and Walt Brown.

The **Dealey Plaza UK** organisation, which has become known as DPUK, first met informally at Charlton Kings just outside Cheltenham, with the official inaugural meeting being held in 1996 at Waltham Abbey in Essex. From small beginnings – the first meeting was attended by 15 people – membership has increased steadily to about 75 today. Included in this number is a member in Ireland, another in France and 12 in the United States. The objectives of the group include bringing together interested people for the mutual exchange of views, opinions and information. The group seeks to assist the worldwide research community in the search for the truth of what happened in Dealey Plaza on 22 November 1963, the planning behind it, the execution of it and the aftermath. Another of its aims is to establish and maintain contact with other groups with similar aims, particularly those in the United States, such as JFK Lancer and COPA, and, of course, other groups in the United Kingdom.

In 2000, a website was created; it was taken in hand and further developed by the present webmaster, Bernard Wilds, in 2007. Plans are afoot for the establishment of a forum to facilitate better communication between members, as well as encouraging more material for publication.

The group inaugurated a journal named *The Dealey Plaza Echo* as long ago as 1996 and it has been circulated to members three times each year since. With articles from eminent researchers from the UK and the United States, the stature and the status of the *Echo* has gone from strength to strength. At the end of each year, the content of the journals is added to the Mary Ferrell website.

Since 2003, DPUK has held a seminar in beautiful Canterbury. The Canterbury seminar has, across the years, featured speakers such as George Michael Evica, Sherry Gutierrez, Larry Hancock, Nancy Weiford, David Talbot and Russ Baker, as well as Alaric Rosman and Chris Scally. Those who attend can mix business with pleasure in an Italian restaurant on the first night, when the discussion is wide and general. The following day, a Saturday, is a day full of presentations, followed by an open forum. Saturday night is banquet night at a local venue, and Sunday features more presentations, a further open forum and finally an auction.

A contingent of DPUK members attends the annual memorial of the assassination in Dallas in November each year. This offers another opportunity to meet old friends and obtain an updating on this and that. More importantly, it contributes to the solidification of the links between those who mourn in America and those who mourn in Britain.

The DPUK organisation is based in the south of England, centred largely on London, which tends to exclude those who live further north. With soaring costs of motoring and escalating train fares, those in the North find it hard if not impossible to take part in the activities of the organisation. The latest news, however, is that meetings are projected in Bath and York, which represents a big step forward.

* * *

It is unthinkable to represent the activities of those in Britain without drawing attention to the work of **John Simkin**. Simkin is basically a dedicated historian. He is a man of broad experience in industry and, among other things, a huge depth of knowledge of the background to the murder of President Kennedy. I recommend readers to sample his work by visiting **Spartacus Educational** on the net, where they will find that a great deal has been going on unheralded. This does not mean I agree with all that you will read, but what you read will be worth reading.

20

THE ASSASSINATION
RECORDS REVIEW BOARD

ONE OF THE BIGGEST SURGES IN POTENTIAL FOR development relating to the investigation into the death of President Kennedy came as a consequence of the impact made by the Oliver Stone movie *JFK* and through the efforts of COPA. There is no doubt that Stone's dynamic film prodded the government and the various agencies hard, and the public, rightly, expected a response. The momentous decision by government to release documents relevant to the assassination from various agencies holding vital documentation ought to have exposed all that we needed to start pointing fingers and attributing blame. I think, however, that we were all cleverly short-changed.

To begin with, take the documents released by the Dallas Police Department. What exactly did they reveal? Who did they expose? I know well that they revealed the identities and details relating to the three tramps who were arrested in a rail freight box shortly after the assassination, for instance, who had puzzled researchers from the time of the assassination, because I have got copies of the arrest sheets. But then, they did not penetrate much beyond the obvious and did not get into who they really were and what they were doing when they were arrested, and they did not answer the questions raised by those who had carefully analysed the photographs of them which had been published. I was at first much inclined to accept that they were, as they said, just three tramps, but, as an instance to inspire doubt, another look at a picture of them highlights how much the one at the back of the three (in the picture we show) resembles CIA agent E. Howard

Hunt. The question arises were they arrested or being given a safe conduct from Dallas?

70. The 'three tramps' arrested in a railway car. But there has been much speculation about who they really were. For instance, the one at the back (seen between heads) looks remarkably like CIA agent E. Howard Hunt. The others have hair recently cut, are well shod and were 'arrested' by officers wearing insignia which did not belong to the Dallas Police. Also, when did Dallas police officers start carrying rifles?

(Courtesy National Archives)

The important evidence relating to what transpired in conversation between Oswald and John Elrod, another man found in the vicinity and who was placed in the same cell as Oswald at Dallas police headquarters, has not received much trumpeting, but could be important. What Elrod had to say was kept secret until the release of the documents. Oswald's denial of the accusations made against him in those particular conversations is worth knowing about.

The contents of files in monstrous proportions were promised for release and indeed were released. So much so that a special, temporary agency of government had to be set up to disseminate such input and make it available to all interested parties. Sterling work was carried out by those employed by that agency, which became known as the Assassination Records Review Board (ARRB). The multiplicity of documents derived from CIA files and elsewhere did not, however, for most of us, give us the vital clues we hoped for, though there is no doubt they provided a colossal fund of interesting related information.

Taking a backwards view, in terms of essentials, I cannot really see that we learned much more than we knew before. A frustrating example of this relates to the release of the notes taken by Captain Will Fritz during his interrogation of Lee Harvey Oswald. The few pages released could not possibly account for his 12 hours of interrogation and they contained much of what we had previously learned from FBI notes released long before. What happened to the rest? And why was there no stenographer present taking down statements, or even a tape recorder? I find it incredible that a tape recorder or some other type of recording machine was not in fact switched on, taking down every word said, which perhaps one day will be revealed. I read somewhere about a conversation between interested parties in which it was claimed that such a tape recording *did* exist. My guess is that it is there, perhaps, waiting to make someone a fortune.

In spite of all the hard work which went into the organising and running of the ARRB, it seems clear that of the millions of documents consigned to the vast number of files relating to the assassination of President Kennedy, we got only those documents which the holders were prepared to let go. Even the ARRB itself held back material deemed to be too sensitive for release. And the millions of documents retained in the CIA and other files, what about them? Do we ever get to see them?

I have an awful feeling that the decision on the part of the government to release a deluge of documents to satisfy the demands of the people will prove to go down as a massively unwelcome damp squib, signalling another triumph for those determined to bury the truth. For researchers, this means back to the drawing board, back to the various sources of input we have ourselves achieved finding, and an acceptance that we are far away from that golden era when the data we need will fall from the skies.

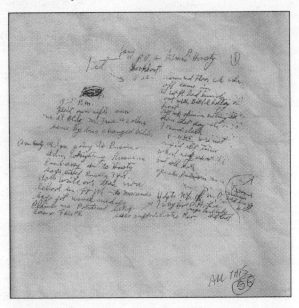

(1)

1st 11-22
B.O. + James P. Hosty
Jame W Bookout

3:15 p.m.
Didn't own rifle saw
one at Bldg M. True + 2 others
home by bus changed britches

Ans Hosty adm going to Russia
adm wrighting Russian
Embassy + to Hosty
says lived Russia 3 yrs.
Does write over then now
school in Ft W. - to Marines
says got usual medals
claims no political belief
belongs Fair Pl
Hdqts NY off N.O.
says supports Castro Rev.

claims 2nd floor Coke when
off came in
to 1st floor had lunch
out with Bill Shelley in
front
lft wk opinion nothing be
done that day etc.
? punch clock
8-4:45 wre not
rigid abt time
wked reg 1st Fl
but all over
speaks Russian

?Why live O.H. Lee
says landlady did that

Terminate interview
with line up
4:15

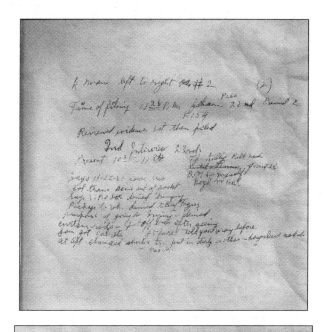

4 man left to right as #2

(2)

Time of filing 11:26 pm Johnson Pres 22nd   Precinct 2
                F154
Received evidence 1st then filed

2nd Interview 23rd
Present 10:35-11:34
T.J. Kelly Robt Nash
Grant ??
B.O + myself
Boyd + Hall

Says 11-22-63 rode bus
got trans same out of pocket
says 1 p.o. box denied bringing
package to wk. Denied telling Frazier
purpose of going to Irving - denied
curtain rods - got off bus after seeing
jam got cab etc .85 fare told you wrong before
at apt. Changed shirts + tr. Put in dirty clothes - long sleeve red sh
          + gray tr.

morning 23rd.
says 11-21-63 say two negr came in
one Jr. + short negro - ask ? for lunch says cheese
sandwiches + apple

says doesn't pay cash for wife staying with Mrs. Payne
denies owning rifle in garage or elsewhere admits other
things these

Came there 63 - N.O.
Says no visitors at apt. Claims never order
owns ???? for gun
denies belonging to Com party
says bgt gun 7 mo Ft W. didn't know what Place.
ams to grest ant questioning
Arv. July 62 from U.S.S.R. Int by F.B.I. Ft W
says Hard + Soft meth etc   Buddy
says on interview of Payne by F.B.I. He thought she was intimidated

Desires to talk to Mr. Abt. I ask who says Smith act att. 4

Says did live N.O. 4706 Magazine St. Frem Apt.
Wked Wm B. Riley Co 640
says nothing against Pres does not want to talk further - No Pahy at time in past had refused
Oswald A.C.L.U. member he says says Mrs. Payne was too. I ask abt organization he says to pay lawyer fees when needed
B.O. ask abt Heidel selective s. card - adm having would not admit signature - wouldn't say why he had it. Says add. Book has names of Russian Emigrants he visits - denied shooting Pres says didn't know Gov. shot

(4

Desires to talk to Mr. Abt. I ask who
says Smith act att.
Says did live N.O. 4706 Magazine St. Frem Apt.
Wked Wm B. Riley Co 640
says nothing against Pres does not want to
talk further - No Pahy at time in past had
refused
Oswald A.C.L.U. member he says says
Mrs. Payne was too. I ask abt organization
he says to pay lawyer fees when needed
B.O. asks about Heidel selective s. Card - adm having
would not admit signature - wouldn't say
why he had it. Says add. Book has names of Russian
Emigrants he visits - denies shooting Pres says didn't know
Gov. shot

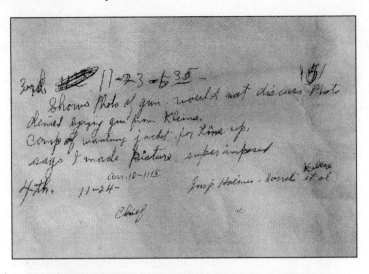

3rd 11-23 - 6:35   (5)

Shows photo of gun. Would not discuss photo
denies buying gun from Kleins.
Comp of wanting jacket for line up.
Says I made picture super imposed

                    arr 10-11:15
4th.   11-24   Insp Holmes - Sorrels - Kelley et al
                        Chief

71. The images shown on pages 168 to 172 reflect the total of what was released from the 12 hours of questioning of Oswald conducted by Captain Will Fritz. They tell us little we had not gleaned from elsewhere, and as for this questioning taking 12 hours, it inspires us to ask what happened to the rest. Most importantly, Oswald did not establish his CIA, FBI or ONI credentials in the foregoing. Or did Fritz ignore them?

Form 141- AFFIDAVIT—General   David Johnston Exhibit 3

IN THE NAME AND BY THE AUTHORITY OF THE STATE OF TEXAS

PERSONALLY APPEARED before me the undersigned authority this affiant, who after being by me duly sworn, deposes and says your Affiant has good reason to believe and does believe that one

Lee Harvey Oswald

hereinafter styled Defendant, heretofore on or about the _22nd_ day of _November_ D. 19 _63_ in the County of Dallas and State of Texas, did unlawfully _then and there_ _voluntarily_ _and with Malice Aforethought kill_ _J.D. Tippitt by shooting him with a_ _gun_

Against the peace and dignity of the State.   David Johnston Exhibit No. 3

Sworn to and subscribed before me this the

_22nd_ day of _November_ A. D. 19 _63_

W. F. Alexander

Assistant Criminal District Attorney of Dallas County, Texas.

                                          Affiant.

JOHNSTON EXHIBIT No. 3

72. Oswald in makeshift press conference (top, courtesy National Archives) and Oswald arrest sheet for shooting Officer Tippit (bottom, Warren Report, courtesy National Archives). The picture above shows Oswald being questioned in a makeshift press conference and the document beneath shows that he was first arrested for the murder of Officer J.D. Tippit, which raises the question of how much time elapsed before he was rearrested for the murder of President Kennedy, and did he know before he was thrust into his 'press conference'? Then a close look at the arrest sheet reveals he was listed as a murderer of the worst possible kind, having killed Tippit, they said, with 'malice aforethought'.

The arrest document was signed by Will Fritz.

Very little of what we really need to know about the assassination, and about who killed the president and why, has derived from government agencies. Rather more they serve to deter us and throw us off the scent. The credit for the massive progress which has been made in the unravelling of the greatest mystery presented to us in modern history must go to individual searchers for truth. And I am happy to record that it would seem that younger people are coming forward to replace those we are losing due to the ravages of time.

I recall a disturbing snatch of something I was reading recently. It related to such political assassinations which occurred in a number of those countries not as advanced as those in the West, involving people less able to defend whatever degree of democracy they had achieved. For such an assassination to take place in the United States was surely not possible, unbelievable, unthinkable . . .

21

THE MEDIA

THE CONTRIBUTION TO THE INVESTIGATION INTO the assassination of President Kennedy by the media in all its varied forms is undeniably unequalled. No other event in history of such enormous political proportions has been filmed, photographed, televised, recorded and written about, and treated in this way. I deal with a number of the books written on the subject in the appropriate places in this book, but also specifically in Chapter 15.

The key piece of evidence in relation to the investigation of exactly when and exactly where the president was shot came in the form of what has become known as the Zapruder film. Abraham Zapruder was a tailor and dressmaker with premises near Dealey Plaza. Whether he thought the weather unsuitable for shooting movie film that day – it had been raining early on – or whether he had just forgotten to bring his camera to work with him we are not sure, but he found himself wishing he had it with him. A member of his staff persuaded him to return home to bring it and he was glad he did. Having established himself in a premier position on the wall by the concrete pergola in Elm Street, he was set to get some magnificent footage. As the motorcade approached, he set his camera moving and, regardless of bangs, noises and other distractions, he kept it going continuously for more than 26 seconds, a long take in the circumstances. The results were extraordinary. Without realising at that moment what he was doing, he had filmed the entire period of the shooting of the president in one unbroken sequence. The remarkable footage was first sold to Time–Life for a sum said to be $230,000. A copy was provided for the FBI and was subsequently supplied to the Warren Commission. Unfortunately for the Warren Commission, there was no way it could be used as evidence against Lee Harvey Oswald.

As time went by, controversies were raised relating to the Zapruder footage. In a version issued at one time, it was readily noticed that two frames were missing, apparently edited out, which Time–Life denied had occurred. But could there have been a reason for the two frames being removed, frames Z155 and Z156?

These were not the only frames to disappear. A splice in the film was identified at frame Z207, and frames Z208, Z209, Z210 and Z211 were removed. Time–Life offered the explanation that a junior member of staff, entrusted with the enlargement of the film, had had an accident which had caused the loss of the frames. For an established, top-rated magazine publisher to leave an incredibly costly and historically valuable film in the hands of someone less than fully experienced and reliable stretched the imagination. Some investigators and researchers found it exceeded their belief. The disbelievers were to obtain their justification years later when the missing frames were discovered in an FBI file. The significance of the removal of these frames was not understood until the time of the House Assassinations Committee, which reported in 1979, when it was established that a fourth shot had been fired at the president. (The Warren Commission had asserted that there were only three.)

At the time of the HSCA investigation, prominent photographic researcher Robert Groden, who gave evidence to the Committee, was heavily involved with matching shots fired to the incredible acoustics evidence submitted by professors Aschkenasy and Weiss (see Chapter 16). He claimed that the point at which the frames were removed appeared to coincide exactly with retired USAF Major Philip Willis coming into shot on the opposite side of the road. It was precisely at the moment the major lowered his camera after taking a still picture. The frames would have shown the moment his lens clicked, permitting a cross-check with the

Zapruder frames, and would have shown that another shot was indeed fired at the president at a point earlier than admitted by the Warren Commission. The anxiety of the commission in denying any more than three shots being fired related to their assertion that Lee Harvey Oswald, alone and unaided, had shot and killed the president, and they knew it was physically impossible for him to fire more than three shots in the time frame of the shooting. A fourth shot shattered this assertion.

The copy the Warren Commission received was said to be quite substandard, this being thought to affect their understanding of its content. However, the individual frames of the movie, also supplied to the commission, were enlarged, printed and numbered. The sequence was muddled by the FBI, who supplied two frames in reverse order. These particular frames showed the president's head snap back at the point of the fatal shot, which the movie appeared to suggest came from the front. The changed order of the frames suggested the head was snapping forward, which was exactly what the Warren Commission wanted: a shot from behind, from the rifle of Lee Harvey Oswald. Strange? Suspicious? Simply an error, said the FBI.

Another anomaly was claimed by Jack White, an important and astute expert in assassination photographs, who believed retouching had taken place to darken the rear of the president's hair in the frames following the fatal shot. Regardless of what the film showed, the commission conceded nothing in respect of decisions already reached relating to their own blow-by-blow account of what they were asserting happened during those few seconds. This was in spite of the obvious challenge of the visual evidence, which indicated the necessity for a reappraisal.

The Zapruder film was analysed thoroughly, being reproduced in a series of single frames. As time went on, these were enhanced and appeared in magazines around the world. The American people would wait 12 years before the film was transmitted on US television, though a copy was secured for screening at the New Orleans trial in which District Attorney Jim Garrison brought a case against prominent citizen Clay Shaw for being involved in 'a conspiracy', without specifying that it was a conspiracy to kill the president he had in mind. What with the mysterious deaths of intended witnesses and other impediments, Garrison, who brought into the open an enormous amount of useful data, was thwarted in his attempt to get a conviction and his case failed. The impact of the Zapruder screening was incalculable, however, **underlining how much about the assassination the American people, and indeed the world, were being prevented from knowing**.

73. New Orleans District Attorney Jim Garrison. (Courtesy Peggy Stewart)

Without this incredible continuous filmed record of the shooting of President Kennedy in Elm Street, perception of the whole affair would have been quite different. The most remarkable thing about this chance 8-mm colour amateur film is that it had no break in its continuity. Restored, it is a single stretch of film, unedited: it shows exactly what was there to be shown. Over the years, this film has been improved beyond measure in the various upgradings it has received. Eventually, it was separated into individual frames to receive the most updated, digitised treatment before being restored to its original form, so that it runs as a movie again. The difference in clarity of the end product is quite astounding.

74. Three frames from the Zapruder film: immediately before the fatal shot; the shot which killed President Kennedy; immediately after the fatal shot. Note where Mrs Kennedy is. Had this shot come from behind, as Warren asserted, her face would have been drenched in blood and brains.

(© Sixth Floor Museum, Dallas)

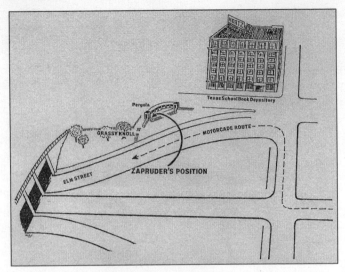

75. Sketch showing Zapruder's vantage point for filming. He stood on a low wall appended to the pergola. (Matthew Smith Collection)

Interestingly, perhaps suffering from a fatigue induced by challenges to the footage and the responsibility for holding it, Time–Life eventually sold the film to Zapruder's heirs for one dollar.

Not as much importance has been attributed to a sequence of moving film taken from the opposite side of the road, the *inside* of Dealey Plaza. Known as the Nix film, in black and white, it is true that it does not tell us as much as the Zapruder footage, but it adds considerably to our overall knowledge of events. The Orville Nix film recorded the president being hit, corresponding to the Zapruder footage. It also captured on film the area behind the motorcade, adjacent to the grassy knoll, and showed movement there, including someone running up the steps and disappearing into the car park. Attempts to get more from the film have not shown anything more remarkable than that which was first obtained.

There were quite a few others with movie cameras operating in Dealey Plaza that day. Located at the junction of Main and

Houston, Robert Hughes tracked the motorcade as it swept into Houston and turned into Elm Street. The special feature of his film, therefore, became the sixth-floor window at the end of the sequence, which, arguably, showed no one standing there. In their anxiety to dismiss the evidence of this film, the Warren Commission came perilously close to exonerating Lee Harvey Oswald. To get themselves out of difficulty, they declared that the film was shot at 12.20 p.m. This represented unbelievably obvious manipulation of evidence, since the timing of the film was established by the presence of the motorcade. The presidential car was in shot. Not surprisingly, however, the Warren Commission opted not to use the relevant still frame from the movie. A further look would have shown a figure at the next window to the one they claimed the shots had come from. This is interesting because the sixth floor was one long, continuous room with windows at regular distances apart, but with no dividing walls. Besides that, both windows also featured in a still picture taken by Jack A. Weaver a few seconds before the shooting began. It also showed a figure standing in the window next to the so-called 'assassin's window'.

On the subject of who was standing at which window and when, three eyewitnesses identified two figures, one with a rifle, standing at the sixth-floor 'assassin's window'. The time was established as 12.24 p.m., six minutes exactly before the shooting began. One of those seen was described as dark-skinned, perhaps black or Mexican, and he was wearing a white shirt. The other was white but no other features were noted. The witnesses thought they were seeing Secret Service personnel.

Charles L. Bronson was another who filmed from a location in Houston Street. He mixed taking 8-mm movie footage and 35-mm slides. He believed he had captured the Texas School Book Depository on film and thought he might have actually caught the sniper in action. He also filmed, with other valuable details, the moment the fatal bullet struck the president. In all, this amounted to a remarkable treasure trove. The FBI sent two special agents to view the film and they declared that Bronson had not, in fact, filmed the building the shots came from. This was quite wrong. The film showed the Texas building, including the sixth-floor window, in 92 frames. It was what it didn't show that would rob the film of interest to the FBI: Oswald was not visible anywhere in the movie. The fatal shot was observed and considered by the FBI special agents, but, they said, it was not clear enough to be useful.

We can now be sure that many pictures taken that day showed the 'assassin's window'. Leaving aside the various examples of which some arguably show either *two* figures at the window or *no* figures in evidence, it becomes remarkable that not one has turned up which claims to identify Lee Harvey Oswald being there.

There was extremely valuable visual evidence to be obtained in footage taken by several of the others with movie cameras. Marie Muchmore caught the moment when the president's head snapped back in response to the final shot. Activity on the grassy knoll was filmed by both F.M. Bell and John Martin. Bell's film showed onlookers racing up the knoll immediately after the shooting stopped. It would appear they clearly perceived that there was a shooter or shooters up there somewhere. At the same time, Martin's film showed several figures running away from the knoll. Could the shooters have been among them? None of these films was viewed by the Warren Commission. Considering the content of this group of films, all of which ran directly in opposition to the line the Warren Commission was taking, this would seem to be another instance of the commission having closed its mind to evidence which opposed it.

One or two mysteries pertain to the pictures taken of the events in Elm Street on that day. A movie camera much superior to Abraham Zapruder's was used by the mysterious 'Babushka Lady', as she became known, who filmed from the inside of Dealey Plaza, the other side of the street to Zapruder, as Nix had done. She filmed what was likely to become the superlative complement to Zapruder's footage. When the sound of the shots died away, however, her film, a cassette, was confiscated by an FBI agent. She has not heard from the FBI from that day to this. Enquiries resulted in her being told that the FBI knew nothing about her film. The Babushka Lady, so-called because of her babushka headscarf, proved to be the attractive Beverly Oliver, whom I met on several occasions during visits to Dallas. I spoke to her while preparing this book to ask if there had been any developments regarding what was prospective dynamic footage of great historical importance. Apart from the vital influence it might have had in relation to the truth of the events as they occurred in Elm Street, it was potentially worth no less than the attributed value of the Zapruder film, which amounts to millions of dollars. First, she told me that she had identified from photographs that Regis Kennedy was the FBI agent who made the confiscation. She had also learned that Seth Kantor, author of *The Ruby Cover-Up*, had told Finnish author Tim Mikkeonin that he should visit a vault in the ATI Building in New York, where he would see what was purported to be several copies (whatever that means) of the movie she had taken on display. He said he did so, saw them and passed the word back to Beverly.

76. The Babushka Lady, identified as Beverly Oliver. She told me she knows the name of the FBI agent who took her film and that it has never been returned.

Another mystery relates to the still pictures taken by Canadian photographer Norman Similas, who was a Toronto journalist. He returned to Canada with a whole series of pictures taken throughout the ambush on Elm Street. His pictures included one which showed the sixth-floor window, with two men in evidence, one holding a rifle. His paper, the *Toronto Telegram*, incredibly, decided not to use them. All of the pictures were returned to Similas, except for the shot of the sixth-floor window. They were accompanied by a generous cheque. Mystery surrounds the *Telegram's* passing up photographs of such a historic event on the one hand, but a further puzzle was created by their retaining the crucial picture of the sixth-floor window. And the questions which must follow are, obviously, where did it go and why?

77. Lee Harvey Oswald. Known as the 'backyard picture'. Marina Oswald tells me she did in fact take it. What is more telling is what happened to it afterwards. (See fig. 78 for related comparison photos.) (Courtesy National Archives)

There were many pictures taken at other times which were extremely pertinent to the killing of the president, perhaps the most famous of them all being the 'backyard photographs', which Marina Oswald assures me personally, the very day of writing this, she had taken. She claims, however, that she took one photograph. She did not account for the second photograph, however. I have always believed them to be fakes and Oswald himself declared them so. This does not mean that both are not right and that the picture was tampered with. At the end of the day, neither does it mean that his CIA paymasters who ordered him to buy a rifle by mail order did not also order him to display it in a photograph. Since he was being prepared as a patsy in the assassination scenario, that would exactly fit the role he was given. That copies turned up here and there in different contexts would only support this line of thinking. Detective Inspector Malcolm Thompson, a British forensic expert, examined copies of the pictures and declared them fakes. Retouching had certainly taken place, Thompson said, but not carefully enough. He thought the chin had been added to Oswald's face. In addition to the nose shadow being at a different angle to the body shadow, which had already been observed, he identified a further discrepancy in the shadow of the rifle Oswald held.

Considering that the motorcade, in total, was covered by literally hundreds of cameras of various kinds, those giving still pictures, slides, motion pictures and television, it might be said that what they produced, at the end of the day, was disappointing in respect of unmasking the killers of President Kennedy. On the other hand, when the vigilance of the Dallas police force and agents of the FBI and those dedicated to suppressing the truth are put into the mix, it might be remarkable how much visual data we actually have. I have no need to add that there were dark forces at work on that day.

78. From various prints: compare the pictures 2, 3 and 4 with the real Oswald, picture 1. (Courtesy National Archives)

* * *

My own experience of contributing to the media has been very mixed. I collaborated as consultant to the German television production *Assassination of the Century* for ZDF, the result being a strikingly good programme, greatly applauded in Germany. It was screened also in France, Belgium and Soviet Russia and, as I also appeared in the programme, I suddenly became an international spokesman on the subject.

I did not fare so well in Britain, however. I took a proposal for a series of six one-hour programmes on the subject to the programme controller, no less, of Central Television, who, as I already knew, was deeply interested in the JFK assassination. He listened to me attentively and said I should consult the head of his documentary department, which I did. In turn, he told me that if I secured the interest of a young producer whom he would send to meet me, it was on. I entertained the producer he sent for the better part of a working day and he left with his feet two inches from the ground. It was on, and I was appointed consultant.

The only problem with this was that I was never consulted. At the outset they were interested to contact a researcher in the United States whom I knew, and they got the benefit of this. They were happy for me to point them towards researchers who would form the key contributors to the programmes. As for consultation beyond this point, the answer is there was literally none. I was never consulted on any score about anything in the programmes, neither content nor any other aspect. I do remember, however, being in their London offices the night before the screening of the final part was scheduled. The man I was speaking to was their chief finance officer, who asked me if I knew what was in the final instalment. I replied that I did not and he told me that the producer intended naming the names of three snipers who shot at the president. The people he mentioned, three Frenchmen, had been suggested to me some years previously, but I had rejected the story. **My reaction to hearing what they intended to broadcast was to tell him that they would be sued.**

In fact, a national scandal broke, with the French government up in arms at such an accusation. This was, literally, front-page news. The three men named were accounted for by the government, no less: two were in different prisons in France and the third was on the high seas in a French minesweeper vessel at the time of the assassination. Threats of law suits on the part of the families of those accused ensued, but everything suddenly went quiet and it dropped out of the news. It is my guess that Central 'bought off' those planning lawsuits. From that day to this, they never told me what happened.

Yet they persist in naming me as a consultant in versions of the programmes showing via the Internet at the time of writing this. May I make it absolutely clear that my only involvement in this series was in persuading Central Television to undertake the major six-part series, and providing names and data relating to those they should contact. I was never consulted on any aspect of the content of the series. There is a tailpiece to this story, however – a real sting in the tail. Several years after *The Men Who Killed Kennedy* was released, I submitted other material to ITV, obtaining a reaction from the person I had approached that he had been warned 'from above' that he should know that I was the consultant to *The Men Who Killed Kennedy*. I think it is called being blackballed! Needless to say, my proposal went nowhere. My work, though featured on the BBC and by independent producers, has never been accepted by ITV since.

My most recent approach to ITV was in the middle of 2012, when I submitted a proposal with material for another major series, which I thought appropriate to the commemoration of the 50th anniversary of the assassination. I wrote a lengthy, personal and private letter to the head of factual programmes explaining fully what I had experienced regarding the production of *The Men Who Killed Kennedy* series. The company did not see its way to discuss my material at all. They simply rejected it. The personal and private letter I wrote was never even acknowledged, let alone answered.

* * *

The press and television have certainly not stopped attempting to influence people on the subject of the assassination, however. Their opinions are forever pressed upon those who read or watch. Television features all kinds of programmes with all kinds of theories, many based on inaccuracies. Newer features are particularly unimpressive, especially where they dramatise – and therefore, to some extent, fictionalise – what happened. This is very persuasive to audiences, especially the growing number of those who have no background knowledge of events.

Newspapers often let loose writers who are quite anti-Kennedy, attempting, it would appear, to promote the 'sweep it under the carpet' movement or, alternatively, the pro-Warren, re-establishment movement. Though I do not read all the US press and certainly not the Dallas press on a regular basis, I was unlucky enough to pick up a couple of editions of newspapers when in the United States commemorating the 30th anniversary of the assassination. I found it hard to stomach the blatant attempts to present the memory of President Kennedy in the worst possible light. I noted a few examples.

The *Dallas Morning News* of 21 November 1993: author G. Paterson is quoted in an article in this Sunday edition exhorting

Americans to 'reckon with a past that has not always matched [their image] of Kennedy as their young, fallen hero who never had a chance. Actually he had his chance and he failed.'

In the *Atlanta Journal* of 23 November 1993, Jon Carroll writes on the persistence of the 'fraudulent Kennedy mystique':

> Kennedy was the first great fraud of the post-modern era. He was the surprised and grateful object of a mass delusion . . . John F. Kennedy was a bit-player, insignificant historically, unimpressive intellectually, unappetising morally. **And it matters not at all who shot him** [my emphasis]. . . . The Kennedy mystique changed the way America thought about its presidents, and it changed it for the worse . . . Camelot . . . Why the hell did we need that?

79. Press cutting, *Daily Express*. Even elements of the British press joined in.

Then, of course, when the Gerald Posner book was released in 1993, the press in general gave it every ounce of support it could muster. In fact, the publicity that book received from the press across the world was more than impressive. No book on the assassination ever achieved anything like the exposure it received, and *Case Closed*, even as a virulently pro-Warren publication and, most certainly, anti-conspiracy volume, hardly justified the trumpeting. It suggested that the Establishment had set its sights on demolishing the memory of Kennedy once and for all. If this was so, it most certainly did not succeed. To my knowledge, Posner was not known as a Kennedy researcher; he had not written a book on the subject before

Case Closed and nor has he published another one since.

At the time his book was published, I was invited by the CBC (Canadian Broadcasting Corporation) to oppose Gerald Posner in a broadcast marking the 30th anniversary of the assassination. It was their prime spot for such programmes, and for it they transmitted me from Dallas and Posner from Washington. It was noticed that immediately prior to the broadcast they broadcast a lengthy live interview with a surviving, voluble member of the Warren Commission. They followed straight on with Posner and myself, and I found myself in deep trouble. Posner speaks rapidly, whereas I have a slow, deliberate delivery, which placed me at an enormous disadvantage. More than this, however, the interviewer went to Posner first throughout and effectively came to me only to comment on what he had said. I think the broadcaster, knowingly or unknowingly, had weighted its programming very heavily in one direction. It seemed to me that the two programmes taken together distinctly amounted to bias.

Having read Posner's book in preparation for the programme, I had quotes and topics I wished to confront him with. I never had the chance, for instance, to ask him why he featured the computer study programmed by Failure Analysis of California which produced the result that, effectively, Lee Harvey Oswald was guilty of killing the president but failed to mention that the same company also programmed a twin study which opposed the Warren findings and produced the opposite result.

22

SUSPECTS (PART ONE)

FOLLOWING THE ASSASSINATION, SLOWLY, THE initial fears that war might be imminent with either Russia or Cuba or both eventually dissipated. As time progressed and a war had not materialised, the tensions eased and people were able to realise for themselves the fallacy in the notion of an imminent communist threat. Those countries might be said to have been officially declared not guilty by the House Committee on Assassinations when it reported in 1979.

John F. Kennedy made a great many friends among the people, but he made a considerable number of enemies in other directions. Among his staff there were a number of people hostile to his ideas and his ways and methods. In the Pentagon, any support for the new president was soon lost amid the disappointment and frustration of being continually bypassed by what soon developed into an administration that sought peace and in the thinking of which hostilities came last. Here they were: the most powerful military force in the world and not permitted so much as to flex its muscles.

The making of a major film entitled *Seven Days in May* from a book by Fletcher Knebel and Charles W. Bailey II which featured a fictitious story about the generals ousting the president and taking over the government of the country had not come as a surprise to Kennedy. The book, extremely popular in the country at large, was dynamite in Washington. It was said that Kennedy vacated the White House for a weekend to facilitate the making of the picture, indicating his anxiety to bring the story further to public notice. Remarkably, at a meeting with President Khrushchev, the Russian president noted Kennedy's misgivings regarding the dangers that might emanate from the military. Fortunately, this scenario did not become a reality.

Kennedy had just cause for being suspicious of the military, however. Shortly after he became president, he discovered that the chairman of the Joint Chiefs of Staff, General Lyman Lemnitzer, had submitted a secret plan to Robert McNamara, who was Secretary of Defense. The proposal was to justify an invasion of Cuba by organising 'terrorist' activities against America, which, in fact, would be carried out by US military and intelligence personnel. It involved exploding plastic bombs and staging the shooting down of a civil airliner emanating from the US by a 'Cuban' plane. The plan was named Operation Northwoods, and Kennedy disposed of it. He also disposed of the services of General Lyman Lemnitzer as chairman of the Joint Chiefs of Staff.

Whatever was felt in the Pentagon was equally felt among those who enabled them to operate, however. There was a unique rapport between those involved in the war machine and the countrywide industrial providers of their needs. This had become known as the military-industrial complex. Dwight D. Eisenhower spoke of this in his outgoing speech as president and might have been delivering a warning directly to his successor when he said: 'The conjunction of an immense military establishment and a large arms industry is new in the American experience. We must guard against the acquisition of unwarranted influence, whether sought or unsought, by the military-industrial complex.'

President Kennedy came into conflict with the steel-makers over anti-inflationary measures on which he sought cooperation. The steelworkers' union, at Kennedy's request, had limited their upcoming demand for a wage increase for the labour force to a modest ten cents per hour. As part of the same anti-inflationary strategy, he had also written to the leaders of the steel industry indicating that their profit expectations were healthy and that increases in the price of steel were unwarranted. Within days of the agreement with the steelworkers, the leaders of steel increased their prices by six dollars a ton. It goes without saying that the steelworkers' union was inflamed, customers horrified and the president severely embarrassed. The president responded tartly to the leaders of the industry in a speech in which he lambasted them publicly for placing personal power and profit before public responsibility and showing utter contempt for the interests of 185 million Americans.

The oilmen were another power-group angered by his interest, which constituted a threat to their depletion tax allowances. Special benefits had been granted at a time when prospectors were risking huge sums of money digging for oil which, more often than not, failed to materialise. To encourage them to continue investment, which was seen to be vital to the country, very generous tax allowances had been granted. These allowances had survived even though, in the meantime, the oilmen had become rich beyond avarice, and Kennedy had their allowances in his sights for revision. Their role in the military-industrial complex was obvious: the military was entirely dependent on plentiful refined oil to make its wheels turn.

* * *

The Mafia was another group distinctly unhappy with Kennedy and his new administration. In the first place, wheeling and dealing which had gone on in Chicago between the president's father, Joe, and Mafia figures had led the mafiosi to believe – justified or unjustified – that they would be beneficiaries of the Kennedy son becoming president. I am not convinced by the stories which circulated that Sam Giancana and company had produced crucial votes sufficient to put Jack Kennedy into the White House. As Harold Weisberg put it to me, 'Mayor Daley always produced the vote for the Democrats.' Why should the Mafia become involved?

Of much greater concern was that the attorney general, the newly appointed Robert Kennedy, brother of the president, was having enormous success inspiring law-enforcement agencies throughout America in putting Mafia figures behind bars. This was on a scale never before known and success begat success.

Instead of hand-wringing, more and more had the courage to bring prosecutions which previously would have been considered a waste of time and money. Now they were succeeding and the Mafia was shaken to its very foundations. Small wonder that when Jimmy Hoffa heard the news of the president's death he is recorded as saying, 'Have you heard the good news? They killed the SOB. This means Bobby is out as attorney general.' His words clearly reflected that the real danger to the Mafia came from Robert rather than the president. Some mafiosi argued astutely that if Bobby Kennedy had become the target for assassination the president would have brought down the fires of hell on the Mafia. Hoffa had, it appears, advocated JFK as a better target than Robert Kennedy, arguing that 'when you cut down the tree, the branches fall with it'.

80. President Kennedy with Robert, his attorney general brother.
(Courtesy John F. Kennedy Library)

Some think that when Jack Ruby shot Oswald the Mafia might have dispatched him to carry out his task, perhaps to cover their backs with regard to any involvement they might have had in the assassination. Frankly, I do not accept this. In view of what we later learned, if the Mafia was involved, though not impossible, it is hard to see how. One writer claimed they had been the shooters, which does not sit comfortably with anyone's idea of the ways and methods of the mafiosi. They certainly were not renowned for outstanding marksmanship. It should be said, however, that the writer was not alone in his assertion. There was a second, similar, theory raised much later that the CIA had brought in Mafia snipers to carry out the assassination.

But then there were a number of theories based on quotations from Carlos Marcello, Santo Trafficante and Jimmy Hoffa, none of which succeeded in convincing those people who heard them. With the notable exception of David E. Scheim, who wrote *The Mafia Killed President Kennedy*, the claims had few convinced supporters among the ranks of the researchers. The biggest problem, in the main, was that evidence of a cover-up became more and more apparent, and, whatever capabilities they might have had, the Mafia distinctly did not have clout in that direction.

* * *

Although Cuba, as a political entity, was exonerated from suspicion of being responsible for the assassination, this did not prevent many from thinking that shooters had been imported from Cuba, and there was a torrent of extremely interesting stories supporting this idea, but, again, it appeared they were short on evidence and long on speculation, based on the obvious suspicion of Cuban involvement on the grounds of the country's anti-American position. Some, however, have never changed their minds on Cubans being behind the assassination. The experience of Sylvia Odio might well be an example of what has supported this suspicion.

It was during September, two months prior to the assassination, that, in her Dallas home, Cuban-born Sylvia Odio was visited by three strangers. Sylvia and her younger sister, Annie, were alone in the house and she was, therefore, extremely cautious about unknown visitors. She kept them strictly on the other side of the chained door at first. Two of the strangers were Latin Americans and one American. When one of the Latin Americans spoke knowledgeably of her father, imprisoned for anti-Castro politics, and said they were members of the Junta Revolucionaria, she became interested enough to let them into her house. Their understanding of Cuban affairs impressed her. They soon made it known that they were seeking funds for their revolutionary activities. They gave their names and introduced the silent American as Leon Oswald. They did not obtain any funding and left after a brief meeting. Sylvia Odio had sensed there was something odd about her visitors. The following day, she received a telephone call from one of the Latin Americans, a Leopoldo, which may have underlined her misgivings. He asked her, 'What did you think of the American?', to which she said she had no particular opinion. 'Well, you know, he's a Marine, an ex-Marine and an expert marksman. He would be a tremendous asset to anyone, except that you never know how to take him . . . He could go either way. You know our idea is to introduce him to the underground in Cuba, because he is great, he is kind of nuts. The Americans say we Cubans don't have any guts. He says we should have shot President Kennedy after the Bay of Pigs. He says we should do something like that.'

There was no further contact from any of them but, watching television at the time of the assassination, Sylvia Odio had no difficulty identifying 'Leon' Oswald with Lee Harvey Oswald.

The meaning of this episode has eluded all who have tried to make complete sense out of it, but a couple of things can be explained. The silent 'Oswald' appeared to be present for the sake of appearance. It facilitated the telephone call the following day, in which Oswald was clearly being advertised as involved in the assassination of President Kennedy a few weeks later. This was during the time a 'false Oswald' was seen in various places attracting attention to himself, as faithfully recorded by Richard H. Popkin in his book *The Second Oswald*.

It is entirely possible the plan was that in taking 'Oswald' to the daughter of a prominent Cuban revolutionary, they appeared to be inviting the forthcoming assassination to be linked to Cuba and Cubans, 'not so gutless, they would have us believe, because they had followed "Oswald's" advice, with him leading the way'. The stories told and the 'connections' revealed leading to Cuban involvement have already occupied the pages of entire books.

* * *

In what I have so far written on this subject I might be thought to be suggesting that somewhere along the line there was the involvement of military figures, unhappy with Kennedy's 'inertia', as they saw it. The actual carrying out of the assassination was, by all accounts, a classic ambush, which would certainly make military involvement a believable scenario. Mafia figures also, in one way or another, were deemed to be involved and, on that basis, I would not argue. It appears that there was also input from Cubans or sources with Cuban influence.

Then there is the CIA. The next chapter leads us to consider the strong suspicion which has surrounded the CIA, which, from the beginning, had people wondering and which became, to many researchers and members of the public, the front-runner among suspects.

23

SUSPECTS (PART TWO):
THE CENTRAL INTELLIGENCE AGENCY

THE HOSTILE ATTITUDE OF THE CIA TOWARDS
President Kennedy was not a secret. Kennedy came to reciprocate
the hostility, and Senator Mike Mansfield, to whom he stated his
intention to 'tear [the CIA] into a thousand pieces and scatter it
to the winds', did not, it would appear, consider the words for
his ears alone. It should be remembered that the divide between
the president and the elected government on the one hand and
the CIA on the other was not something originated for President
Kennedy. The CIA had been formed by President Harry S. Truman,
who had apparently watched in dismay at the so-called development
of the Agency. After John F. Kennedy was killed, though long
retired, Truman spoke his mind on the subject:

> For some time I have been disturbed by the way the CIA has been
> diverted from its original assignment. It has become an operational
> arm and at times a policy-making arm of the government. I never
> had any thought . . . when I set up the CIA that it would be
> injected into peacetime cloak-and-dagger operations. Some of the
> complications and embarrassment that I think we have experienced
> are in part attributable to the fact that this quiet intelligence arm
> of the President has become so removed from its intended role.

There was no doubt that Kennedy had come to realise soon after
his election to the Presidency that the CIA considered themselves
above and apart from the elected government. His was a baptism
of fire, in having had the details of the projected invasion of Cuba

thrust at him before he had had time to find out where to hang his hat. This was to be a CIA invasion. It had been planned by the CIA to be carried out by Cuban dissidents, refugees and others who had fled Cuba on Castro taking power. The CIA had recruited them, clothed them, fed them, trained them and equipped them. The CIA had organised their transit to a Bay of Pigs landing point, organised air cover, such as it was, organised supply ships, the whole works. What they had not organised was the president and his support for their scheme. Kennedy's predecessor, Dwight D. Eisenhower, believed he had authorised the formation of a guerrilla band who would be sent to Cuba. He apparently had no idea of the proportions to which the scheme had been expanded, though it is suspected that the man he had put in charge of it, Richard Nixon, may have done. Kennedy reluctantly agreed to the proposed invasion when pressed on the basis that everything was 'ready to go' and would not keep.

Kennedy had distinct reservations, however, of which he made no secret. This was to be Cuban against Cuban. There would be no US support given and America would not be going to war against Cuba on the operation's coat-tails. There would be no involvement of US personnel whatsoever, the president stipulated. Of course, this was largely ignored by the CIA, whose agents were much in evidence directing operations. By all indications, they thought that if push came to shove they could always twist the arm of the 'new boy'. If that was the case, they were terribly wrong. From the beginning, the so-called invasion went awry. Incredibly, it was said to have been doomed to failure by poor and incorrect basic intelligence upon which they acted.

In desperation, they sent a radio message to Washington for air backup, under which umbrella they would withdraw. They claimed Kennedy had agreed to this, altough this is extremely doubtful. Even though he had almost certainly not done so, under extreme pressure he ordered the essential withdrawal cover to be provided. Unfortunately, the aircraft designated to see them out arrived one hour after it was due. This was likely caused by an error in calculating time-zone differences. The consequences were disastrous.

Blood flowed freely, some of which was that of agents who should not have been there. The outcome was that the CIA placed the entire blame for their fiasco on President Kennedy and his brother Robert, who was deputising for him during part of the time involved. I am not sure whether it was bravely or foolishly, but the president accepted the blame. There is no doubt, however, that he was acutely aware of the CIA's hostility towards him.

When Cuba received missiles from Russia, which it erected in what was considered a deliberate threat to America, the famous 'eyeball-to-eyeball' confrontation with Khrushchev took place. The world held its breath and, eventually, the Russian president yielded. As part of the Cuban missiles settlement, President Kennedy agreed there would be no more attempts to invade Cuba, nor any more attempts on Castro's life. Unbelievably, the CIA blatantly disregarded the president's promises and planned in collaboration with prominent Mafia figures further attempts to kill Castro. When Kennedy learned of this, he was furious. Further to this, it was also revealed that the CIA had, after the Bay of Pigs fiasco, created new training camps and planned a second invasion of Cuba. Kennedy responded by sending in the FBI and the police to dismantle the camps and destroy the armaments they found there.

Needless to say, the relationship between the president and the CIA went from bad to worse. In one case, Kennedy suspected they had been responsible for the murder of a foreign leader which he had expressly forbidden. In another, he had been assured by the CIA of the innocence of an American academic arrested in the USSR for spying. A personal appeal from Kennedy to President Khrushchev on the man's behalf led to him being released. Upon the professor's return to America, he was invited to meet the president and revealed to him that he had, in fact, been working for the CIA in Russia. This could only suggest to Kennedy that Khrushchev knew more of what was happening in America than he did. Such events hacked at the roots of confidence in government from every point of view. Long before the deep and meaningful speech on the subject from Harry S. Truman, David Wise and

Thomas B. Ross, of the *New York Herald Tribune*, saw clearly what was going on and wrote:

> There are two governments in the United States today. One is visible. The other is invisible. The first is the government people read about in the newspapers and children study in their civics books. The second . . . invisible government, gathers intelligence, conducts espionage, and plans and executes secret operations all over the globe . . . Major decisions involving war or peace are taking place out of public view. An informed citizen might come to suspect that the foreign policy of the United States often works publicly in one direction and secretly through the invisible government in just the opposite direction.

Such insight was, therefore, not exclusive to 'insiders'. Here were two journalists who perceived what was happening and were bold enough to speak out. They could not have been alone in reading the signs. Undoubtedly, John F. Kennedy knew precisely what time of day it was. Small wonder that 'CIA' sprang into so many minds as the chief suspect when John F. Kennedy was assassinated.

* * *

Many years later, millions watched the Oliver Stone movie *JFK* and wondered who the shadowy military man was who was central to his version of events. Stone later revealed that the man was L. Fletcher Prouty, who was a colonel in the USAAF. He could not have done better. Prouty was high up in the 'those who know' league and in possession of data which he was determined to bring out into the open. He wrote several books, one of which was *JFK: The CIA, Vietnam and the Plot to Assassinate John F. Kennedy* and another *The Secret Team: The CIA and Its Allies in Control of the United States and the World*, in which he shared what he knew of that which was not intended to be known outside certain privileged circles.

L. Fletcher Prouty was chief of special operations for the Joint

Chiefs of Staff. During Kennedy's time in office, he had been the focal point officer between the CIA and the Pentagon. He was in New Zealand when the news of the assassination was received and spoke out about how amazed he was to find in a newspaper that Lee Harvey Oswald was already named as the killer. They also had a photograph of Oswald. Prouty was further astonished to learn that full details of who Oswald was, his 'defection' and his time in Russia, being pro-Castro and having a Russian wife, complete with a photograph of a smartly dressed Oswald, were transmitted on the international news wire soon after, if not before, he was arrested by Dallas Police.

Like the FBI, the CIA filtered what was supplied to the Warren Commission. James Jesus Angleton, who was the CIA's counter-intelligence chief, was understood to have telephoned FBI man Bill Sullivan to rehearse questions and answers in readiness for submission to the Warren Commission. The CIA, skilled in such matters, made sure the Warren Commission heard only what it wanted them to hear.

Any consideration of the complicity of CIA agents in the murder of President Kennedy is undoubtedly complicated by the knowledge that trying to get the truth from that Agency is difficult beyond belief. They are skilled at 'dirty tricks', deceit, lies and covering their tracks. The CIA has been top of the suspects list virtually since the day the president was killed. It constitutes another group, like those we have already mentioned, which most researchers believe was involved in the assassination in one way or another. I was privileged in being given 'sound-as-a-dollar' information relating to this by a person who ranks as an outstanding first-hand witness, which I feature in some detail in Chapter 35.

Kennedy, daily aware of the menace of the CIA to United States government, knew they considered themselves the originators and executives of American foreign policy, regardless of the president and the elected government. Kennedy had taken steps to bring them into line by the issuance of orders which completely spiked their guns. They continued as though nothing had happened until the assassination took place and afterwards.

Meanwhile, it appears everyone suspected CIA involvement all along, except – by virtue of their 'exoneration' by the House Assassinations Committee – for the American government.

24

SUSPECTS (PART THREE):
THE MILITARY-INDUSTRIAL COMPLEX

THERE IS NOT THE SLIGHTEST DOUBT THAT THE Establishment, made up of industrialists and other big-business people, were frustrated and extremely unhappy with President Kennedy, not to mention somewhat in fear of what he might do next. Their frustration and unhappiness derived from a variety of causes. The manufacturers of warplanes, armaments and the other many accoutrements of war had no outlet for their manufactures, since Kennedy resolutely sought other ways in international policies than going to war. Included were those identified as belonging to the military-industrial complex, ranging from such as the steel industry to the vast range and number of light industries and other business houses which supplied them. To their ranks should be added the oilmen, whose product was essential to fuel the military vehicles, tanks, planes and everything they made that moved and throbbed. Additionally, the oilmen had another pertinent reason for disliking the president. He was looking at the very special tax allowances they enjoyed with a view to bringing them into line with other businesses. These tax breaks had made billionaires out of millionaires, and they did not like the prospect of a change.

The Kennedy administration had revealed a tendency towards a fundamental shift in government priorities. Hitherto, the well-being of the Establishment had taken pride of place, first in the queue for consideration. Put into simple terms, Kennedy was placing the best interests of the people ahead of those of big business, and it had begun to show and to be felt. As we have observed elsewhere, President Kennedy had no qualms in taking on whoever or whatever he saw enjoying an unwarranted advantage, especially if the workers were penalised as a consequence, and even more especially if the advantage to the perpetrators was the satisfaction of greed. The steel industry was an outstanding example of this. Industrialists at large feared the steel dispute was the thin end of the wedge which would bring in government prices and wage controls, distinctly socialist and to be avoided at all costs.

Developments since the 'removal' of President Kennedy underline how right he was and illustrate how well aimed were his intentions. I listened to a rerun of a speech made by Robert Kennedy Jr in New York on May Day of 2007, in which he speaks of 'the corporate takeover of our government and the domination of a free press'. He speaks of a negative and indolent press in the United States, points a finger at the government showing an obligation to shareholders rather than the people and gives examples of the government accommodating big business in response to their donations.

The Establishment did not expect Kennedy to become president, of course, and when he did it was by the smallest of margins. His win came as quite a shock to many, especially those in big business who regarded him as a completely unknown quantity, an outsider. Kennedy's whole attitude to disadvantaged Americans, for instance, such as the black population who, in general terms, were regarded by many as inferiors, second-class citizens, came as another shock. He stood for equality, which for some translated as socialism; to others, he was, in any case, considered an out-and-out socialist, and socialism, in their book, amounted to a form of communism, their biggest dread. Fortunately, many ordinary Americans did not see it that way, and they welcomed this young man who was vigorous, capable of original thought and who brought with him a breath of fresh air, which, as they saw it, was much wanted in politics.

There was no doubt that Kennedy stuck out his chin when it came to giving voice to his vision of a version of the welfare state in which there would be provision for the poor, the disadvantaged, the sick and the elderly. And the fact that his policies were, generally, acceptable to if not popular with most ordinary Americans, as might have been expected, resulted in support for him increasing by leaps and bounds, which provided another reason for the Establishment to worry: at the next election it would not be a tiny margin that would see him to a second term. John F. Kennedy was to be no flash in the pan. And then, in the back of the minds of some was the question, after John F., what about Bobby Kennedy and then Edward?

There is no doubt that a deal of the uncertainty and indeed suspicion surrounding Kennedy when he became president derived from the fact that he was sponsored and bankrolled by Joe, his father. Joe was a millionaire over and over again. His background included politics in a big way; he had backed Roosevelt in his efforts to unscramble the dire economic problems of the '30s. His success in this led to his appointment as American ambassador to London during the Second World War. At this stage, he likely had ambitions to become president himself one day.

In London, however, he seriously blotted his copybook. He did not like Winston Churchill and he was somewhat scornful of the Queen. Furthermore, he is on record as expressing the belief that Hitler would win the war. Could there be any other way to attract unpopularity? He found one. He observed that those ships which brought lend-lease essentials to Britain would be returning to the US empty. Having made a fortune out of bootleg liquor during Prohibition and still very much in the business, he bought supplies of liquor to occupy the empty ships returning home, from which he would add to his fortune.

His other business dealings included funding a Hollywood studio, and his scandalous affair with film star Gloria Swanson did not go down well. Neither did his association with Chicago-based Mafia figures. Overall, he was not well liked in business circles and there were those nervous of him becoming 'the power behind the throne'. But there was no cause for fear. Though perhaps it was not apparent at the outset, President Kennedy was his own man and not remotely likely to be pursuing an agenda pressed on him by his father. He was to prove such fears quite unfounded easily in what he did and how he did it. But Establishment fears were not so readily dismissed, and the new path he was following, as advertised in his policies, attracted an opposition great enough to encompass a group who were anxious to get rid of him.

In a startling book entitled *Farewell America*, which was published as early as 1968, James Hepburn wrote, 'Big business grew more and more concerned about the tendencies of the Kennedy administration, and industrialists aren't the type of people to sit around and chew their fingernails.' Small wonder his book was published in Liechtenstein, no doubt because he could not find anyone to take it on in the United States of America. This was a daring thing to say in the context, and it was not by any means the only daring thing he had to say.

Some readers will recall a movie released in 1973, a feature film entitled *Executive Action* which purported to be no more than a fictional account of a conspiracy to kill the president. It also was daring in its day, portraying a group of like-minded businessmen who sit round a long table, much in the style of a board meeting, and discuss how to get rid of the 'unacceptable' and 'un-American' president. The storyline was based on Mark Lane's book *Rush to Judgment*. The screenplay was by Dalton Trumbo, based on a story by Donald Freed and Mark Lane. It featured Burt Lancaster and Robert Ryan, two top stars at the time, in leading roles and therefore ranked as a major movie. 'Executive action', by the way, is a term coined by the CIA in the '50s, and the man appointed to organise the assassination (played by Lancaster) is said to be a black-operations specialist who has previously worked for the CIA.

I have never forgotten the image of that 'board meeting', and it would come as no surprise to me if that proved to be how the involvement of big business in the assassination was set up. But the question has to be asked: was there a connection between big business and the CIA? Indeed there was. CIA agents acted as the eyes and ears of big business in foreign lands. It was the inspiration for the vigorous words written by Jim Hougan in *Spooks*:

> Whether it's computers, hamburgers, newspapers, or jets, America's Paladin spooks are increasingly likely to have a hand in it (and sometimes a strong arm as well) . . . Profit, rather than patriotism, is their assignment. Laws are broken: smears, bag jobs, bribes, wiretaps, deception operations, currency scams, industrial espionage, tax frauds, and even assassination programs have been planned and carried out by contract agents of the business world.

I have been aware for a long time that CIA agents met with representatives of US big-business concerns to report on market potential, political considerations and many other valuable aspects affecting overseas commerce. It would be no stretch of the imagination to think their discussions might revolve around the difficulties for businessmen emanating from the policies of President Kennedy and the hatred of CIA agents for JFK, particularly after the Bay of Pigs debacle. It would be no surprise if this contact between the CIA and Establishment moguls through the meetings between staff and agents resulted in their cooperation. The details of their respective feelings – and maybe plans – of the agents to whom they had been talking being relayed upwards to their superiors in the boardrooms, would not come as any surprise. It might account for who eventually sat round that boardroom table (à la *Executive Action*) debating the availability of large sums of money dedicated to the 'removal' of what they saw as the cause of their problems.

Those in the big-business community, which would, of course, include the industrialists, had liaisons with more than CIA agents. Their contacts and their influence went far and wide. It must be apparent to many associated with the armed forces, for instance, that the president was mown down in a classic ambush. Snipers were located in a number of positions around the point where he was killed and shooting from various directions. That part of the plan does not sound as though it emanated from the CIA planners or, say, Mafia planners either. It sounds like the contribution of a military man, and a very influential military man at that. Perhaps there was one sitting at the boardroom table whose suggestion was thrust forward to those who would be carrying out the execution, for it was nothing short of that.

25

PARKLAND HOSPITAL:
THE PROCEDURES

By Colin McSween

Colin McSween studied human biology, physiology and pathology for his degree in mortuary science, and later forensic odontology and microbiology in infectious disease.

AS SOON AS THE PRESIDENT HAD BEEN SHOT, DALLAS Police Chief Jesse Curry, in an unmarked car leading the presidential limousine, ordered his dispatcher to notify Parkland Memorial Hospital of the shooting and that they were on their way there. The confirmation to Chief Curry from dispatch was at 12.32 p.m. CST.

In response, a stat call went over Parkland's PA system for Dr Tom Shires, who was away speaking at a medical conference in Galveston, Texas. Aware of his absence, several other doctors headed to the emergency department. Hospital staff cleared the emergency area, in particular Major Medicine, of anyone deemed non-essential.

Although the motorcade had largely disintegrated after the shooting, the first group of some eight vehicles arrived at Parkland's emergency entrance by 12.38 p.m. One of the vehicles to get detached from the motorcade bore the president's personal physician, Dr George G. Burkley. He, along with other members of the president's staff, had wound up at the Trade Mart where the president was scheduled to speak. A police officer found out who he was, placed him in his police car and rushed him to Parkland Hospital.

81. The scene at Parkland Hospital. (Courtesy National Archives)

The curious at Parkland Hospital attempted to get near the presidential car to see what had happened. Mrs Kennedy did her best to shield her husband, to keep anyone from seeing his wounds. She had spent the trip from Dealey Plaza to Parkland trying to hold his shattered head together and wanted privacy, trying to prevent others from seeing the gruesome disfigurement inflicted by the bullet(s).

Motorcycle policeman H.B. McLain had flanked the left side of the motorcade six to eight vehicle lengths behind the president but had caught up to Chief Curry's car on Stemmons Freeway while en route to Parkland. He now stood at the left side of the president's car, where he saw pieces of cranial debris (scalp, skull and brain) scattered about the limousine's rear passenger compartment. Along with Officer McLain stood presidential aides David Powers and Kenneth O'Donnell and agents including Clint Hill, who had climbed onto the presidential car after the fatal head shot(s) and was still in the limousine for the first several seconds at Parkland. This human shield, supported by a number of police officers, was effective in keeping the curious at bay.

In the jump seat immediately in front of the president, Texas governor John Connally knew he was seriously wounded but also knew the president's injury was infinitely worse, as he had pieces of the president's brain on his clothing, and knew he'd have to move before anyone could get to the president. The governor ignored his wife's plea to be still and instead tried to get out of the way. In his effort to stand up, the governor instinctively inhaled and in doing so he drew slivers of his fractured fifth rib back into his chest and cried out, 'My God, it hurts!' as he dropped back into his seat.

Those around Mrs Kennedy were trying to get her to let them take the president into the hospital, where he could be looked at by medical personnel. Mrs Kennedy said, 'But, Mr Hill, you know he's dead.' Clint Hill replied to the effect, 'They've got to try.' Hill had removed his own suit jacket and placed it over the president. Mrs Kennedy used the jacket to cover the president's head and shoulders.

The governor was quickly lifted out of the car and taken to Trauma Room 2 (TR2) for triage and then to the surgical suite on the second floor. With the jump seats now folded and out of the way, President Kennedy was lifted and placed on a gurney by Dave Powers and Secret Service agents Clint Hill and Roy Kellerman. Mrs Kennedy was assisted by Officer McLain, who lifted her out of the rear passenger compartment as she reached to keep Hill's jacket around the president's head. She took a position holding onto the right-hand side rail of the gurney. People inside the hospital saw her running in this pose, escorted by a ring of men in suits and Officer McLain.

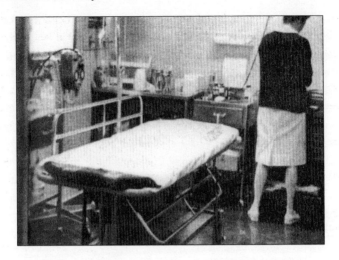

82. Trauma Room 1, where they took President Kennedy.
(Courtesy Colin McSween)

The President's Wounds

Two wounds were noted, one in the anterior (front) neck in the lower third, slightly beneath the Adam's apple (thyroid cartilage). This wound was variably described as neat, punctuated, perforating, penetrating, smooth, tucked inward, etc. Dr Malcolm Perry said it was no larger than 3.5 to 5 mm in greatest diameter. It exhibited a bleeding that medical experts described as 'exuding' (def. 'sweating'). This was a type of bleeding not unlike what you'd see with a puncture wound caused by a nail or similar smaller instrument of injury.

The other wound was in the occipital (rearmost area) and parietal (upper side or 'crown') of the skull. As some of the doctors later described it, 'occipitoparietal', which is a deliberate conjoined term (back and upper side of the skull). The term 'occipito' placed in front of 'parietal' is no mistake. The preference or prefix position in the conjoined term is given to the area of greatest defect. The skull wound was described as avulsed, blasted, blasted out, and the brain (encephalon) injury was described as herniated, torn, macerated, etc.

The hole in the back and upper right side of the skull was not only large enough for physicians to see the areas of the brain that were effectively destroyed and/or missing but also large enough to allow the entire cerebellum (approximately half the size of a large peach) normally located at the extreme rear and lower aspect thereof of the skull to fall out onto the trauma cart during treatment in Trauma Room 1 (TR1). This was far larger than any alleged entry wound.

Triage and Trauma Treatment

By 12.43 p.m., President Kennedy was in TR1 in the care of Dr James Carrico, who expeditiously conducted his own triage* in assessing the wounds while rapidly initiating emergency trauma treatments and resuscitation efforts on the president. His views of the president's condition are perhaps the most significant, as he was the first physician to see the president immediately after the shooting, and although Dr Kemp Clark, director of Parkland's neurological surgery, entered the room some minutes after Dr Carrico and several other doctors, Dr Clark's report mirrors closest the admission notes of Dr Carrico. The latter was the only physician to detect a heartbeat, which soon faded in the ensuing minutes as the blood pressure was so low as to be non-existent, due to severe exsanguination (blood loss), so as to preclude cardiac arrest (heart stoppage).

The basic steps of primary trauma are similar to the ABCs of emergency first aid: airway, breathing and circulation. Many of the attending physicians in TR1 noted that the president was making what is called 'agonal respirations' or 'spasmodic respirations' ('spasmodic' implies a jerky, irregular but definite attempt to breathe). 'Agonal' is a term pertaining to the approach of death,

---

* Triage is an assessment of the more evident and serious injuries in terms of immediate threat to the survivability of a patient. Although the many physicians who saw the president had felt that he was in fact 'moribund' (near or nearing death), they were fully professionally committed to doing what they could in their trauma treatment to maintain the basic remaining vital signs even if there was little or no hope of getting their patient stabilised.

which lends itself further yet to the term that so many of the doctors used in stating that the president was 'moribund'.

The reader may find it odd that the president was still able to be breathing in spite of having nearly one half of his brain blasted out, but the lingering efforts at breathing were possible because that which had been blasted out was portions of the voluntary, volitional or intellectual matter (portions of the right side of the cerebrum and all of the cerebellum, which had been detached). The portion of the brain which regulates breathing is the medulla oblongata which is a portion of the brain stem (not part of the cerebrum or the cerebellum) and is non-volitional or non-intellectual, thus not requiring any level of consciousness of the patient in order to function. However, in President Kennedy's situation this was being seriously compromised due to the tremendous loss of blood and the severe ravages committed on all of the adjacent tissues comprising his skull and brain. If the blood became deprived of vital oxygen and the blood stopped circulating, which eventually did occur, somatic death would result.

Dr Carrico initiated treatment of the immediate issues of concern as fast as nurses cut the president's clothing and peeled it out of the way. The airway was of immediate concern, as the president was making some effort to breathe (albeit autonomically), but it was clear some assistance had to be provided. A Bennett respirator was at the ready in TR1. A cuffed endotracheal tube (or orotracheal tube) was inserted via the mouth and beyond the pharynx (throat) and into the trachea (windpipe). It was evident to Dr Carrico that there was a small anterior (frontal) wound in the lower third of the president's neck. Dr Perry later described it as from 3.5 to 5 mm in greatest diameter. Oswald's ammunition was 6.5 mm in diameter.

The discovery made when they inserted the endotracheal (orotracheal) tube is interesting. Mind you, none of the attending physicians was a forensic pathologist, and nor were they trying to find such things. However, their notes recorded that same day reveal some amazing data. The tube reached the trachea (airway/ windpipe) then passed the larynx (vocal cords); as it reached immediately below the larynx, the tube met with blasted 'ragged' tissue. This is significant for this reason: the end of the tube would have tended to glide along the inside of the frontal surface of the interior of the trachea. If there was blasted or ragged tissue in that location and there was a corresponding small, neat, punctuated, penetrating wound on the outside surface of the neck, this was most likely a wound inflicted from the front and not from the rear, where the president's accused assassin was allegedly located.

Once the end of the tube was positioned at a point that they felt was sufficiently past the area of injury in order to work, they inflated the cuff in order to provide the best possible seal so as to affect an uninterrupted flow of oxygen to the president's lungs. The Bennett respirator was attached to the tube so as to 'assist' the president's breathing or respirations and not to 'provide respirations' as the Bennett respirator was not a 'life-support' machine but was rather a 'positive ventilation' apparatus, much like a sleep-apnoea machine. This might well suffice, provided that the seal created by the endotracheal tube's inflated cuff held adequately, and provided the president managed to continue making some effort to breathe, as spasmodic as it was. TR1 at this time was nearly filled by several other doctors, all of whom had been alerted either by the stat call or by fellow doctors or nurses. The otherwise sufficiently sized room was at capacity or beyond, but there was work for almost everyone, and they managed to find a location where their skills were put to work.

Some of them performed 'cut downs', which are deep incisions made to access some of the larger veins in order to insert larger flexible IV needles (polyethylene catheters) than those with which we are, perhaps, familiar. This was done in order to provide a rapid and large-volume infusion of blood and other required life-sustaining liquids that had been for the most part lost due to the massive bleeding sustained from the head shot. In President Kennedy's case, the sites selected were his right and left ankles at the lateral aspects and his left anterior forearm nearer the wrist. To increase the best possible results of the infusion of blood and Ringer's lactated solution, the trauma cart was adjusted so as to effect a Trendelenburg position. This places the body in a head-end-downward position so as to result in a more rapid delivery of the vital infused fluids to the areas of the body where the injuries have been sustained and the vital organs which had been deprived of their vital blood and fluid balance.

The president's blood was drawn for type and cross-match and whole units of blood quickly arrived (by delivery van). Dr Carrico was already aware of some aspects of the president's medical history, in particular his adrenal insufficiency, and diligently included 300 cc of hydrocortisone to the president along with the infused fluids.

As frustrating as this may seem now in retrospect, the doctors were not there to perform a forensic task and so were not concerned with locating bullets nor proving or establishing trajectories. Their entire focus and primary concern was trying to resuscitate the president, to keep him alive so as to provide every conceivable advantage perhaps towards getting his vital signs working and stabilising – if there were any chance of that.

Interestingly, the Secret Service had recruited ambulance attendants Aubrey Rike and Dennis McGuire for the purpose of transferring the president to a Catholic hospital in the event that the doctors managed to get him stabilised. These two men were seated with Mrs Kennedy immediately outside of TR1.

It soon became evident that the cuffed endotracheal tube was proving to be insufficient and the president's respirations were failing. It was also evident that there were internal thoracic (chest) injuries resulting from the anterior throat bullet wound. There was, as stated later by Dr Perry, 'evidence of blood and air in the upper mediastinum [upper mid-chest and extending into what some might call the lower neck]'.

One would think that 'air in the chest' might be normal, given that that's where the lungs are, but whereas air within the bronchial tree (the lungs' air passages and air sacs) is normal, air in the pleural spaces or elsewhere in the chest is not normal. It is generally referred to as 'pneumothoracis' (air in the chest or lung spaces) and can very quickly become life-threatening, as this misplaced air will continue to accumulate, eventually creating enough pressure on the outer surfaces of the lungs to prevent them from inflating. Another evidence of this 'air' was manifest in a condition known as subcutaneous emphysema, which presented as palpable air bubbles trapped beneath the skin.

Many of the Parkland doctors felt that the shot that had hit the president in the neck had ranged downward into his chest. But at no time was the president ever turned onto his side(s) nor was he turned over for further examination of his posterior surfaces while under the care of the Parkland physicians, as many of them felt that this bullet had not transited the body or exited. Furthermore, they were not in a position to perform surgery, as such surgery is never undertaken unless the vital signs can be more or less stabilised. At this juncture, their task was to do what they could to maintain whatever rapidly fading signs of life remained.

In order to counter the pneumothoracis, two small incisions were made in the upper anterior chest slightly above each nipple. These incisions were made sufficiently deep to perforate the anterior pleurae, facilitating the insertion of two chest tubes (one to each of the two lung spaces) in order to enable the displaced air to escape and allow the best chance for the lungs to be able to fully inflate. The opposite or free ends of the tubes were placed in underwater sealed drainage to create a vacuum to draw the 'air' off.

In order to provide a more thorough avenue for the delivery of oxygen to the air spaces in the lungs, two changes were made. The endotracheal tube was exchanged for a tracheotomy. A tracheotomy is an invasive procedure – an incision is made in the front of the neck and through the superficial subcutaneous muscles in order to access the trachea, which is in turn then opened to allow the placement of a breathing tube.

Discussion and debate has ensued about the location and direction in which Dr Malcolm Perry made his incision: whether it was transverse (from side to side/crosswise) or otherwise. Aubrey Rike, the man who casketed the president, told me many times over some 20 years that to the best of his recollection the incision ran vertically (straight up and down, and not transverse). Further discussion has raged for years over how large an incision is deemed 'normal' for such a procedure. In my own experience, tracheotomy incisions tend to vary in size and in direction from one extreme to another depending upon any number of anomalies or other obstacles encountered.

The president's tracheotomy incision may have been made larger than in other circumstances on account of there being damaged tissue and perhaps bruising in the immediate area due to the bullet wound in that location. There was in fact a wound noted more to the right of centre, which had caused the trachea to be slightly bent or deviated to one side. Dr Malcolm Perry said he made his incision at the location of the wound. The argument tends to revolve around the size of the external incision in the skin, but should more realistically and reasonably focus on the size of the opening made in the trachea itself, and not the size of the photographically visible incision at the surface of the skin on the front of the neck. (Observations made by persons such as Paul O'Connor, who attended the autopsy, tend to be more telling in this regard, at least in terms of what was observable at that later juncture.)

Dr Perry was assisted by doctors Charles Baxter and Robert McClelland in performing the tracheotomy. Anaesthetist Dr Marion 'Pepper' Jenkins made the decision to replace the Bennett respirator with a Heidbrink anaesthesia machine, which he had brought from the department of anaesthesia and which was then hooked up to the tracheotomy tube. The reason for an anaesthesia machine wasn't because the president was conscious or alert and therefore requiring anaesthetic medication; the machine was employed because it had a 'bellows' – a 'bag' or 'balloon' which could be manually operated by attending medical personnel to provide measured, deliberate respirations to the president's lungs.

The head wound, which ultimately proved to be the fatal injury, was a large defect in the upper right-hand side of the head which extended into the rearmost portion of the skull. To help the reader understand this location, imagine lying back to rest on a sofa or recliner and placing your hands, palm side up, against the back of your head for added support. Keeping your right hand where it is at the rearmost location and your thumb where it is in line with the base of the back of the skull, relax your fingers allowing them to move so the pinky finger is at a point about an inch from the top and rear of your right ear. That essentially covers the blasted, avulsed wound area described by the Parkland physicians.

Although we can be reasonably certain that the throat wound was caused by an incoming projectile/bullet fired from a point somewhere in front of the president, the exact location of an entry wound on the president's head seems to have remained an undetermined factor in TR1. The Dallas/Parkland doctors were physicians devoted and trained to provide every means of life-sustaining resuscitative medical treatments with an eye towards (hopefully) stabilising the patient. None of these men were trained forensic pathologists, nor were they there to ascertain entry wounds and exit wounds or trajectories of bullets, etc. Any such determining factors would be left to the expertise of the Dallas County Medical Examiner.

They all had the same feeling, based on prior similar experience: that when the president died, Dr Earl Rose, Dallas County Medical Examiner, would conduct a proper forensic examination on the remains. However, as we have known for the 50 years that have passed since that time, that was not the plan of the federal agents who took charge of the situation in Dallas that day in 1963, and whose actions were against the laws of the land at that time.

However, speculation has raged on over those long years, in part because Dr McClelland mentioned in his written report that afternoon that the president had a bullet wound in his 'left temple'. When I met with Dr McClelland some years ago and again in his home in 2010, he said that as he entered TR1 he didn't see any wound at the front of the head, but that Dr Jenkins told him there was a wound in the left temple. In fact, what had happened was that Dr Jenkins was alongside the left side of the table and was operating the 'bag' on the anaesthesia machine by hand. As

Dr McClelland neared the head end of the table, Dr Jenkins inclined his own forehead towards the left side of the president's head and said, 'Bob, there's a bullet hole there.' Dr McClelland told me that he had simply taken that to mean that there was a bullet hole at that location, in the left temple. Dr McClelland went on to say that there was so much blood that unless they had washed it away, which they didn't do, a wound of entry on the head would not have been exposed or revealed. In writing his report later on that same afternoon, Dr McClelland had straightforwardly given Dr Jenkins the benefit of the doubt. I asked Dr McClelland if it might have been the right temple and said that if Dr Jenkins had been facing the president perhaps this might have been a simple error – that if he'd been facing the president, the president's right might have become the doctor's left in his perception. Dr McClelland disagreed on this point but said Dr Jenkins later denied having ever said anything about an entrance wound at all. Dr McClelland went on to say that there was no doubt in his mind that the large, ragged, avulsed occipitoparietal wound at the back of the head was without any question the exit wound, and that for his own reasons he has over the many years since come to believe that the bullet had entered the front right temple.

83. Dr McClelland demonstrates on Colin McSween.
(Courtesy Colin McSween)

The head wound had exhibited profuse bleeding throughout the course of treatment undertaken on the president. 'Profuse' meaning great, abundant, free, seemingly coming from everywhere. Others described it as being due to vast multifocal vascular disruption. Both cerebral and cerebellar tissue were noted to be 'extruding' from the wound. In fact, the cerebellum actually slid out of the great defect and onto the emergency cart during treatment. Some say that this occurred during the closed-chest cardiac massage.

The entire time that President Kennedy had been in TR1, he had been in the supine (back down) position and his head turned to his left. The only time that his head had been anywhere near a face-up pose was during the two to three minutes while the tracheotomy was performed. Other than during that brief interval, every effort was made to staunch the flow of blood from the large, gaping skull wound.

Manual closed-chest massage had been employed by both doctors Clark and Perry, but to no avail. The only things this had succeeded in doing were to (a) generate a palpable pulse in some of the proximal and some of the more distal arteries, which proved to be unsustainable without this manual action and (b) create an even heavier blood flow out of the skull wound. A cardiotachioscope had been connected when Dr Perry had initiated the chest compressions, but this machine indicated electrical silence of the heart, that cardiac arrest had occurred due to the massive blood loss.

The only evidence of 'life' was illusory at best and was due only to the 'respirations' made possible by the functioning anaesthesia machine. The president's death had occurred at some point between 12.53 and 12.55 p.m. CST. Dr Kemp Clark made the official pronouncement of death as being at 1.00 p.m. CST and presidential press secretary Malcolm Kilduff went with that time in his televised announcement, which he made minutes after 1.30 pm. This was at the behest of Vice-President Johnson, who insisted he was allowed to get back to the presidential plane, Air Force One, before Kennedy's death was announced.

84. Malcolm Kilduff, press aide to President Kennedy, was present at Parkland Hospital and afterwards had no doubt about where the fatal bullet struck.

In the wake of the departure of President Kennedy's body from Parkland, many of the doctors commented on the possibility that the throat wound was the entry point of a projectile which had then somehow managed to make the exit defect that they saw on the back of the head. This was reverberated in numerous newspapers. The genuine possibility of this, however, from an anatomic perspective is extremely unlikely without far greater internal injuries to the interior of the throat at least being inflicted, which would have been clearly detectable during the insertion of the orotracheal tube.

Two facts remain to this day in so far as the Parkland doctors were able to ascertain (notwithstanding the number of comments made otherwise over the many long years since) and that is that on that day and at that time of the early afternoon of Friday, 22 November 1963, in the written depositions made that same day, the throat wound was perceived by those who'd seen it before Dr Perry's tracheotomy incision as an entrance wound and the large defect at the back of the head had been perceived as a wound of exit. For those not familiar with medicolegal protocols, this is frustrating. No one, least of all the medical staff at Parkland, nor the local law-enforcement people, could have foreseen the illegal hijacking of the president's body from the lawful, duly appointed custody of the Dallas County authorities.

Those of the doctors and nurses who'd attended the president had absolute confidence that in accordance with the laws as they were at the time that Dr Earl Rose, Dallas County medical examiner, would perform his complete forensic post-mortem examination and any and all such determinations pertaining to trajectories' entry wounds and exit wounds would be made clear.

Sadly, when Dr Earl Rose stood the gap in the corridor of Parkland Hospital to prevent the federal authorities from making their unorthodox departure, he was quite simply picked up by a federal agent. This man lifted him off his feet and set him aside as one might a grandfather clock. Then the agent, as soon as he had set the good doctor down on his feet again, insultingly waved one menacing finger back and forth in the doctor's face as though to say, 'No you don't!' This account of the extremely offensive incident was recounted by Dr Rose himself to Dr McClelland on the day it happened.

From that moment of that day through the Bethesda Naval Hospital autopsy to this day, the remains of the 35th President of the United States have been assigned to the 24-hour guarded protective custody of the US military.

85. Colin McSween played the part of Bill Greer, the president's driver, in a reconstruction of the assassination for an episode of *The X-Files*.
(Courtesy Colin McSween)

26

TROUBLE AT PARKLAND

IT IS QUITE IMPORTANT THAT WE UNDERSTAND what transpired between the work at Parkland Hospital and Bethesda Memorial Hospital, where the autopsy was carried out. Events moved quickly after the president had been declared dead. To put it bluntly, as recounted above, a row broke out between the Secret Service agents present and those representing the hospital authorities over where the autopsy was to be held.

If fisticuffs did not take place at this point, it came very near to it. The Secret Service agents made ready to take the coffin in which the president's body had been placed away to Washington for autopsy, while Dallas County medical examiner Earl Rose was adamant that the body should remain in Dallas for autopsy. According to the law, he was quite right, and he knew it. But for reasons about which we are left guessing, the Secret Service agents had decided otherwise.

A full-blown argument took place, a most unseemly affair, especially with Jacqueline Kennedy still nearby in the hospital while it was all going on. Texas law said that the 'chain of evidence' could not be broken and removal of the body would break that law. This chain had to be maintained to preserve the rights of the assassin, which included access to the findings of an impartial post-mortem examination. To support his assertions, Earl Rose sent for a JP to pronounce on the subject. However, while Judge Theron Ward was taking his time in considering the situation, matters went from bad to worse.

The indignant Earl Rose was manhandled out of the way in the ensuing row, with Agent Roy Kellerman and General Godfrey

McHugh, the president's Air Force aide, getting hot under the collar. It was indeed approaching the point where it looked as if fisticuffs might take place, with a police officer who was observing all this beginning to finger his gun. An end was put to a situation with particularly ugly potential with the command, 'Wheel it out!' and the coffin was wheeled out of the hospital to a waiting hearse. Regardless of the law, the Secret Service had decided.

The essential release-of-body documents were quickly scrambled together and made available just before the hearse moved off. It would seem, however, that those who had assumed command were going with or without the necessary papers. Inside the hospital, Earl Rose indignantly fumed. His position was based not on a personal wish, a whim or on some invented rule, but on the law, which it was his duty to uphold. The Secret Service individuals were breaking the law, and they must have known it.

The outcome of this episode raised many questions, including two extremely important ones. First, why were the Texas officials so determined to retain the body, since rules might well have been bent if not broken in circumstances such as this? And second, why were the government officials so determined it should not remain in Dallas for autopsy, thereby causing enormous upset, offending a number of well-meaning people and breaking the law to boot?

Perhaps it was that those *behind* the rigid instructions given to the Secret Service agents did not trust what might happen in an autopsy carried out at Dallas, where the president was, in general, unpopular, even hated by some. On the other hand, perhaps it had nothing to do with that at all. What happened after this point has become a matter of considerable speculation. It might be said to relate to the findings of an important researcher, David Lifton, or the implications of the conclusions he drew.

David Lifton wrote a book, *Best Evidence*, after equipping himself with an enormous amount of background knowledge in the form of medical studies which he undertook. Reviewing the work of the doctors at Parkland Hospital and noting, for instance, the size of the president's head wounds as recorded by them, he then compared them with the measurements and other data provided by the autopsy doctors at Bethesda Military Hospital. In simple terms, what he saw persuaded him that the wounds had been tampered with by someone acting for the conspirators between leaving Parkland and reaching Bethesda, resulting in a degree of support being created for the 'shot from behind' theory. This, he believed, was likely to have happened on Air Force One as the body was flown to Washington.

In spite of Lifton's work on this being greatly admired, his findings in some respects have been hotly disputed. I have sat on the fence for years on this one, but I concede that, for starters, the essential weaknesses, as I see them, come minimally on three counts. The first is that it would have taken a skilled surgeon to carry out the alterations to the wound which Lifton identified and there was no hint of such a person being present during the flight. Second, access to the body could only have been achieved with the complicity of special agents Sibert and O'Neill, who had been given instructions to stay at all times with the body, and is therefore most unlikely. Third, the motion of the plane during the flight would militate against any surgery being carried out. On these grounds, I reject what he has claimed, but I feel sure his contribution is there to be confirmed in another explanation. In any case, make no mistake, Lifton's achievements in other aspects of the work he carried out renders it a most valuable contribution.

Returning to the determination of the federal government to retain control of the body and what happened afterwards, what we are next to read might well give us the insight we require to understand a great deal more of the complexities involved in these events.

27

THE AUTOPSY OF PRESIDENT KENNEDY

by William Matson Law
Author of
In the Eye of History

ACCORDING TO THE OFFICIAL VERSION OF EVENTS, on the night of 22 November 1963, after the casket containing the president's remains was unloaded from Air Force One and placed aboard a grey Navy ambulance for the forty-minute drive from Andrews Air Force Base to Bethesda, it was accompanied in the third car of the motorcade by an entourage of two FBI agents, James W. Sibert and Francis X. O'Neill, who were placed there under the order of J. Edgar Hoover, head of the FBI. Their instructions were to stay with Kennedy's remains at all times, recover any evidence found during the autopsy and then take it to the FBI laboratory in Washington DC.

I interviewed James Sibert at his home in Florida in 2001 and Sibert gave a description of being in the motorcade:

Suitland Parkway is an overpass, a series of them, and every one of those overpasses was lined with people. Of course, it was on the radio and television. And all I can remember is, near dusk, people with handkerchiefs to their eyes crying.

Another witness described the grounds at Bethesda Naval Hospital as 'a solid mass of humanity, people standing shoulder to shoulder, back to back. It was unbelievable. Something I will never forget.' (More on the interviews with agents Sibert and O'Neill follows in Chapter 28.)

The grey Navy ambulance went through the main gate and pulled up in front of the hospital. Jacqueline Kennedy got out of the vehicle along with Robert Kennedy, and others alighted from different cars in the motorcade. They crossed the marble lobby and vanished into the dark-brown elevator. Godfrey McHugh stayed by the coffin for a full five minutes. McHugh, Greer, Kellerman and the coffin were left among the motionless spectators. William Manchester, in his history of the assassination, *Death of a President*, passes this off as 'a muddle of a failure in inter-service communication'.

The president's body was placed on autopsy table number 1. The sheet that encased the body was removed and Kennedy was now nude except for a bloody sheet wrapped around the head. The head remained wrapped until the normal preliminary examination was complete, with scars, bruising and other markings on the body noted and recorded on an autopsy face sheet. The head was unwrapped at that point and personnel were told to leave the morgue and go into the anteroom while X-rays were taken. There were at least eleven X-rays taken during this time. Pictures were also taken of Kennedy's body throughout the autopsy. Twenty-two 4 x 5 in. colour photographs and eighteen 4 x 5 in. black-and-white photographs are in the official record. There was also one roll of 120 film containing five exposures taken by medical photographer Floyd Reibie. The photographs and X-rays were turned over to Secret Service man Roy Kellerman.

The autopsy of record begins with the first incision on the body being made at 8.15 p.m. A few minutes later, a discussion begins amongst the doctors about a limited versus full autopsy. Dr Burkley, Kennedy's personal physician, tells the doctors that Mrs Kennedy has given her permission for a limited autopsy, but after an argument between the doctors, permission is finally granted to do the full autopsy. After the 'Y' incision is made and the abdomen is opened up, the ribcage and breastbone are removed to expose the internal organs. The organs are removed and weighed. Upon further examination of the body, it is found that there is a wound at about the knot of the tie in the president's throat. Dr James Humes notes that it is between 7 and 8 cm in length, with widely irregular gaping edges. The doctors throughout the autopsy believed this wound had been made by a tracheotomy. The large wound at the rear of Kennedy's head is approximately 2.5 cm laterally to the right and slightly above the external occipital protuberance. The wound, presumably of exit, is through the top of the skull, involving chiefly the parietal bone but extending into the temporal and occipital regions. Dr J. Thornton Boswell records the hole in the skull as being roughly rectangular, with dimensions of 10 cm x 17 cm. The brain is removed and preserved for further study.

There is a wound in the president's back near the base of the back of the neck, about 5.5 in. (14 cm) from the tip of the right shoulder joint and 5.5 in. below the tip of the right mastoid process. The wound is relatively small, sharply delineated and with clean edges. The wound is probed and Dr Humes sticks his little finger into it. The doctors are not able to find any definite path. They are at a loss as to why they can find no large bullet fragments in Kennedy's body. Third-class X-ray technician Jerrol Custer is brought in to take X-rays and Dr James Ebersole is called in to direct the taking of full-body X-rays. No large fragments are found. An FBI agent leaves the morgue to call the FBI laboratory to tell those in authority that no bullets have been found in Kennedy's body. The FBI agent is then told by laboratory personnel that a whole bullet has been found on a stretcher at Parkland Hospital.

The agent returns to the autopsy room and tells the doctors about the bullet that has been found in Dallas. Humes, Boswell and Dr Pierre Finck agree that this explains where the bullet went that caused the back wound.

At about midnight, an agent of either the FBI or Secret Service enters the morgue with two bone fragments. One of these bone fragments has bevelling on the edge that matches a notch on the large defect in the skull that was interpreted as completing the circumference of a bullet hole in the skull where a bullet had fragmented during exit from the top of the skull. It was on this basis that Dr Humes concluded that the pattern was clear . . . One bullet had entered the president's back and worked its way out of the body during external cardiac massage in Dallas and a second high-velocity bullet had entered the rear of the skull and fragmented prior to exit through the top of the skull. Humes attributed the death of the president to a gunshot wound to the head. The autopsy completed, morticians from Gawler's Funeral Home did cosmetology work on Kennedy's remains, taking nearly three hours. The body was dressed in a blue-grey suit, black shoes, black socks and a blue tie with a slight pattern of light dots. It was then wheeled into the anteroom and placed in a waiting coffin purchased from Gawler's Funeral Home, the first casket, the 400-lb Britannia provided at Parkland Hospital, having been damaged in transit. The body was then driven to the White House to lie in state.

* * *

There is a myriad of problems with the official version of the history of President John F. Kennedy's autopsy. Dennis Duane David was chief of the day the evening of 22 November 1963. He was given instructions to be at the loading dock at the back of the Bethesda morgue with six or seven enlisted men. In David's words, 'We just stood there for five, ten minutes, and about 6:30, 6:35 a black hearse pulled up and backed up to the jetty. We sat the casket down in the middle of the floor and then they came back out. At about five minutes to seven or five after seven, somewhere in that time frame, [I] went up to the second floor of the main building and, looking down, saw the flashing red lights of a DC police car pull in at the front of Bethesda Naval Hospital, with a grey Navy ambulance close behind, and an entourage of official cars. Admiral Calvin Galloway got out of the vehicle, while Jackie Kennedy got out of the back of the ambulance.' He recognised some of the people who got out of the official cars: Robert McNamara, Robert Kennedy and some people who he believed were senators.

David was standing looking down 'right at the front door when Mrs Kennedy and McNamara and others came in, and I can still see that dress and the pillbox hat, blood on her dress and on her skirt'. David's face and voice filled with emotion and tears came to his eyes while describing the scene to me. 'They came across the lobby, went right under where I was standing and into the elevator. Then I turned around and watched the elevator till it hit the 17th floor, which was the presidential suite.' If Dennis David's experiences at Bethesda set the stage for a shell game with these remains, the testimonies of medical corpsmen Paul Kelly O'Connor and James Curtis Jenkins opened a Pandora's box that the conspirators and those who believe Oswald did it alone have never been able to close.

Paul O'Connor has for years told of his helping to take the body of Jack Kennedy from a cheap metal shipping casket. He was instructed to report to the morgue and set up all of the equipment for the autopsy of President Kennedy. O'Connor remembers that

'a crew of hospital corpsmen and a higher-ranking corpsman brought in a plain pinkish-grey casket, what I call a shipping casket. It was not ornate. It was not damaged. It was just a pinkish-grey casket . . . the kind you ship bodies home from places like Vietnam in.'

86. An ornate casket of the type and description
used for the body of President Kennedy.

87. A shipping casket of the type also used for the body of the president.
But when was the body placed in it?

O'Connor had worked in funeral homes from a very early age
and, working at Bethesda, he had had experience involving at
least 50 to 60 autopsies by 1963. He recalled, 'Inside the casket
was a body-bag. We unzipped it quickly. Inside was a nude body
with a bloody sheet wrapped around the head of the body.' Six
or seven others helped O'Connor lift the body onto the first
autopsy table.

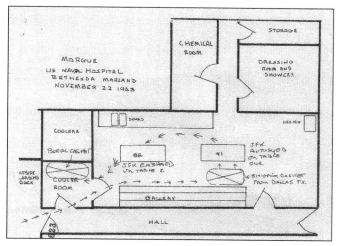

88. Diagram of the areas in which the autopsy took place.
(Courtesy Paul O'Connor)

O'Connor was 'astounded to look down and see that half of President Kennedy's head was half blown off. Part of the top, back and side of Kennedy's head were gone, the scalp was macerated and torn.' O'Connor then looked straight down into the cranium and saw the president's brains were absent from the head.

In a normal autopsy, you make a cut with a scalpel from ear to ear, across the top of the head, pull back the scalp towards the front and towards the back, take a bone saw and cut around the cranium and take the top of the skull off, opening up the dura, the thick membrane that encases the brain, then slowly lift up the front part of the skull where the optical nerves come into the brain, snip those off, then go to the rear of the skull and pull the back of the brain up and reach in with a pair of long scissors to cut the spinal cord. The brain is then put in a bucket of formalin solution with a gauze sling lying on top for the brain to rest on during the hardening process, so that it can later be sectioned for examination.

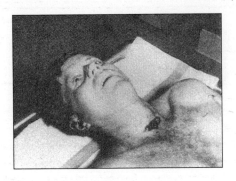

89. A picture taken of the president during the autopsy.
(Courtesy National Archives)

O'Connor did not have to do this procedure that night because there was no brain to be removed. 'There was no need for me to open up the cranium because the cranium was completely shattered.' O'Connor went on to describe the wound in Kennedy's throat: 'The wound was a big gash. It looked very sloppy. Very ugly.' O'Connor said that they did not dissect the neck and 'were told to go on to other things'. The fact that the president's neck was not dissected was very disturbing. The prosectors, doctors James Humes, Jim Boswell and Pierre Finck, brought in from the Armed Forces Institute School of Pathology, should have dissected the neck to find the path of the bullet that made the wound, and it should have been a part of the normal autopsy procedure.

90. Paul O'Connor. (Courtesy William Matson Law)

TOP SECRET `193`

The Chairman. Of course there are so many Spanish-speaking people down in Texas.

Mr. Rankin. In the area.

The Chairman. That she might have gotten it from someone else.

Mr. Rankin. Then there is a great range of material in regard to the wounds, and the autopsy and this point of exit or entrance of the bullet in the front of the neck, and that all has to be developed much more than we have at the present time.

We have an explanation there in the autopsy that probably a fragment came out the front of the neck, but with the elevation the shot must have come from, and the angle, it seems quite apparent now, since we have the picture of where the bullet entered in the back, that the bullet entered below the shoulder blade to the right of the backbone, which is below the place where the picture shows the bullet came out in the neckband of the shirt in front, and the bullet, according to the autopsy didn't strike any bone at all, that particular bullet, and go through.

So that how it could turn and ―

Rep. Boggs. I thought I read that bullet just went in a finger's length.

Mr. Rankin. That is what they first said. They reached in and they could feel where it came, it didn't go any further than that, about part of the finger or something, part of the autopsy, and then they proceeded to reconstruct where they thought

91. An interesting document relating to questions raised by J. Lee Rankin (of the Warren Commission) which seem to contradict the commission's assertion that the 'magic bullet' did what they said it had done.

In an interview with O'Connor, he said that the first thing that usually happened during a normal autopsy was to weigh and measure the body before checking for any scars, contusions and other abnormalities. This procedure was never deviated from – until the night of 22 November. Therefore, the bullet wound in the president's back was not found until some time in the later stages of the autopsy. The wound was to the right of the spinal column, about three inches down and an inch or two to the right of the seventh cervical vertebra. O'Connor said that Dr Humes took one of his fingers and put it into the bullet wound in the back and the bullet-wound track: 'It didn't go anywhere,' said O'Connor. Humes putting his finger in the bullet wound made the wound larger than it was when first noticed. 'There was a very big argument, a lot of consternation that he shouldn't have stuck his finger in the hole.' Dr Finck at that point took a malleable metal non-rigid probe and tried to trace the track of the bullet, but it only went in about 'an inch, an inch and a quarter'. They did not know the track of the bullet until, in O'Connor's words,

'we eviscerated [disembowelled] the body later. That's what happened at that time: We traced the bullet wound down and found that it did not traverse the body. It did not go in one side and come out the other side of the body.'

This is an important point. The single-bullet theory rests on one bullet going through two men, i.e. the bullet enters President Kennedy's back, comes up, goes out the front of Kennedy's neck, goes into Governor Connally's back, smashes a rib, comes out the governor's chest under his right nipple, slams into his right wrist, breaking the bone, and goes into his left thigh. If this scenario is not true, then you have more than one shooter, and hence a conspiracy.

James Curtis Jenkins, Paul O'Connor's partner in the Bethesda morgue, was in the morgue proper when Kennedy's body was brought in and put on the floor. He does not have a clear memory of the casket coming through the door, but he does remember that the casket was marked with the word 'Government'. The clearest memories Jenkins had were of when the body was placed on the table. He was not specifically involved in taking the president's body out of the shipping casket. Therefore Jenkins did not remember the body being inside a body-bag. Jenkins told me during an interview with him that when the body was placed on the table it was wrapped in sheets. 'I remember the towels.' Jenkins remembered that Dr Humes took the towels and threw them 'on the floor against the wall'. Jenkins later had to clean up the mess.

When asked about the wound to the president's head, he said that the size

'would be difficult to estimate because a lot of the hair was still attached to the skull fragments – the skull was fragmented. But I would say if you take your hand and put the heel of your thumb behind your [right] ear, that would cover the basic part of the wound, with the open hole in this area.'

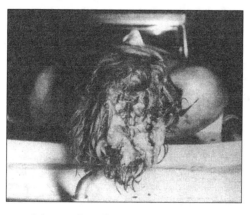

92. The rear of the president's head, photographed during the autopsy.
(Courtesy National Archives)

After the head was unwrapped, the autopsy face sheet was started. A face sheet has drawings, front and back, of a body. The body is examined for scars, wounds, etc. Measurements are taken on the body of the deceased and then placed on the drawings of the autopsy face sheet correlating in exact measure to the body. Jenkins helped the prosectors with the face sheet, filling in some of the measurements and weights of the organs. 'Boswell continued, too, with me writing what Dr Boswell said.' Jenkins has said that they moved Kennedy's body around when the X-rays were taken. 'We set the body up; we rolled the body over on its side to do the AP laterals.' Jenkins said most of the X-rays were taken in the head area and the upper body. Jenkins remembered that Humes and Boswell were both standing at the head of the table looking down on the head and Dr Finck 'was closest to me. I was at his right shoulder.' Jenkins said that the doctors were 'speculating about a lot of things'. There was an apparent hole above Kennedy's right ear, with some grey matter on it, and the doctors were speculating that the grey matter was lead from a bullet. Jenkins said that it was his impression that the hole above the right ear was an entry wound – in the right side of President Kennedy's head.

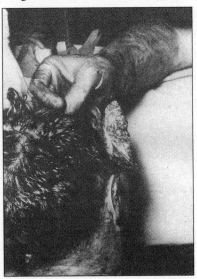

93. In this picture was the intention to hold the hair in place, covering the gaping head wound while the picture was taken?
(Courtesy National Archives)

When I first interviewed Jenkins in 1998, I told him that in depositions by Humes and Boswell, given before the Records Review Board, they said that they had made decisions the night of Kennedy's autopsy where bullets had entered and exited Kennedy's body. Jenkins said:

'To my knowledge, no . . . I came out of that autopsy that night and I was sure that the bullet entered the right side of the head and exited in this area [Jenkins reached up and touched the back of his head above his right ear] and that there was a bullet wound around the scapula in the back.'

This is explosive testimony from a man who was there – and I absolutely believe in Jenkins' veracity.

Jenkins went on to say that the wound in President Kennedy's back was at T4, the fourth thoracic vertebra. Jenkins does not believe that the bullet that supposedly went into Kennedy's back could have come out Kennedy's throat:

'I wouldn't think so because it was below [the throat wound]. Later in the autopsy, I helped Dr Boswell remove the organs from the body and we were sectioning the organs and weighing them. Dr Humes and Dr Finck were trying to probe that wound.'

Jenkins went on to say that Humes first probed the back one with his little finger. 'Humes has big hands and is a big man.' Then a probe was used. 'I could see his finger and I could see the probes behind the pleural area in the back, and it never did break into the pleural cavity. The wound actually went down and stopped.' If this is true, and I believe Jenkins is telling us what he saw, it underlines that the single-bullet theory was not possible.

Jim Jenkins then told me that the autopsy doctors did not find any bullet: 'We didn't find any bullet fragments. The bullet fragments were the ones that were brought in after the autopsy started.' There was more to Jim Jenkins' experiences that night in the Bethesda morgue. For me, sitting across from him while he was telling me of what he experienced that night so long ago, watching his emotions play over his face, it was one of the most spellbinding – and unnerving – interviews I have ever carried out.

The earlier mention of Paul Kelly O'Connor came to mind. O'Connor's job was to remove brains from cadavers that were brought in for autopsy, but in the case of President Kennedy 'there was no brain to be removed'. Jenkins now told me that after the X-rays were taken, the Y incision made, and the organs removed and weighed, the doctors began to remove the brain. I asked Jim Jenkins who took out the brain.

'That's something that's a little strange. We normally did a skullcap. We didn't really have to do a skullcap on this because as they expanded the wound, it was large enough for the brain to come out, and Dr Humes removed the brain and made a kind of an exclamatory statement. I think what he said was, "The damn thing fell out in my hand."'

I sat there stunned. The brain is encased in the dura, a tough membrane that helps to protect the brain and the fluid around the brain. Once this membrane is removed, the brain is exposed and then the normal steps are taken for the removal of the brain. The brain does not rattle around in the skull. So the statement made by Jenkins vis-à-vis Humes is explosive indeed.

But there was more to come from the memories of Jim Jenkins.

'The brain stem had already been severed and that, with some other statements and other conversations about some areas that were fragmented, along the sagittal suture, looked like – there was some comment that it looked like it had been surgically extended.'

'Surgically extended?' I asked. 'What does that mean?'
Jenkins replied:

'I think what they were talking about was some of the fragmented area up here [top-right of the head], that it looked like it had been cut with a scalpel to expand it a bit. To me that indicated that the brain had been removed and replaced.'

I sat across the table from Jim Jenkins. His tone of voice was soft. He looked straight into my eyes, his face absent of guile. Jenkins continued:

'My impression of the brain was that the damage to the area of the brain, the extensiveness of it, did not quite match the extensiveness of the wound. In other words, the damage to the brain seemed to be a little less than you would expect from [the damage to the skull].'

Jenkins was talking about massive damage to the skull, but minimal damage to the brain – something that is strange to say the least. Jenkins explained to me that after the brain was removed it was taken to the brain bucket.

Jim went on to say,

'Where the brain stem had been severed, it looked almost like it'd been severed on one side to a certain point, then severed on the other side, but not quite at the same level. To me, it was a little bit unusual. But you have to understand, I'm a third-class hospital corpsman, I'm 20 years old and everything in [the autopsy room] could have me shot tomorrow.'

After the brain was taken to the bucket and put into the gauze sling, Jenkins said, a pathology resident came in and helped him put needles into the carotid arteries to help with the hardening process so that the brain could be sectioned later. Jenkins explained:

'They [the internal carotids] were retracted. It was like they had been severed in a short period of time after. When you sever a blood vessel, especially an artery, it retracts. And the longer it is severed, the more it retracts and it was kind of mangled a little bit. So we had problems with that.'

I pulled a document from my briefcase and Jenkins looked at the paper I was holding. 'Where did you get that?' he exclaimed, jerking it out of my hand. It was the House Select Committee on Assassinations' Ida Dox's drawing from a photograph of what is purportedly of President Kennedy's brain. 'This looks like the brain I was handed to infuse that night!' Jenkins was clearly excited.

I was a bit shocked, thinking that Jim had surely seen the drawing before, but as I was to learn later, Jim Jenkins, unlike me, was not obsessed with Kennedy's assassination and had not read a lot – if any – of the literature on the subject.

If there was a shell game going on with President Kennedy's remains, and I believe there was, the fact that there are photographs of a brain that is supposed to be that of John F. Kennedy points to conspiracy. But more on that later. For now, I have some final words from Jim Jenkins:

'I am convinced that John Kennedy was shot at least two times by two separate people, and possibly a third time. Relating to the wound in the back – the entrance wound that I feel was at the right side of the head just above the [right] ear, a little bit forward, and exited in the large expanse at the back [of the head]. Right above, the small entrance wound at the hairline which has been reported . . . I never saw that. I'm not saying it wasn't there, but I never saw it. I had the opportunity to see it. So I think what history needs to understand . . . [is] that this was a cover-up. **For whatever reason . . . but certainly the evidence presented by Humes to the public – from the Warren Commission to the public – was not the evidence that we found at the autopsy.'**

94. Jim Jenkins. (Courtesy William Matson Law)

Sitting across the table from him, watching his face, his body language, feeling the frustration of this man who had witnessed history in the making and carried the pain of knowing his country had lied and kept lying about this dark truth, is something I have not been able to shake to this day. And I know this: if Paul O'Connor and Jim Jenkins opened up a Pandora's box in the Kennedy assassination, then X-ray technician Jerrol Custer and FBI agents James Sibert and Francis O'Neill kicked the box over.

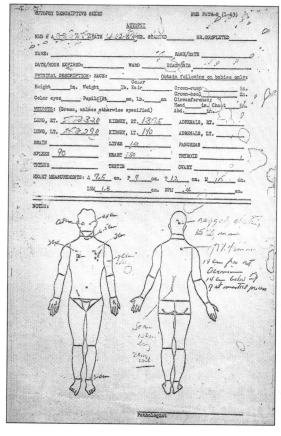

95. The autopsy sheet. (Courtesy National Archives)

* * *

Jerrol Custer was the X-ray technician on call when President Kennedy's remains were brought in for autopsy. He was told by the officer of the day that he was to take a portable X-ray machine and 'a bunch of films' to the morgue. 'They brought in a casket, put the casket down and opened it, so we proceeded to remove the body and place it on the autopsy table.'

Doug Horne, military analyst for the Assassination Records Review Board, believes that it was at this point that agents Sibert and O'Neill, with specific instructions from J. Edgar Hoover to stay with the body at all times, were not, in fact, allowed to stay with the body. In the agents' own FD-302 report, they state: 'Bureau agents assisted in the moving of the casket to the autopsy room. **A tight security was immediately placed around the autopsy room by the Naval facility and the US Secret Service. Bureau agents made contact with Mr Roy Kellerman, the assistant Secret Service agent in charge of the White House detail, and advised him of the Bureau's interest in this matter.**' Doug Horne says this is Bureau speak for being kept out of the autopsy room. If this was indeed the case, the agents were never going to admit to it, embarrassing the Bureau, possibly ending their careers and losing their pension rights. Custer, when asked, made it clear that Kennedy's body was taken out of a metal shipping casket. 'The head was completely covered by a plastic bag and there was a sheet around it. The sheet, of course, was bloodied, but nothing was ever mentioned about that.' Custer and his assistant were then told they could leave and go back to the X-ray department. **The implications of this are enormous. Was this the moment that one, at least, of the autopsy doctors made the changes to the head wounds observed later by Sibert and O'Neill, changes ordered by the conspirators to support that all the shots had come from behind?**

It was a couple of hours later that Custer and his assistant were called back to the morgue and ordered to take X-rays of Kennedy's head. 'We took an AP film [front to rear] and a lateral film [from side to side].' Custer said that at the time he was taking X-rays the morgue was crowded, and in the gallery he saw Secret Service agents. He continued:

> 'I'm sure there were CIA there and a lot of men dressed in suits. We were being watched constantly. There were times when I literally had to scream at people to move. In that close area, you're taking X-rays with a mass-producing ionising radiation and you had to be at a distance of six feet to be safe.'

A degree of confusion caused by differing accounts of the arrival of the casket containing the president's body is readily understood and easily explained, but the implications lead to the unthinkable. The first question to ask is whether the confusion has been caused merely by differing accounts from different observers. The answer to this one is a distinct 'no'. The accounts rendered introduce specific features the sequence of which is not interchangeable.

To start at the beginning, the body of the president was placed in a heavy, ornate coffin at Parkland Hospital and moved to Air Force One for transportation to Washington. The coffin was said to have been damaged in transit and replaced upon arrival in Washington. The body, however, was clearly transferred later to a cheap, pinkish-grey casket of the type usually supplied for the transportation of military personnel killed in action, and this is where complication arises. It involves the fact that **more than one** casket arrived at the Bethesda Memorial Hospital, where the autopsy was to take place.

To avoid additional confusion, it is vital to establish a time frame for the arrival of the various caskets. Casket entry number one is confirmed by Dennis David, who ordered seven or eight enlisted personnel from the medical dental school to unload a metal shipping casket from a black Cadillac hearse at the rear entrance to the morgue at about 6.35 p.m. They carried the casket into the anteroom before departing.

96. Dennis David. (Courtesy William Matson Law)

Casket entry number two was the replacement display casket driven from Andrews Air Force Base and it arrived at about 6.55 p.m. The grey Navy ambulance in which it arrived sat motionless for a few minutes. This, presumably, is the arrival witnessed by Jerrol Custer.

Perhaps the most valuable – and poignant – part of Custer's story is what he told me about seeing Jacqueline Kennedy come into Bethesda Naval Hospital. He had just finished taking X-ray pictures of her husband. 'The morgue was in the basement . . . and our X-ray department was on the fourth floor of the tower. I had to get on an elevator and go up to the main level then go down to the main rotunda [to get to another elevator to the fourth floor].' Custer then said that he 'ran into Jacqueline Kennedy and her entourage'. 'I had a handful of films . . . And you could see them, the flashings going on from guys taking pictures of the Kennedys. In fact, I still remember the bloody suit that she had on.'

This is clearly of huge significance. If Jerrol Custer saw Jacqueline Kennedy coming in the front door of Bethesda Naval Hospital, this would suggest that it would have been at the time that the 'official' grey Navy ambulance, supposedly carrying the remains of John F. Kennedy, pulled up out front of the Naval Center. But according to Custer he had already taken X-rays of the president's body and had a handful that he was taking to the X-ray department to be developed. And that would mean that the display casket in the grey Navy ambulance was empty because John Kennedy's body was already in the morgue laid out on autopsy table number one. This ambulance was, nonetheless, then driven to the rear entrance, where the casket was carried in by Secret Service agents Bill Greer and Roy Kellerman with FBI agents Sibert and O'Neill at about 7.15 p.m. Why the subterfuge was deemed necessary is not clear. We were never told.

There was actually a casket entry number three, by all accounts. It was the one where all the honour guard was present. The joint-service casket team was made up of men from all the branches of the military, each man dressed in his individual attire. This was surely a form of 'window dressing', but nevertheless important, particularly to the participants.

* * *

Where do we go from here? First, the members of the Kennedy family who have had records placed under their protection must reveal these for public scrutiny. Second, as painful as it may be, President Kennedy's remains must be exhumed and re-examined, this time by the top pathologist in the nation. We will then learn about the direction of the gunfire, which will result in a decision on whether a new, thorough investigation is warranted. These would appear to be the essential steps towards this country coming to terms with the nagging questions which have plagued it since Friday, 22 November 1963. **Until then, there can be no expectation of truth for the living, nor justice for the dead, and the indignant spirit of John Fitzgerald Kennedy will continue to call out to us across the abyss of time.**

28

THE SIBERT AND O'NEILL INTERVIEWS

by William Matson Law

THE STORY OF HOW I MANAGED TO GET FORMER FBI
agents James W. Sibert and Francis X. O'Neill, those long-silent
witnesses to the Kennedy autopsy, to talk to me about what they
experienced the night of 22 November 1963 is beyond the scope
of this writing, but suffice it to say it was an amazing journey.
The FBI agents are important in the history of the Kennedy
assassination for a number of reasons, but perhaps the most
important of those reasons is this: every agent of the FBI – every
law-enforcement officer, for that matter – is required to take notes
of any case on which they are working. These agents followed that
protocol on the night of 22 November 1963, and they then wrote
a report based on those notes that became the official basis for
the Kennedy autopsy report. The following is their report, which
has received minor editing, principally to avoid repetition and for
brevity:

**To wit the FBI Sibert and O'Neill report DL 100–10461/
CV**

**A. Autopsy of body of President John Fitzgerald Kennedy
date dictated 11/26/63**

At approximately 3 p.m. on November 22, 1963, following the
announcement of the assassination of the President, it was
ascertained that Air Force One, the President's jet, was returning

from Love Field, Dallas, Texas, flying the body back to Andrews Air Force Base, Camp Springs, Maryland. Special agents Francis X. O'Neill Jr and James W. Sibert proceeded to Andrews Air Force Base to handle any matters which would fall within the jurisdiction of the Federal Bureau of Investigation, inasmuch as it was anticipated that a large group of both military and civilian personnel assigned to the base would congregate at base operations to witness the landing of this flight . . .

At approximately 5.55 p.m., agents were advised by the Hyattsville resident agency that the Bureau had instructed the agents to accompany the body to the national Naval Medical Center, Bethesda, MD, to stay with the body and obtain bullets reportedly in the President's body. Immediately agents contacted Mr James Rowley, the Director of the US Secret Service, identified themselves, and made Mr Rowley aware of aforementioned instructions. Immediately following the plane's landing, Mr Rowley arranged seating for Bureau agents in the third car of the White House motorcade which followed the ambulance containing the President's body to the Naval Medical Center, Bethesda, MD.

On arrival at the Medical Center, the ambulance stopped in front of the main entrance, at which time Mrs Jacqueline Kennedy and Attorney General Robert Kennedy alighted and entered the building. The ambulance was thereafter driven around to the rear entrance, where the President's body was removed and taken into an autopsy room. Bureau agents assisted in the moving of the casket to the autopsy room. A tight security was immediately placed around the autopsy room by the Naval facility and the US Secret Service. [In a later conversation, Jim Sibert said to me, 'I'll tell you something – I don't know – but I think they ran a decoy ambulance out there.'] Bureau agents made contact with Mr Roy Kellerman, the assistant Secret Service agent in charge of the White House detail, and advised him of the Bureau's interest in this matter. He advised that he had already received instructions from Director Rowley as to the presence of Bureau agents. (It will be noted that the affirmed Bureau agents, Mr Roy Kellerman, Mr William Greer, and Mr William O'Leary, Secret Service agents, were the only personnel other than the medical personnel present during the autopsy.)

The following individuals attended the autopsy: Admiral C.B. Holloway, US Naval commanding officer of the Medical Center; Admiral Burkley, US Navy, the President's personal physician; Commander James J. Humes, chief pathologist Bethesda Naval Hospital, who conducted the autopsy; Capt. James H. Stoner Jr, commanding officer US Naval Medical School; Mr John T. Stringer Jr, medical photographer; James H. Ebersole; Lloyd E. Raihe; Dr J.T. Boswell; J.G. Reid; Paul K. O'Connor; J.C. Jenkins; 'Jerrol' F. Custer; Edward F. Reid; and James Metzler.

During the course of the autopsy Lieut. Col. Pierre Finck, US Army, Armed Services Institute of Pathology, arrived to assist Commander Humes in the autopsy. In addition Lieut. Cmdr. Greg Cross and Capt. David Osborne, Chief of Surgery, entered the autopsy room. Major General Weill, Commanding Officer of US Military District, Washington DC, entered the autopsy room to ascertain from the Secret Service arrangements concerning the transportation of the President's body back to the White House. AMC Chester H. Boyers, US Navy, visited the autopsy room during the final stages of such to type receipts given by FBI and Secret Service for items obtained.

At the termination of the autopsy the following personnel from Gawler's funeral home entered the autopsy room to prepare the President's body for burial: John Van Hoesen, Edwin Stroble, Thomas E. Robinson, Mr Hagen. Brigadier General Godfrey McHugh, Air Force Military Aide to the President, was also present, as was Dr George Bakeman, US Navy.

Arrangements were made for the performance of the autopsy by US Navy and Secret Service. The President's body was removed from the casket in which it had been transported and was placed on the autopsy table, at which time the complete body was wrapped in a sheet and the head area contained an additional wrapping, which was saturated with blood. Following the removal of the wrapping, it was ascertained that the President's clothing had been removed and [here they quote directly from Dr Humes] it was also apparent that 'a tracheotomy has been performed, as well as surgery of the head area, namely in the top of the skull [my emphasis]'. All personnel with the exception of medical officers needed in the taking of photographs and X-rays were requested to leave the autopsy room and remain in an adjacent room. Upon completion of X-rays and photographs, the first incision was made at 8.15 p.m. X-rays of the brain area which were developed and returned to the autopsy room disclosed the path of a missile which appeared to enter the back of the skull and the path of the disintegrated fragments could be observed along the right side of the skull. The largest section of this missile, as portrayed by X-ray, appeared to be behind the right frontal sinus. The next largest fragment appeared to be at the rear of the skull at the juncture of the skull bone. The Chief Pathologist advised approximately 40 particles of disintegrated bullet and smudges indicated that the projectile had fragmented while passing through the skull region.

During the autopsy inspection of the area of the brain, fragments of metal were removed by Dr Humes, namely one fragment measuring 7 x 2 mm, which was removed from the right side of the brain. An additional fragment of metal measuring 1 x 3 mm was also removed from this area, both of which were placed in a glass jar containing a black metal top which were thereafter marked for identification and following the signing of a proper receipt were transported by Bureau agents to the FBI laboratory. During the latter stages of this autopsy, Dr Humes located an opening which appeared to be a bullet hole, which was below the shoulders and 2 inches to the right of the midline of the spinal column. This opening was probed by Dr Humes with a finger, at which time it was determined that the trajectory of the missile entered at this point had entered at a downward position of 45 to 60°. Further probing determined that the distance traveled by this missile was a short distance, inasmuch as the end of the opening could be felt with the finger.

Inasmuch as no complete bullet of any size could be located in the brain area and likewise no bullet could be located in the back of any other area of the body, is determined by total body X-rays and an inspection revealing there was no point of exit. The individuals performing the autopsy were at a loss to explain why they could find no bullets. A call was made by Bureau agents to the firearms section of the FBI laboratory, at which time a Charles L. Killian advised that the laboratory had received through Secret Service Agent Richard Johnson a bullet which had reportedly been found on a stretcher in the emergency room of Parkland Hospital, Dallas, Texas. The stretcher had also contained a stethoscope and a pair of rubber gloves. Agent Johnson had advised the laboratory that it had not been ascertained whether or not this was the stretcher which had been used to transport the body of President Kennedy.

Agent Killian further described the bullet as pertaining to a 6.5-mm rifle, which would be approximately a 25-caliber rifle, and that this bullet consisted of a copper alloy, full jacket. Immediately following receipt of this data, the information was made available to Dr Humes, who advised that in his opinion this accounted for no bullet being located which entered the back region and that since external cardiac massage had been performed at Parkland Hospital, it was entirely possible that through such movement the bullet had worked its way out of the point of entry and fallen on the stretcher. Also during the later stages of the autopsy, a piece of skull measuring 10 x 6.5 cm was brought to Dr Humes, who was instructed that it had been removed from the President's skull. Immediately this section of skull was X-rayed, at which time it was determined by Dr Humes that one corner of the section revealed minute metal particles and inspection of the same area disclosed a chipping of the top portion of this piece, both of which indicated that this had been the point of exit on the bullet entering the skull region.

On the basis of the latter two developments, Doctor Humes stated that the pattern was clear that one bullet had entered the President's back and it worked its way out of the body during external cardiac massage and that a second high-velocity bullet had entered the rear of the skull and it fragmented prior to exit to the top of the skull.

Dr Humes further pointed out that X-rays had disclosed numerous fractures in the cranial area, which he attributed to the force generated by the impact of the bullet in its passage through the brain area. He attributed the death of the President to a gunshot wound in the head.

The following is a complete listing of photographs and X-rays taken by medical authorities of the President's body. They were turned over to Mr. Roy Kellerman of the Secret Service. X-rays were developed by the hospital, however, the photographs were delivered to the Secret Service undeveloped: 11 X-rays, 22 4 x 5 colour photographs, 18 black-and-white photographs, and one roll of 120 film containing five exposures. Mr. Kellerman stated these items could be made available to the FBI upon request. The portion of the skull measuring 10 x 6.5 cm was maintained in the custody of Dr Humes, who stated that it also could be made available for further examination. The two metal fragments removed from the brain area were hand-carried by special agents Sibert and O'Neill to the FBI laboratory immediately following the autopsy and were turned over to Special Agent Kurt Frazier.

Surgery of the head area, namely in the top of the skull. We know there was no surgery done in Dallas. There were standard procedures carried out to put Ringer's lactate – in essence, salt water – into the president's body, and closed heart massage was performed by one of the doctors, **but no surgery**. This sentence in the above FD-302 report led researchers of this case to the conclusion that there had been illegal tampering with President Kennedy's remains before his body ever reached Bethesda Naval Hospital.

I followed the path trodden by few before me in interviewing the medical personnel from Bethesda to try to reach whatever truths could be found as far as the autopsy of the president was concerned. I first contacted James Sibert in 1998, hoping I could get him to answer questions concerning the statement in his and O'Neill's FBI Federal Document 302. I discovered where the former agent now lived in Florida and called him at his home in

Fort Myers. I explained who I was and asked if he would answer some questions about what he knew concerning President Kennedy's autopsy.

'Everything I have to say is in the 302 Frank O'Neill and I did. I was contacted by the House Select Committee on Assassinations in the '70s and told them what I could remember. And that was how many years ago now?'

I decided at that point to ask directly about the statement in the FD-302 concerning 'surgery of the head area, namely in the top of the skull'. To my surprise, he answered:

'We found out later that the statement was wrong. One of the doctors said there had been surgery done on the head from the way the wound looked. I wish we would have worded it better. It would've saved some confusion in some books.'

Clearly, Jim Sibert was backtracking.

97. James Sibert indicates the size of the head wound.
(Courtesy William Matson Law)

* * *

I needed to talk to his partner Frank O'Neill, and I asked Sibert if he could put me in contact with him. He gave me a number in Connecticut. O'Neill answered the phone in a brusque, clipped manner, and when I told him who I was and that I would like to ask him some questions about what he had learned at President Kennedy's autopsy, he responded, 'I'm going to call Jim Sibert first . . . As to an interview, I'm going to have to think about it.' Instructing me to call him back within the week, O'Neill hung up the phone.

As it turned out, when I called the two former agents back the next week, both refused to answer my questions about the autopsy. I did manage to get in a question answered by Jim Sibert. I asked, 'When you were shown the autopsy pictures before the Records Review Board – did President Kennedy's body look like what you remember from that night?'

Silence. Then: 'The body looked cleaner than what I remember seeing. Maybe they were taken further along in the autopsy after the mortician started working on it.'

I blurted out, 'No, sir, as far as we know, all the pictures we have were taken at the start of the autopsy.'

This clearly made James Sibert angry, and he said, 'Hell, I'll probably still be getting calls about this when I'm 90.' (I thought to myself that he would, and that it would be me asking the questions.) 'I know you're interested in this,' he said. 'You'll just have to wait till all of the records on this are released.'

With a terse goodbye, Sibert hung up the phone. O'Neill basically told me the same, no interview, but, as with Sibert, he did at least answer one question, which was, 'When you went before the Records Review Board and were shown the Kennedy autopsy photographs, did they look like what you remembered?'

He replied, 'Some of them did, some of them didn't.'

I pressed on. 'Did the president's body look like what you remember?'

O'Neill's angry reply came back: 'No!'

I thanked him and he hung up the phone.

Three years later, I would contact both former agents again.

The manuscript of my book *In the Eye of History* was complete – except for contributions from Sibert and O'Neill. I used the manuscript as a catalyst to ask questions, contacting O'Neill first, and, much to my surprise, they responded. Over a period of several weeks, I was able to ask a number of questions, most of which O'Neill answered. But the most valuable thing the retired agent did was send me a chapter he was working on for a book about his life. It was the chapter on President Kennedy's autopsy – and it was incredible. Here are excerpts from that chapter.

He describes in detail arriving at Bethesda, then he describes the casket. He says it was bronze – in essence, the casket that left Dallas. He describes the body, wrapped in a sheet, with another bloody sheet wrapped around the head. The body, he said, was lying on a plastic-type sheet, to prevent the lining of the casket from becoming soiled with blood. 'His hands were clenched, eyes opened, and his mouth in a grimace.' He and Sibert helped to take the body out of the casket.

He also wrote about the interviews of Kellerman and Greer (driver and passenger in the front seat of President Kennedy's limousine at the time of the shooting in Dallas), noting that they had not had a chance to clean up after the shooting; both men had blood and brain tissue on the backs of their coats, evidence of the force with which the head of the president had, 'for want of a better word, exploded. We left, and came back with a coffin for burial, as the bronze casket had a broken handle, and we did not feel it was appropriate for President Kennedy be buried in a broken coffin.' At some point that night, O'Neill and Sibert 'hastily passed around a sheet of paper and directed that all present write down their names'. After O'Neill tells us about passing paper for signatures, the next paragraph states that 'immediately upon viewing the body it was evident that a tracheotomy may have been performed'. So far, it's close to what was in the FD-302 report. He goes on:

'Humes, viewing the body, indicated that some type of surgical procedure had been done in the head region, possibly cutting of hair, or removal of some slight tissue to view the massive wound in the right rear of the President's head.'

He tells us it was Humes who made the statement '**as well as surgery of the head area, namely in the top of the skull**'. He had admitted this to me in a phone conversation, so I wasn't surprised by this. But the crucial words here are 'possibly cutting of hair, or removal of some slight tissue to view the massive wound in the right rear of the President's head'. **Surely, even a paper pusher such as James J. Humes, who hadn't done an autopsy in years, could tell the difference between a cut from a scalpel and cutting of hair versus tearing from a bullet?**

The most stunning portion of the manuscript on Kennedy that O'Neill had sent was yet to come: 'Humes pointed out the many fragments of bullets or skull that were in the skull cavity. **Parts of the brain were still within the cavity, but not much** [my emphasis].' This fits directly with Paul O'Connor's recollection that when President Kennedy was taken from the casket and the sheets were unwrapped from around the head, there was no brain to be removed, that only fragments were left inside the cranium. I went back to Frank O'Neill's deposition before the Records Review Board on 12 September 1997.

Q: These photographs have been identified as having been taken of President Kennedy's brain at some time after the autopsy – after they have been set in formalin. Can you identify that in any reasonable way as appearing to be the – what the brain looked like of President Kennedy?

A: No.

Q: In what regard does it appear to be different?

A: It appears to be too much.

Q: Could we now look at – let me ask a question, if you could elaborate a little bit on what you mean, 'It appears to be too much.'

A: Well, from this particular photograph here, it would seem that the only section of the brain which is missing is this small section over here. To me, that's not consistent with the way I recall seeing it. I do recall a large amount of what was identified to me as brain matter being on the back of Kellerman's shirt – I mean Kellerman's jacket – and Greer's jacket. And to me, that was a larger portion than that section there. This looks like a complete brain or am I wrong on that? I don't know.

Q: Could we take a look . . . If we could keep this one out for a moment and take a look at the 90 view, which is described as the superior view of the brain, colour photograph number 50. Just so it is clear to you, the basilar view is going to be the brain from the bottom. The superior view is going to be the brain from the top. And what I am showing you now would be the left hemisphere of the brain, and the portion over here is the right hemisphere of the brain. The correlation is the portion down there. Does that look approximately the size of what you recall President Kennedy's brain being when it was removed from the cranium?

A: In all honesty, I can't say that it looks like the brain that I saw, quite frankly. I – as I described before, I did not recall it being that large . . . It could've been, but I can't swear to it on a stack of Bibles that it was.

Clearly O'Neill suspected that it was not Kennedy's brain, which is confirmed by his own words in the chapter on JFK he sent me: 'Parts of the brain were within the cavity, but not much.' He did his best to convey this to the Records Review Board without coming right out and directly saying it. But he came close, as close as Frank O'Neill was able, to saying that something was terribly wrong. One can argue that Paul O'Connor was not in the autopsy room at the time of the brain's removal from the cranium. It is known that O'Connor was out of the room getting things for the doctors from time to time, and he could have missed the brain being removed, but if O'Neill is being truthful, the only time he was out of the room was when the X-rays and pictures were being taken. He and Sibert were in the cooler room looking through the glass window in the door at what was going on in the autopsy room. O'Neill says in his unpublished work (the material was later published in his book *A Fox Among Wolves*) that 'no cutting was done on the body until the X-rays were developed. The X-rays were returned to a small room within the autopsy room and viewed.' O'Neill goes on to say that the head wound was 'massive . . . Humes pointed out to Sibert and myself the gaping wound at the right rear of the President's head and the tremendous damage done to the brain therein.' When Humes was ready for the body to be turned over, O'Neill and Sibert assisted. 'The first thing that everyone noticed was the large scar on the President's back due to an operational procedure.' Jim Sibert is credited by O'Neill with noticing a small hole in the upper right rear of Kennedy's back. O'Neill goes on to record the details of the mystery of the bullet wound but no bullet in evidence. When the news arrived that a bullet had rolled off a stretcher at Parkland Hospital at Dallas, he was most relieved and accepted that it must have been the missing bullet. O'Neill then writes, 'At no time did the autopsy doctors give any other kind of explanation for the back wound. This probably accounts at least in part, for his [Humes'] destroying his original draft notes in his fireplace at his home.'

I marvelled at what O'Neill's unpublished chapter contained. He told me that he does not believe there was any conspiracy to take John F. Kennedy's life. In his manuscript he states, 'There has been no hard evidence to date, nothing to support any conspiracy theories in a court of law, nor a scintilla of fact that would prove otherwise.' Yet he puts the lie to his own words against conspiracy in Kennedy's death by his own belief that the single-bullet theory is not possible. If one bullet did not cause seven wounds sustained by President Kennedy and Governor Connally, going through skin and bone and falling out on a stretcher at Parkland Hospital, almost pristine, there was indeed more than one assassin in Dealey Plaza that day.

The 'surgery of the head area' statement in the field report is responsible for the greatest conspiracy theory ever presented in the history of the JFK assassination. President Kennedy's remains were intercepted at some point by the conspirators and, in effect, there was a pre-autopsy 'autopsy' in order to remove bullets from the body and take the president's brain. After following the trail of paper documents, and interviews with those individuals who handled President Kennedy's remains, I believe this to be true. And despite the denials of James Sibert and Frank O'Neill, their actions on the night of 22 November and the report they left behind confirm that there was indeed a pre-autopsy probing of Kennedy's body. And it was Francis X. O'Neill who, in his own writing, confirmed this. It is now an incontrovertible fact. This passage from O'Neill's unpublished chapter on Kennedy is every bit as explosive as the 'surgery of the head area' statement in the pages of the FD-302 report.

* * *

Mystery after mystery surfaced during the autopsy carried out on the body of President Kennedy, but there was no riddle greater than that of the brain. At one time or another it was said to be completely missing. Special Agent Jim Sibert was asked what he saw when he looked into the cavity on the arrival of the body for autopsy. 'Just a big hole,' he said. Sibert's wife, Esther, asked me, 'You know his brains were blown out of his head?' Jim Jenkins believed the brain was removed before the body was received for autopsy and was subsequently replaced with another. During autopsy, it was noted as small and completely detached, so as to allow it to drop into Dr Humes' hands. It apparently differed in size according to the various descriptions rendered. It did not appear to be the same as the one seen previously. At one time, it was reported to have been given into the charge of the president's brother Senator Robert F. Kennedy, and, finally, to add to the confusion, it was noted in the records of the House Assassinations Committee that it appeared that two brains might have been examined subsequent to the conclusion of the autopsy.

* * *

A number of backtrackings eventually followed the outspokenness of Sibert and O'Neill. Their statement that they had witnessed the arrival of the body of the president at Bethesda, with evidence that the head wounds had been tampered with, was at a later point toned down, for instance. Perhaps they had had time to reflect on the impact this would have; perhaps they had received instructions to soften it from elsewhere. I go with their original statement. Neither of these men was the kind to make the blunders their first statement would have represented. Similarly, when stating **(in writing)** that they had handed in a 'missile' which had been recovered, it would have been decidedly odd if they had become sloppy enough to refer to fragments as a 'missile', as they wanted us later to believe. In other examples of their reports, fragments were called fragments. It is significant that when they decided to modify this it was in respect of a bullet found in President Kennedy's body.

Sibert and O'Neill were excellent observers and their written reports were not expected in any way to be tainted by instances of 'maybe' or 'perhaps'.

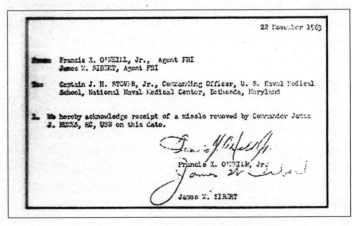

98. Receipt for 'missile'.

BA 89-30
FXO/JWS:df1
3

transportation of the President's body back to the White House. AMC CHESTER H. BOYERS, U. S. Navy, visited the autopsy room during the final stages of such to type receipts given by FBI and Secret Service for items obtained.

At the termination of the autopsy, the following personnel from Gawler's Funeral Home entered the autopsy room to prepare the President's body for burial:

    JOHN VAN HAESEN
    EDWIN STROBLE
    THOMAS ROBINSON
    Mr. HAGEN

Brigidier General GODFREY McHUGH, Air Force Military Aide to the President, was also present, as was Dr. GEORGE BAKEMAN, U. S. Navy.

Arrangements were made for the performance of the autopsy by the U. S. Navy and Secret Service.

The President's body was removed from the casket in which it had been transported and was placed on the autopsy table, at which time the complete body was wrapped in a sheet and the head area contained an additional wrapping which was saturated with blood. Following the removal of the wrapping, it was ascertained that the President's clothing had been removed and it was also apparent that a tracheotomy had been performed, as well as surgery of the head area, namely, in the top of the skull. All personnel with the exception of medical officers needed in the taking of photographs and X-Rays were requested to leave the autopsy room and remain in an adjacent room.

Upon completion of X-Rays and photographs, the first incision was made at 8:15 p.m. X-Rays of the brain area which were developed and returned to the autopsy room disclosed a path of a missile which appeared to enter the back of the skull and the path of the disintegrated fragments could be observed along the right side of the skull. The largest section of this missile as portrayed by X-Ray appeared to be behind the right frontal sinus. The next largest fragment appeared to be at the rear of the skull at the juncture of the skull bone.

The Chief Pathologist advised approximately 40 particles of disintegrated bullet and smudged indicated that the projectile had fragmentized while passing through the skull region.

99. Excerpt from the report of Sibert and O'Neill showing reference to surgery of the head and a tracheotomy.

TREASURY DEPARTMENT
WASHINGTON 25, D.C.

CO-2-34938

Protective Research Section
November 26, 1963

Receipt is acknowledged this date, Nov. 26, 1963, of the following items from Dr. George G. Burkley:

One piece of bronze colored material inadvertently broken in transit from casket in which body was brought from Dallas.

One letter—Certificate of Death of John F. Kennedy—State of Texas—dated Nov. 22, 1963.

One carbon copy of letter dated November 26 from Commanding Officer, U. S. Medical School, concerning law and regulations regarding confidential nature of the events.

One receipt dated Nov. 22, 1963, for bed sheet, surgical drapes, and shroud used to cover the body in transit.

One receipt dated Nov. 22, 1963, regarding a carton of photographic film, undeveloped except for X-rays, delivered to PRS for safekeeping.

An original and six pink copies of Certificate of Death (Nav.Med.N)

One receipt from FBI for a missile removed during the examination of the body.

One letter from University of Texas South West Medical School including report from Dr. Clark and summary of their findings of treatment and examination of the President in the Dallas County Hospital. Said letter of transmittal states that three carbon copies have been retained in that area.

One copy of autopsy report and notes of the examining doctor which is described in letter of transmittal Nov. 25, 1963 by Dr. Gallaway.

100. The Treasury Department accepted the term 'missile'.

29

PEOPLE

THE NUMBER OF PEOPLE ENCOUNTERED IN ANY survey of the events surrounding the assassination is legion. I should say at the start of this chapter that I laud the splendid work of Michael Benson in this connection. His excellent *Who's Who in the JFK Assassination*, in spite of the fact that I am not mentioned in his book (I say with a grin on my face; it was being researched at about the same time as my first book was being written), is an exceptionally valuable aid to anyone interested in the subject at any level. I rush to say, therefore, that I am not entering into any kind of competition with him.

I am being highly selective in focusing on people, some of whom are mentioned in context elsewhere, who for one or more of many reasons merit a closer look. **George Sergei de Mohrenschildt** is certainly one of them. Born into a White Russian noble family, he was a count, entitled to be called 'Baron'. He had links which branched out in many directions. He had been close to the Bouvier family (Jacqueline called him 'Uncle George'. He played with her when she was a child.) It was claimed that in 'another life' during the Second World War he worked for the Nazis, involved in their anti-communist activities, and he spoke Russian fluently.

His general background was that of an intelligence agent. He worked for the CIA training Cuban exiles for the Bay of Pigs invasion and is believed to have been still in the pay of the Agency when he lived with his wife, Jeanne, in Dallas. He was friends with the Paines, the family Marina Oswald moved in with when she and her husband separated. **Ruth and Michael Paine**, who lived in Irving, Texas, were both believed to have had involvements linked to the assassination. It was Ruth who was responsible for Lee Harvey Oswald getting work at the Texas School Book Depository, and it was her station wagon that was thought to have been picking up Oswald or someone like him outside the Texas building immediately after the assassination. It should be said, however, that when this connection arose Oswald staunchly denied Ruth Paine was involved in events in any way.

On the other hand, it was somewhat suspicious that so many 'indicators' of differing kinds turned up at the Paine household, an example being Ruth's report to the Warren Committee of seeing the blanket which had covered Oswald's rifle when it was allegedly stored on the floor in her garage looking flat (and not covering a rifle any more). Michael had connections with the military-industrial complex in that he worked for Bell Helicopter.

De Mohrenschildt, however, had connections all over the place. It is generally accepted that he had links with the CIA, and he helped get Marina into the Paines' house, about which Ruth was known to be happy, and it was no doubt agreed with Michael, her husband. The Baron may have been behind the job Ruth Paine was involved in getting for Oswald at the Texas School Book Depository, and it was known that, somewhat surprisingly, he had direct connections with oil billionaire Clint Murchison, whose eyes and ears he apparently was in Haiti at the time of the assassination. Baron de Mohrenschildt was said to have come into a great deal of money, paid into an overseas account, at the time of the assassination, but, on the face of it, with the moneyed connections he had it would scarcely have attracted attention. One has to wonder, however, is it possible that a closer look at where the money came from would have been importantly revealing?

Clint Murchison was suspected by many of being involved in the assassination of President Kennedy. One of those who was appalled by the idea of Kennedy abolishing the tax depletion allowance to oil producers, he also had business interests in publishing (Henry Holt), real estate, construction and railroads. He was the host of the disputed party held at his home the night before the assassination took place. Disputed only because since that day considerable attempts have been made to prove it did not take place. There is little doubt that the party did, in fact, take place, with guests including Richard Nixon, J. Edgar Hoover, Senator John Tower, oil billionaire H.L. Hunt and Chase Manhattan Bank's John McCloy, the same John McCloy who later became a Warren commissioner.

101. Johnson's mistress, Madeleine Brown. (Courtesy Madeleine Brown)

Also there was **Madeleine Brown**, Johnson's mistress, who told me of the late arrival of **Lyndon B. Johnson**, who came over from Fort Worth, where the Kennedy entourage was established that night, to be at the gathering. Madeleine told me that Nixon, Hoover and Johnson went into conclave, after which Johnson left 'with smoke coming out of his ears'. The following morning, before it was time to join the flight to Dallas Love Field, Johnson rang Madeleine and in the course of the conversation said, 'Those damned Kennedys will not be poking fun at me after today.' This was a clear implication that Johnson was told of the plan to kill the president before the assassination happened, therefore having knowledge before the fact. It did not, however, suggest he had any part in the conspiracy itself, which many believe was the case.

It is interesting that if Johnson was told of the plan to kill the president in the small group that separated in conclave at that party, Richard Nixon and J. Edgar Hoover were also present. And the question nags, who brought the news of the planned assassination? An exceptionally pertinent question if we assume Johnson did not know of it until that time.

The name **E. Howard Hunt** comes up in various contexts relating to the assassination. Hunt was a CIA agent who seemed to be in everything. He was involved in the Bay of Pigs invasion and he was the most likely person Lee Harvey Oswald was writing to in a letter which turned up immediately before the House Assassinations Committee began its work. The letter ran:

Dear Mr Hunt,
I would like information concerning [*sic*] my position.

I am asking only for information. I am suggesting we discuss the matter fully before any steps are taken by me or anyone else.

Thank you,

Lee Harvey Oswald.

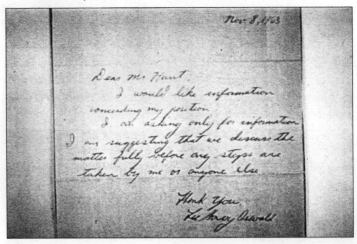

102. Which Hunt? It seems possible it was meant for H.L. Hunt, the oil magnate, but more likely it was for CIA agent E. Howard Hunt.

(Courtesy National Archives)

272

The House Assassinations Committee dismissed the letter without comment, so that whatever was supposed – or hoped – to be achieved in releasing it 12 years after it was written came to nothing. Only two prominent Hunts came to mind: one was the CIA agent and the other **H.L. Hunt**, the oil billionaire. It was considered somewhat curious that H.L. managed to be 'away from home' at the time the assassination took place. A prominent member of the family told me of his departure at that particular time and found it suspicious. Suspicious particularly since he was said to be at the Murchison party the night before?

Domingo Benavides was in his truck near to where Officer Tippit was shot. He ran quickly to the dying officer's side. Asked about the killer, Benavides adamantly refused to identify Oswald. Needless to say, he was not asked to attend the line-up at police headquarters. When Domingo's brother was shot and killed about three months afterwards, he figured his brother had been mistaken for him. He changed his mind and said he identified Oswald at that point.

Benavides witnessed the gunman remove an empty shell from his gun and discard it, throwing another away before leaving. If he saw this happen and would not, until under duress, identify Oswald as the man he saw, it is a strong indication that he clearly did not see Oswald. Benavides tried to call the police from Tippit's car but did not know how to operate the equipment. A man named Bowley, who was driving past, saw him in difficulties and stopped to make the call for him.

The man seen by Domingo Benavides was wearing a beige jacket, he said. Shown a blue jacket and likely trying to be helpful, he identified that as the jacket he saw. Attempts to tie in the actual time of the shooting to the Bowley call to the police department were not successful, due to the fact that Benavides, who was driving his truck when the shots were actually fired, told how he kept his head down and stayed put till the shooting was over. Add to that the period he spent with Tippit and during which he attempted to call the police on Tippit's radio, and the time of the shooting becomes guesswork.

Of three people arrested at the time of the assassination in the Dal-Tex Building, the building across the street from the Book Depository, **Jim Braden** aka **Eugene Hale Brading** was the most interesting. Braden, who was listed as having been arrested on 30 previous occasions, was known to be a Mafia courier, and when questioned about his reasons for being in that place at that time, he stated that he had had an appointment with Lamar Hunt, the son of H.L. Hunt, on oil business. Jim Braden had stayed at the Kabanya Motor Hotel, where Jack Ruby had met with some Chicago friends the night before the president was shot.

103. Jim Braden, Mafia courier with a link to Jack Ruby, said he had an appointment to see Lamar Hunt, son of H.L. Hunt. Interesting?

Remarkably, Braden was not detained for further questioning by the police, who might have been seen as 'skating around' to avoid the involvement of others. Could it have been Lamar or H.L. Hunt, for instance? Or perhaps Jack Ruby, who was required to be 'available' by whoever sent him to kill Lee Harvey Oswald? Curious? It was profoundly more curious when Braden was identified in Los Angeles five years later at the time Senator Robert Kennedy was gunned down.

Police Chief Jesse Curry had to accept responsibility for the unaccountable APB put out on Lee Harvey Oswald only minutes after he had left the Texas School Book Depository. His explanation that the staff had been assembled and a roll call taken and that

Oswald was the only one missing simply did not hold water. In the first place, it would have taken quite some time to bring together the staff still remaining in the building and even more time to check who was present and who wasn't. Furthermore, it was reported that Oswald was not the only member of staff who had quit for the day at that point.

Curry also had to bear the ultimate responsibility for the failure of the Dallas Police Department to protect Lee Harvey Oswald from being gunned down by Jack Ruby on police premises. Curry had a great many failings to answer for. The fact that Jack Ruby got to where he was at the particular time Oswald was due for transfer to the county jail was one of them. It was said that Ruby must have had help from some responsible person in the police department to get to his position, and it has even been suggested how this was done. If anyone in the police department assisted Ruby in any way, responsibility, again, was laid ultimately at Curry's door.

Curry could not be said completely to have favoured the conspiracy aspect of the assassination, however. It will be recalled that when he was asked by reporters if they had an eyewitness to Oswald firing from the sixth-floor window, in spite of the testimony of Howard Brennan, he replied, 'No, sir. We do not.' Brennan's testimony proved to be extremely dubious, and it appeared Curry was not impressed. Futhermore, in an interview with Tom Johnson, a former aide to Lyndon B. Johnson, he told him, 'We don't have any proof that Oswald fired the rifle, and never did. Nobody's yet been able to put him in that building with a gun in his hand.'

Without it necessarily reflecting on Jesse Curry, however, there is little doubt that members of the Dallas Police Department appeared to have been subverted to acting on behalf of the conspirators on the day Kennedy died.

Mystery surrounds the chief pilot attached to Huntsville Penitentiary. **John Ian Crawford** had connections with Jack Ruby and, it is believed, through him with the Bay of Pigs CIA survivors. Crawford is suspected of being the pilot who would be at the controls of the small aircraft being sought by CIA agents from

Wayne January. (See Chapter 35.) Since that particular small aircraft was not forthcoming and since the frustrated agents were believed to have secured a plane for their 'mission' from another aircraft company, Crawford may have been the pilot selected to fly Oswald to Cuba, another flight aborted. However, Crawford was one of those who disappeared then died a mysterious death. (The known details are featured in Chapter 31.)

Mary Dowling was a waitress at Dobbs Restaurant on North Beckley, near where Lee Harvey Oswald boarded. She told of an interesting event on the Wednesday before the assassination took place. Oswald normally came in for breakfast each morning between 7 a.m. and 7.30 a.m., but on that day he came in at about 10 a.m. He made a fuss because his eggs were not cooked to his satisfaction and finished up swearing. This did not escape the attention of a police officer who was in the restaurant at that time. The officer, who just happened to be J.D. Tippit, made no move to intervene.

The question arises, if Oswald and Tippit had not previously met, was this a prearranged way of them identifying one another, since Tippit, it appears, was due to ferry Oswald to Red Bird airfield two days afterwards? Tippit was the only police officer in the restaurant at that time and Oswald was the only one sounding off about his eggs, which was unusual for him. This connects to events described in Chapter 35.

It is worth a note in passing that Oswald apparently earned a reputation for himself when on cookhouse duties in the Marines for his expertise – with eggs.

Gordon Shanklin and **James P. Hosty** were two FBI agents located in Dallas. Shanklin was the special agent in charge of the Dallas office and Hosty was assigned to monitor Marina Oswald, a foreign national.

Lee Harvey Oswald is believed to have worked for the FBI in addition to the CIA and, possibly, the Office of Naval Intelligence. It was quite common for agents to work for more than one agency. A few days before the assassination took place, Oswald stepped into the Dallas FBI office and asked for Agent Hosty. Hosty was not in the office at that time, and Oswald therefore left a note in an envelope for him with the receptionist. 'Get this to him,' he snapped and left. The note and its contents were never heard of again until 1975, when an FBI employee mentioned it to a journalist. The time was right for the note to be probed by first the Senate Intelligence Committee and then the House Assassinations Committee, both of which sought to know its contents.

104. FBI agent James P. Hosty.

James Hosty admitted receiving the note and said the contents referred to a matter concerning Marina Oswald which had irritated Oswald. He told how he had put the note in a file, where it lay until Oswald was shot and killed, whereupon Gordon Shanklin became 'agitated and upset' and called Hosty into his office. It was the note from Oswald which was bothering him. The note had found its way to Shanklin's desk drawer and, taking it out, he gave it to Hosty, saying, 'Oswald's dead now. There can be no trial. Here, get rid of this.' Hosty took the note and tore it up, but that was not enough for Shanklin. 'No!' he said. 'Get it out of here. I don't even want it in this office. Get rid of it.' Hosty duly obliged, throwing the pieces of the note into the toilet and flushing them away.

It hardly needs saying that Shanklin's reaction to what was claimed to be a somewhat innocuous note was very much over the top. When questioned, Shanklin denied any knowledge of it. If the agent in charge of the Dallas office had no knowledge of it, how was it known of at the Bureau's headquarters, where Assistant Director William Sullivan referred to 'an internal problem' concerning a note from Lee Harvey Oswald? Kenneth Howe was another agent assigned to the Dallas office and saw the note in Hosty's tray. He asked Gordon Shanklin about it and was rebuffed. 'He didn't want to discuss it with me.' It appeared that the decision to destroy the note came from headquarters to 'avoid embarrassment to the Bureau'. That in itself is exceptionally interesting.

The note, which had been lying about for all to see in a filing tray, became a hot potato, but why? Was it because of the president being killed? It seemed clear that it was an extra-hot potato after Lee Harvey Oswald was murdered. Those seeking the truth about it all have speculated that Oswald, doing his job for the FBI, had come across indications that the president was to be assassinated and he let them know at once. True or not, we do not know, but that scenario would certainly account for all the reactions to a mystifying note. It would also explain Shanklin's words to Hosty when he said, 'Oswald's dead now. There can be no trial. Here, get rid of this.'

It might have been thought that after his retirement Agent Hosty would have more to say on the subject of the note. Not so, but he did hint that there was more to learn about Oswald's connections with intelligence. Hosty wrote a book in his retirement, but those hoping for revelations regarding the note from Oswald were doomed to disappointment.

30

SILENCED!

> The available evidence does not establish anything about the nature
> of these deaths which would indicate that the deaths were in some
> manner, either direct or peripheral, caused by the assassination of
> President Kennedy or by any aspect of the subsequent investigation.

Jacqueline Hess, who took over the House Assassinations
Committee's 'mysterious deaths project', made this declaration,
which was probably intended to put an immediate end to assertions
that people who had knowledge relative to the assassination or
who possibly had useful information were being killed. For those
who looked around and saw people they knew who were connected
in some way with what had happened unexpectedly or unaccountably
dying, however, it was not very convincing.

It was even less convincing when they added to their number
those they read about in their newspapers. Some died by violence,
some in accidents, others by what appeared to be natural causes,
and this is not to mention those said to have taken their own
lives. One way or another, an amazing count of 'connected' or
'related' deaths mounted up.

Two days before the assassination, Rose Cheramie, who had at
one time worked for Jack Ruby, was taken to hospital by Lieutenant
Francis Frugé, a Louisiana state police officer, after having been
thrown out of a car and suffering minor injuries. At the time he
picked her up, she appeared drugged or under the influence of
drugs, but she was able to give an account of a conversation overheard
between two Latin types with whom she had travelled on a car
journey from Florida to Dallas. It included discussing a plot to kill

President Kennedy. She repeated that Kennedy was to be killed in Dallas to the hospital doctors, who, confirming that she was lucid and 'without psychosis', passed on the information to the House Assassinations Committee in the '70s. On the day of the assassination, however, Lieutenant Frugé had taken Rose Cheramie into custody for further questioning. Frugé got in touch with Captain Will Fritz, who was in charge of the investigation into the assassination, at Dallas police headquarters. Fritz told him he wasn't interested.

105. Rose Cheramie. Captain Fritz wasn't interested in hearing her testimony.

The frustrated Rose Cheramie made another attempt to tell what she knew to the FBI in 1965, but soon afterwards she was picked up once more by the roadside, apparently having been, once again, thrown from a car. This time she was dead. A driver giving the name of Tyler reported that though he had run over her head, he had tried, unsuccessfully, to avoid her. The police took down details of where he lived, but, on checking, found there was no such address. There was certainly something for them to investigate, however. At the hospital, Cheramie was operated on for eight hours and resultant hospital records showed a wound to her right forehead which might have been caused by a bullet fired at close range.

Questions arise from this story, as well they might from all the accounts we give of mysterious and untimely deaths. In this particular case, had Rose Cheramie overheard the intention to assassinate the president from a conversation between two of the expert marksmen brought in by the CIA to shoot the president? Had Will Fritz missed an opportunity to disentangle the whole plan by ignoring the diligent Lieutenant Frugé? Or was there no intention of heeding any information which did not point the finger at Lee Harvey Oswald?

The deaths had started early. Two days before the assassination, Karyn Kupcinet lifted the telephone to speak to a long-distance operator and screamed that President Kennedy was going to be killed. Two days after the assassination, she was found dead at her home. She was 23 years of age. The killers were never found.

Mrs Earlene Roberts was one of those they said died of a heart attack. Mrs Roberts was Lee Harvey Oswald's landlady, who last saw him when he called to change before setting off to meet Officer Tippit at Oak Cliff. She also reported the police car which stopped outside her house, pipping its horn. To her memory, the number of the police car she had noted was similar to that of Tippit's vehicle, which indeed was the only police vehicle in that area following the assassination. But she did not live long enough to settle a proved identification. It would have opened up a whole new can of worms had she established seeing Tippit's car outside her house signalling to Lee Oswald.

A heart attack was also said to be the cause of the death of Jack Ruby's lawyer, Tom Howard. Ruby had claimed his motive for shooting Oswald was to prevent Jacqueline Kennedy from having to endure the expected trial for murder of Lee Harvey Oswald. He confessed that Tom Howard had suggested this in order to obtain sympathy. In seeking reasons for his death, however, the privileged information Ruby may have given Howard, a much bigger consideration, has to enter the equation.

Tom Howard had appeared as if by magic at the side of Jack Ruby when he shot and killed Lee Harvey Oswald, and this did not escape notice. One who said it looked as though Howard had been primed to be there was journalist Bill Hunter. He was later shot and killed in a mishap in a police station in California. Hunter was one of two who, together, interviewed Tom Howard. The second journalist was Jim Koethe. He lost his life to an assassin when he stepped out of his shower. He was killed by a karate chop to his throat. If Howard was killed because he had privileged information from Ruby, did both journalists he had talked to die because he had shared that information with them?

106. Tom Howard, Ruby's lawyer. What secrets
did he have? Died of a heart attack.

107. Bill Hunter, journalist, interviewed Tom Howard.
Died in a shooting mishap.

108. Jim Koethe, journalist, also interviewed Tom Howard.
Killed by a karate chop to the throat.

Warren Reynolds worked at his car lot near to where the Tippit shooting took place. He witnessed a man fleeing the scene of the crime and running right past the car lot and, crucially, stated that it was not Lee Harvey Oswald. He was shot at and wounded in the head and later 'changed his mind' and said that it was Oswald he had seen. The man arrested and accused of shooting him was Darrell Wayne Garner, who was given an alibi by showgirl Nancy Jane Mooney. Garner was released, but Nancy Jane was picked up by police for a minor offence. After only an hour in a cell, she was found hanged by her toreador trousers. Garner died of an overdose a few years later. Nancy Jane Mooney was one of four showgirls who died violent deaths, all linked by two things: they all knew Jack Ruby and they all worked at his Carousel Club. Of these, Marilyn Magyar is believed to have been murdered by her husband, although it came to light that she was planning to write a book on the assassination; another was Karen Bennett Carlin, who was shot and killed in a Houston hotel room.

Another who worked for Ruby was the wife of Thomas 'Hank' Killam, who was said to know of a link between Ruby and Oswald.

Killam was found in an alley with his throat cut. Before his death, he had reportedly said to his brother, 'I am a dead man, but I have run as far as I am running.'

The cab driver who had taken Lee Harvey Oswald home from the Texas School Book Depository when he left after the assassination was William Whaley. He died in a traffic accident while driving his taxi, something that happens extremely rarely to cab drivers. Another to die in a road accident was James Worrell, who witnessed a man running away from the rear door of the Book Depository building after the assassination. The man wore a dark sports coat and, after his hasty departure, slowed down to a walk and made off down Houston Street, said Worrell. The man he described was distinctly not Lee Harvey Oswald.

Yet another to die in a road accident was Lee Bowers. Bowers, a railroad worker, was located at the tower behind the grassy knoll and had a clear view of the parking area behind the picket fence. Bowers knew that entry to the area had been forbidden by the police some 30 minutes before the assassination took place. From his vantage point, however, he had witnessed three cars enter the area during the 'closed' period. One was a blue-and-white Oldsmobile, spattered with red mud and showing a 'Goldwater for President' sticker; the car circled the area and left. The driver of the second car to enter the forbidden area appeared to be holding something to his mouth, maybe a microphone, said Bowers. This was a black Ford, which probed for several minutes more than the first car and left. The third car was a Chevrolet, another showing a 'Goldwater' sticker and also spattered with red mud. It spent longer still circling the area, passing quite close to the railroad tower where Bowers was. He commented that before driving slowly away it stopped at the spot where the assassination took place.

109. Lee Bowers. Had a vantage point to oversee the car park behind the grassy knoll. Died in a road accident.

110. The tower in which Bowers was located.

Bowers had more to offer. He told a Warren Commission counsel of 'something which had attracted my eye', and made to expand on it. Counsel came in with an unrelated question and that was as far as Bowers got with his statement. He picked up from that point at a later date, however, when questioned by researcher Mark Lane. He described a flash of light or smoke which took place in front of him on the embankment: an important witness statement. When 41-year-old Lee Bowers' car left the road, causing his death, the doctors commented that he appeared to have been in a state of 'strange shock' at the time of his death.

Two others with contributions to make to the investigation suffered violent deaths. One was Gary Underhill, a CIA agent who said he had inside knowledge relating to the assassination. Found with a bullet in his head, he was claimed to have committed suicide, but it is odd for a right-handed man to shoot himself behind the left ear. The other was Harold Russell, who witnessed the escape of Officer Tippit's killer. In July 1965, when out partying at a bar with friends, he became hysterical and said he was going to be killed, causing concern about his state of mind among those present. His anxious friends decided to call the police, which, curiously, became the cause of his death. A brawl broke out and one of the attending police officers struck Russell on his head. He died shortly afterwards from his injuries.

These were not all of the 'mysterious deaths' which occurred during the period following the assassination. It must be asked how many deaths and what manner of dying would have impressed the House Assassinations Committee's investigator, Ms Hess. It had long since passed the point where it would have been easier to recognise a pattern of killings related to those with contributions related to the assassination than *not* to recognise such a pattern. This situation was not lost on a (London) *Sunday Times* actuary who looked at the number of material witnesses who had died at a point not long after the assassination and calculated the odds against that group of people dying from any causes in that period of time. He quoted an astounding one hundred thousand trillion to one against. At the time of the Hess pronouncements based on the deaths of 21 people quoted to her, objections were raised against this and brought an apology from the *Sunday Times*. One is left to wonder if the dropping of the odd nought or two from their calculation would have made any difference to the truth which was being underlined.

What would Ms Hess have said after the death toll went up

steeply when Jim Garrison conducted his case against Clay Shaw? The eccentric Dave Ferrie was one who died before Garrison could obtain the testimony he was seeking from him. His friend Eladio del Valle died also, found shot through the heart and with his skull split open. Garrison did obtain evidence from Clyde Johnson, who was later shot to death, but was too late to get to Robert Perrin, who died of arsenic poisoning. He had wanted to interview Dr Mary Sherman, who was shot to death, her corpse being found with a kitchen knife plunged into it. The murderer sought to conceal what had happened by setting fire to her bed. Nicholas Chetta, New Orleans coroner, conducted autopsies on Ferrie, Perrin and Sherman: he died of a heart attack while his assistant, Dr Henry Delaune, was murdered a little later. From the beginning, Garrison had Guy Banister in his sights as a star witness but he had died long before he got his case into court. Even the discharged Clay Shaw died in apparently mysterious circumstances a while later, in 1974.

Then we wonder whether Ms Hess had looked into the fresh crop of deaths in the mid-to-late '70s, when the House Assassinations Committee, the very agency which had appointed her to carry out her study, was in session. George de Mohrenschildt was one – another suicide, they said – and the notorious Sam Giancana was another. His death was distinctly not a suicide. Giancana had already appeared before the committee. His sidekick, the equally notorious Johnny Roselli, who was about to be questioned by the committee, was killed before testifying. He was found floating off the coast of Florida in an oil drum, while another of Giancana's hit men, Charles Nicoletti, was found riddled with bullets in a blazing car.

To the suspicious deaths tally has to be added six FBI officials who died within six months of each other and included William Sullivan, Hoover's right-hand man, who was very much involved with the FBI investigation into the assassination. Sullivan was listed to appear for questioning before the House Assassinations Committee but died in a hunting accident before he could do so.

Then there were others. Bill Chesher, said to know of a link between Ruby and Oswald, died of a heart attack in 1964. The tormented Roger Craig, who has been mentioned elsewhere, was said to have killed himself. Albert Guy Bogard, a car salesman who was on record as having shown cars to a man calling himself Lee Harvey Oswald on 9 November and claiming he recklessly test-drove one of them, also died. When Oswald's picture appeared on television, he said it was not the man who had been looking at his cars. It could not have been Oswald, of course, since he could not drive. Bogard gave evidence to the Warren Commission and afterwards was beaten up so badly his injuries cost him a protracted stay in hospital. The Warren Commission found he had been dealing with a 'false' Oswald, someone purporting to be him, but they never looked into who it might have been impersonating him. Albert Bogard was found dead in a car parked in a cemetery with all windows closed and a pipe running from the exhaust to the inside of the car. He was 41 years of age.

It will be recalled that star journalist Dorothy Kilgallen and her friend Mrs Earl T. Smith also died mysteriously. Returning to her home after her interview with Jack Ruby, Dorothy Kilgallen confided to her friend that she was going to break the assassination mystery 'wide open'; she was found dead a few days afterwards, while Mrs Earl T. Smith died two days later. Both, it was decided, had taken their own lives.

Congressman Hale Boggs, member of the Warren Commission and who later became House majority leader, began, eventually, to voice doubts about the Warren findings. In 1972, he disappeared on a plane which was on a flight over Alaska.

It would appear that Jack Ruby himself is another addition to the list, dying of cancer, which he claimed had been introduced by means of an injection administered by a mysterious doctor nobody had ever heard of. And not overlooked is the man who died at Ruby's hands, the man who was deprived of the chance to defend himself, Lee Harvey Oswald.

A catalogue of coincidences?

31

LOOSE ENDS

ONE HAS NOT FAR TO LOOK IN THE HUGE VOLUME of facts identified by researchers during the 50 years of the investigation to find a huge accumulation of unexplained events. Some would rate as 'interesting' and some 'curious'; some would be likely to conceal truths which would contribute to our understanding of the larger truth, while others would be listed under the 'utterly mysterious' category. I cannot promise I have them all here, but the following are examples, the first belonging in the last category.

A deep mystery surrounds what happened to a pilot named John Crawford. He lived in a trailer at the airport where he had his plane. On 17 April 1969, he was having a late-evening meal with some friends and their two children. Some kind of emergency arose, causing them all to rush to Crawford's plane, which had been hurriedly brought out of its hangar. All five of them, with the airport manager, took off in the plane, which unaccountably crashed, killing everyone on board.

Police examined the trailer carefully, finding, for instance, the coffee pot still on the lit stove. The plates contained uneaten food and the coffee cups still had coffee in them. In this uncanny situation, the stereo was still playing, and when the cars belonging to the three men present were examined, the keys were in the ignition in all three. On the seat of one car there was even the purse of the only woman in the group.

The connection with the assassination relates to the question of who was scheduled to fly the small aircraft revving up and ready to go found at the perimeter fence of Red Bird airfield (see

Chapter 35), which was thought to be the means of Oswald 'escaping'. Was it Crawford? As it happens, Crawford was also a friend of Jack Ruby and Wesley Frazier, who gave Lee Harvey Oswald a lift to work on the day of the assassination.

The Crawford and party mystery is a subject on which no progress has been made since the event. No one, to my knowledge, has come forward with an explanation. A genuine, totally puzzling *Marie Celeste* scenario.

Julia Ann Mercer had her eyes wide open when she drove down Elm Street, along what became the scene of the assassination. The traffic was snarled up because a green pick-up truck was illegally parked half on the pavement on the right side of the road at the foot of the grassy knoll. She stopped behind it, waiting to pass, and saw a man remove what answered to being a brown rifle case – she gave approximate measurements – from the tool compartment of the vehicle. He carried it up to the top of the knoll. She clearly described him. As she pulled round the truck, she looked into the cab and saw a man, white with fair brown hair, about 40, heavyset and wearing a green jacket. Looking ahead of her, she saw three police officers atop the railway overpass bridge and assumed therefore that she had witnessed a Secret Service man getting into position in preparation for the motorcade.

She knew she would have to report what she had seen when the news of the assassination broke, and she contacted the sheriff's office. After telling what she had seen, she was asked to go and sign an affidavit, which she did. The next day, she was visited by FBI agents who showed her a lot of photographs, from which she was able to identify the driver of the green truck. Though she had no idea who he was, she was astounded the following day to see pictures of him on television shooting Lee Harvey Oswald.

Question: did the fact that Ruby was not taken in for questioning relate to the 'need' to keep him in circulation long enough to shoot Oswald next day? Question two: Why did the police alter Mercer's statement in such ways as to throw investigators off the scent? Question three: Why did the police allow such vital evidence to be subject to an interview with a single officer? For this to constitute a police department investigation into highly relevant testimony was unthinkable, and to add to the indications that they were doing their best to ignore it, they finally filed the single officer's 'findings' on 9 December, 17 days after the date of the assassination. Final question: Why did the Warren Commission not want to probe this evidence?

Abraham Bolden was the first African American to be appointed to the US Secret Service White House detail. He had learned of a plot to kill President Kennedy on a scheduled Chicago visit and was anxious to tell what he knew. The plot had been foiled and it derailed Warren's Lee Harvey Oswald as the lone killer, since Oswald was certainly not involved in the Chicago affair. Bolden was arrested on charges of seeking a bribe from a counterfeiter, Joseph Spagnoli, in return for passing on secret information. Bolden received a six-year jail sentence and, despite Spagnoli admitting he had lied, he was made to serve the whole term. More? Spagnoli later claimed he had lied at the behest of prosecutor Richard Sykes.

Of all things, a mystery surrounds the ballistics evidence relating to the bullets which killed Officer J.D. Tippit. In the first place, the empty shell cases picked up at the scene of the shooting were apparently only there by kind permission of the killer. Witnessed by Dominic Benavides, he appeared to deliberately throw them where they would be found. Two of the empty shell cases were Winchesters and two were Remingtons. This presented the first problem, since Oswald's gun did not eject empty shell cases. The recovered cases were not finished causing problems though. Benavides placed two of them in a cigarette box and gave them to Officer J.M. Poe, who dutifully showed them to Sergeant Gerald R. Hill. Hill told Poe to be sure to mark them for evidence with his initials, 'JMP', which he stated he did. Hill introduced a note of doubt when he said he recollected seeing three shell cases in the cigarette box, but confusion followed when Poe could not find his mark on any of four shell cases shown him. Sergeant Barnes, to whom Poe had given the cigarette packet containing the spent shells, marked them also with a 'B', but on examining those put forward as evidence could not find his initial either. Another two shell cases found at the scene by Barbara Davis and Virginia R. Davis were handed over, but when asked to identify them later, they could not. The Warren commissioners now had four shell cases said to have been found at the scene of the crime which were totally worthless as evidence.

When it came to the bullets recovered from Officer Tippit's body, the situation did not improve. Three were Western Winchesters and the fourth a Remington, which did not match the empty cases found. The FBI firearms specialist Cortlandt Cunningham was sent only one bullet by the Dallas Police Department to examine. Cunningham reported to the Warren Commission:

> 'They reportedly said this was the only bullet that was recovered, or that they had. Later, at the request of this Commission, we went back to the Dallas Police Department and found in their files that they actually had three other bullets.'

Cunningham reported that it was not possible to tell from the distorted bullets which gun had fired them. The Warren Commission therefore decided to have a second opinion and engaged Joseph D. Nicol, an expert with the Illinois police, to carry out further tests. He found that in the case of one of the bullets there were 'sufficient individual characteristics' to conclude that the projectile was fired from the same gun as the test projectiles, presumably fired from Oswald's revolver.

By the time the three additional bullets had been discovered by Cortlandt Cunningham in the Dallas Police files it was March 1964, and four months had elapsed from the time of the assassination. At this point a very pertinent question was asked by commissioner Congressman Boggs: 'What proof do we have, though, that these are the bullets?' To my knowledge, there was no answer to that question, nor any investigation into the ludicrous Keystone Cops behaviour of the Dallas Police Department regarding the straightforward, everyday procedure of preserving evidence for eventual presentation of the officers. Nevertheless, despite evidence that did not add up in any direction, the Warren Commission decided Officer Tippit had been killed by Lee Harvey Oswald.

Remember the Mauser rifle which was found on the sixth floor of the Depository building? That magically turned into the Mannlicher-Carcano 'owned' by Lee Harvey Oswald and was claimed to be the weapon which killed President Kennedy. We never heard any more about the rifle brought down by a police officer from the roof of the same building, which was referred to as 'the assassin's rifle' even though it had no telescopic sight.

Then Donald B. Thomas, the scientist who carried out the definitive analysis of the content of the Dictabelt tapes in the US Forensic Science Society journal in 2001, claimed that his analysis showed that the final bullet fired, the one which killed President Kennedy, was consistent with the shot having come from a weapon of .30 calibre. This was a vital contribution which has gone virtually unnoticed. It introduced a new dimension into the consideration of the weaponry used.

But then one thing connects with another. Immediately after the shot in question had been fired in Dealey Plaza, a police officer on duty there, Inspector Herbert Sawyer, radioed a message in to headquarters regarding a man wanted for questioning. It ran: 'The wanted person is a slender white male about 30, 5 ft 10 in., 165 lb, carrying what looked to be a .30-30 or some type of Winchester.' Inspector Sawyer reported that the information had come from one of his officers. Fully explored, this would have considerably weakened any case against Oswald and might, in fact, have resulted in complete exoneration. The officer was never identified and the rifle never heard of again.

What happened to the pavement and the road sign? Breneman and West were the surveyors who carried out the Dealey Plaza survey requested by the FBI for the Warren Commission. During their work, they observed a chip in the pavement on the kerb. They also noted a stress mark on a road sign made by a bullet on it. The pavement area was quickly replaced and the sign taken down. The sign, I discovered, was removed to the basement of the School Book Depository, from where it vanished and has never been seen again. Was this evidence of other bullets flying around in addition to those which hit the president? And was this evidence another instance of cover-up?

Why would the Mannlicher-Carcano rifle said to have been fired by Lee Harvey Oswald, who was right-handed, have been found upon examination to have been adapted for use by a left-handed person? It also required three shims for the sight to become effective.

32

JIM GARRISON: ON THE TRAIL OF THE ASSASSINS

THE GENERAL FEELING AMONG RESEARCHERS AT the time Jim Garrison, district attorney for New Orleans, brought his action against Clay Shaw, in the hope of unravelling the secrets of the conspiracy to kill Kennedy, was that it was regrettable and that he set the enquiry back. I, for one, do not agree. From the outset, I was convinced Garrison had got onto something that he could not let go of. By now, it is likely that all his detractors would agree he was right.

Utterly convinced that at least some of the evidence of a conspiracy was to be found in New Orleans, in January 1969 he brought an action against Clay Shaw, a New Orleans businessman, whom he indicted for conspiracy to assassinate President Kennedy. He claimed Shaw worked for the CIA, and, in a nutshell, he failed to prove this. His case was thrown out and he consequently lost his job as district attorney. We now know he was right all along. Shaw did work for the CIA and this was, eventually, confirmed by no less than the head of the CIA, Richard Helms. Shaw had consistently lied, as might be expected of any agent of the CIA. Garrison had a group of activists in his sights. He believed that they, including Shaw, were involved in planning the murder of the president, and, as one thing would lead to another, he pursued his objective with everything he had to reach that point.

111. Clay Shaw was unsuccessfully prosecuted by Jim Garrison; it was the only prosecution ever attempted of a suspected participant in the assassination.

112. CIA director Richard Helms admitted long after the case failed that Garrison had been right all along: Clay Shaw *did* work for the CIA.

He did not trust Lyndon Johnson and made that clear, so there was no hope of support from Washington. Some might argue that this lack of cooperation was at the root of the failure of his case. From the beginning, I have said that what he did might be described as finding a loose thread which he pulled as hard as he could in the hope that it would expose the conspiracy. That he did not succeed did not mean he was wrong, and, considering he had all the cards stacked against him in attempting what he did, he did well.

It was striking that many of those Garrison wished to interview during the hearing of the case he brought against Shaw suddenly died one way or another. David Ferrie supposedly died of a ruptured blood vessel within the same hour as his close friend Eladio del Valle, whom Garrison also wanted to question. Del Valle was shot and had his head split, presumably with an axe. Robert Perrin, the husband of Nancy Perrin, who testified before the Warren Commission, was on Garrison's list for questioning, but he died of arsenic poisoning. Another desired witness was Dr Mary Sherman, who was shot in the head before her bedclothes were set alight. Nicholas Chetta, coroner of New Orleans, who conducted autopsies on the bodies of Ferrie, Perrin and Sherman, later suffered a heart attack and died, while his assistant, Dr Henry Delaune, was murdered a few months afterwards. Another who was 'removed' was Clyde Johnson, who had knowledge of the relationship between Jack Ruby, Clay Shaw and Oswald. He told Garrison what he knew but did not survive to testify in court, the victim of a shotgun attack.

113. David Ferrie died before Garrison could bring him to court.

These were not his only setbacks. The district attorney's office was repeatedly infiltrated, documents disappeared and the media were relentless in a bitter campaign against him personally and the case he was pressing. He claimed he was denounced by the president, the attorney general and the chief justice. There was a policy of non-cooperation. Small wonder Garrison's case collapsed.

During his prosecution, however, he secured a copy of the Zapruder film, which was projected in the courtroom. This was spectacular. The reaction to it was electric and it caused the film to be made available for transmission on television, when America was shocked. It was not screened on television, however, until 12 years after Kennedy was killed.

David Ferrie, who had links to Clay Shaw, was a former Eastern Airlines pilot who had links also with the underworld, the CIA and the anti-Castro movement. Ferrie was at the heart of the activities being investigated by Garrison, and came under fresh scrutiny when he was said to have been the pilot involved in flying the hit squad out of Dallas. This was not the case (see Chapter 35), but since it is not unlikely that the Douglas DC-3 in which they left Red Bird airfield at Dallas made a stop at Houston and Ferrie was believed to be thereabouts at the time, it is possible that he piloted the plane from Houston to wherever it went. Oswald had met Ferrie as a young teenager in the Civil Air Patrol, with which Ferrie was involved, and he must have rubbed shoulders with him again in New Orleans while being handled by the Guy Banister crowd.

114. New Orleans District Attorney Jim Garrison. (Courtesy Peggy Stewart)

In his book *On the Trail of the Assassins*, Jim Garrison specifies disinformation as being the last essential element required for a successful *coup d'état* and speaks of the flood of disinformation in the major media supporting the cover-up and ratification of the assassination. He points to the CIA and claims that journalists who were ostensibly working for the media in general were on the payroll of the Agency for the dissembling of data so that their propaganda was supported. **The CIA subsidised the publication of more than 1,000 books,** he said. In support of this, he quotes Richard Barnet, the co-director of the Institute for Policy Studies, who wrote:

> The stock in trade of the intelligence underworld is deceit. Its purpose is to create contrived realities, to make things appear other than they are for the purposes of manipulation and subversion. More than two hundred agents pose as businessmen abroad. The CIA has admitted it has had more than thirty journalists on its payroll since World War II. 'Proprietary' corporations – Air America and other agency fronts, fake foundations, student organisations, church organisations, and so forth – are all part of the false-bottom world that has ended up confusing the American people as much as it has confounded foreign governments.

Jim Garrison failed in his attempt to be re-elected as district attorney, mainly as a result of trumped-up charges against him which he had to fight. It has to be said that he was not the laid-back, pensive character portrayed in the film *JFK*; he was known as a flamboyant individual who had a penchant for showmanship. This did not detract in any way from his competence as a district attorney, but it made him a better target for those anxious to discredit him. He was accused of receiving pay-offs from pinball-machine operators, which he vigorously denied. In a case brought against him, attempts to bring witnesses to accuse him failed over and over again, culminating in the prosecution's 'big gun', Pershing Gervais, an old and valued friend of Garrison, who claimed he had paid him $150,000, being put on the stand. Under cross-examination, however, Gervais had to admit to a previous confession to a journalist that he had been coerced by the Justice Department to tell lies about his old friend to incriminate him in the pinball scandal. He had said it was 'a total, complete political frame-up, absolutely'. Since it was also exposed in court that a sound recording used in evidence against Garrison was found, by an expert witness, to have been spliced together from comments made at different times, the case collapsed and was dismissed.

While all this was happening, the electioneering for the post of district attorney was in full swing. Garrison had no time to compete and thus the election was lost. Unbelievably, it appears that the government were so sure they would convict Garrison in the case he was fighting in court that the tax authorities instituted proceedings against him for non-payment of tax on the pay-offs he was proved not to have received. That is what is called a classic example of adding insult to injury.

In a foreword Garrison wrote to Harold Weisberg's *Oswald in New Orleans*, he said:

> 'The American people have suffered two tragedies. In addition to the assassination of the President by dishonorable men, our national integrity is being assassinated by honorable men. It does not matter what the rationale is – whether to calm the public or to protect our image – the fact remains that the truth is being concealed.'

Jim Garrison became a distinguished judge of the Louisiana Court of Appeal.

33

THE IMPEDIMENTS

DURING THE 50 YEARS WE HAVE EXAMINED THE investigation into the assassination, it has become crystal clear that there were forces determined to prevent the truth from being known. The Warren Commission, we know, was the first of those forces, shielded by the vital necessity to defuse the tense uncertainty which was everywhere in evidence both in the United States and elsewhere in the world. Lee Harvey Oswald, it seems, was offered up on the basis of 'it is better for one man to die . . .' But if the Warren Commission contributed to bringing about calm and reason, an important achievement, it certainly did not satisfactorily investigate the assassination of President Kennedy. The commission made little if any attempt to find out who really killed him or why he was killed.

From the outset, the cards were stacked against an honest and impartial investigation. First, Earl Warren, known as a man of the highest integrity, in fact had a somewhat dubious background in certain respects. He was, for instance, said to make political deals and was not above treating innocent parties as guilty if he believed it suited the good of the country. And it is not that those selected to serve under him believed he was the right person for the job. His only real supporter was Allen Dulles, one-time head of the CIA, who was fired by JFK after the Bay of Pigs episode. Why, of all people, Dulles ever qualified to become a commission member is something of a mystery, but then one or two others are also considered doubtful choices. Representative John J. McCloy, with Dulles, dominated the procedures in the commission. They were largely responsible for the appointment of J. Lee Rankin as general counsel. This made up a compact team who contrived to direct proceedings. Though it was not made anything of, at the outset Dulles made a gift of a paperback book to every commission member. The subject was American assassinations and the author argued that they were always the work of a lone, crazy creature!

115. Allen Dulles, the CIA chief fired by Kennedy
after the Bay of Pigs invasion.

Gerald Ford, later Richard Nixon's vice-president and who became president when Nixon resigned, had at one time participated in an attempt to impeach Warren. In his role as a Warren commissioner, he now appeared to be in relationship with the FBI. Later, he wrote a book, breaking all the rules to use knowledge he had obtained while a member of the Warren Commission. The CIA and the FBI were filtering information to the Warren Commission, retaining what they did not want the commissioners to know. Neither was going to tell us the truth; that is quite clear, for all the reasons we give elsewhere in this book.

The Warren Commission had the enormous benefit of support from the media. We recount elsewhere the fact that all branches of the media appeared to close ranks in defence of the Warren investigation, and indeed in the promotion of it, making it virtually impossible for those who detected shortcomings – and some of them glaring ones – to find a voice to reach the people. Refusal to comply on the part of authors, researchers and investigators brought down very serious ignominy on the owners of the voices and those rare people who might be bold enough to provide the means by which they could speak to the public. This, to some businesses, could spell ruination. Though I am not aware of any dark, shadowy manipulation of the media to establish the protective attitude they adopted, that attitude nevertheless was there and it became a major culprit in the prevention of honest and open criticism. We might be reminded, nevertheless, that any such manipulation would hardly have been publicised.

The vital questions of why and by whom President Kennedy was killed have been left to private individuals, citizens primarily from America but also from other, mainly European countries, and Britain in particular. The American government has been notably reticent on the subject. It appears that to them the case was closed from the beginning. They had the answers, or at least those they wanted.

There were those among the senators and representatives who were not satisfied with that position, however, and their creditable efforts resulted in the establishment of the House Assassinations Committee in the '70s. The House Assassinations Committee was originally intended to be a thorough independent investigation, and the intention was entirely creditworthy, but in all the wrangling which went on at the outset – a story in itself – it was clearly hijacked by the CIA, no doubt supported by the FBI. It then gave all the indications of being another attempt to shore up the discredited Warren Report. In fact, by the time those who were determined to see that it was not an independent investigation had finished their wrangling and 'repositioning', we were lucky to get something worth having from the few months left for actual investigative work.

When the results of the acoustics testing of the Dallas Police Dictabelts were, with some reluctance, announced, they effectively established as a fact that there had been a conspiracy to kill the president, which was probably already believed by most around the world, although it was staunchly denied by the US government. This represented a major broadside at Warren, and the results were challenged. They were challenged by no less than the Justice

Department of the United States government. A new analysis ordered by the Justice Department, costly as it was to the taxpayer, was found to be erroneous: an expensive damp squib. The original submitted to the House Assassinations Committee was found to be correct. And just in case there were any lingering doubts, the only other scientific analysis, using even better and the most advanced equipment and techniques, carried out by Donald B. Thomas and reported in 2001, confirmed this.

Documents held by the CIA, and probably the FBI also, would have been of enormous help to researchers if we had all been on the same side. When I say that, I mean that the researcher-investigators were on one side and the CIA and the FBI were definitely on the other. Even when it was decreed that millions of documents should be released via the Assassination Records Review Board, it appeared to me that, before a handover, every document had been scrutinised for 'suitability to be released', while any dynamite residing in the official files is still there – that is, unless it has been destroyed. This in no way lessens our gratitude to the team who dealt with the mind-boggling avalanche of paper unleashed upon them, or our appreciation for what they achieved.

Exactly how much meaningful information was ignored, diverted or buried by the CIA we will never know. The original remit of the CIA, of course, clearly marked it out as designated to relate to intelligence matters in foreign countries. The fact that it became involved in the assassination investigation as it did was further evidence of it going its own way, making its own rules. But then, the FBI, responsible for combating crime at home, could not exactly hold its head up. In fact, it could not hold its head up at all when it came to contributions it made towards finding the truth about the murder of President Kennedy. Examples abound of the FBI being complicit in withholding information, refusing to accept pertinent witness statements and threatening those who held valuable information.

An example of skulduggery of a different kind which comes to mind is the telex received by William Walter. A TWX message transmitted from Washington DC reached the New Orleans office of the FBI and was received and read by William S. Walter. Dated 17 November and marked 'URGENT', it baldly stated that it was suspected an attempt would be made to assassinate President Kennedy in Dallas on 22 November 1963, and instructions on procedures were then given. The FBI disclaimed all knowledge of the telex. Walters went to pull the copy, which had been placed in a file, and was nonplussed to discover it was missing. His reaction was: 'They had a system established to make damn sure there was no record of some of those sensitive matters, especially when it became an embarrassing situation.' Walters had his own system, however, which was superior to that of the FBI: he had kept his own copy, a photograph of which we show (see fig. 116).

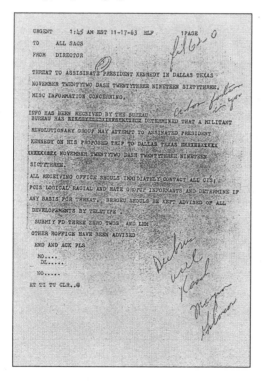

116. TWX message received by William Walters in the New Orleans FBI office five days before Kennedy was assassinated.

He was outspoken on another pertinent issue, also. When the FBI declared that Lee Harvey Oswald had never worked for them, Walters asserted he had *actually seen* documents proving this wrong and that, in fact, he did work for the Bureau. Remarkably, 17 November, the date the TWX message was sent, was just about the time the disputed note was left by Lee Harvey Oswald for Agent Hosty at the Dallas office. There has been speculation that it may have been a warning of the same kind. After all, Oswald worked for the CIA, the FBI and possibly other intelligence agencies. He was a government man until he was elected patsy.

Jim Garrison spoke of the cover-up on the part of the government beginning at Parkland Hospital when Secret Service agents took charge of the body of the president, ensuring it went back into the hands of representatives of the federal government immediately. He had, by the time he was making this assertion, ample evidence that the conspirators were being backed all the way by that government. After all, an autopsy carried out in Texas would have revealed that shots had come from behind and from the front, and a conspiracy would have been proven from the beginning.

Among those who have been disillusioned by the evidence of deceptions following the murder of President Kennedy, there are those who believe that the assassination was, in fact, government-inspired. That might be a hard one to swallow, though the assassination of President Kennedy is difficult not to describe as a *coup d'état*. By all appearances, that is exactly what it was, and 50 years of individuals left to soldier on to find the truth while the government either impedes them or tries to ignore them only reinforces that.

34

THE CONSPIRACY

THE READER MAY THINK THE CONTENTS OF THIS chapter are speculative. You will be forgiven for thinking so, but wait and see if you think that the case when I have finished. My research methods, as I have said in earlier books, have included the perception of 'patterns of evidence'. Evidence given by knowledgeable eyewitnesses would usually be preferred, and I agree with that, but sometimes eyewitnesses are not there. Also, sometimes such evidence is, perhaps unconsciously, biased and sometimes, for one reason or another, it is not remembered in the exact terms from which a researcher would profit. However, a *pattern* of evidence is either there or it is not there, and it is fixed, not subject to errors or bias, and therefore I maintain that observed patterns of evidence are in no way speculative.

When Lee Harvey Oswald left the Book Depository after the assassination, he first made for 'home'. Home at that time was the boarding house in North Beckley in which he had a room. Mrs Earlene Roberts, his landlady, heard him come in and moments later heard a motor horn beeping outside. Looking to find out who it was, she saw a police car which bore a number reminiscent of the number of Officer Tippit's car. Assuming for a moment it was Tippit in the car outside the house, it crossed my mind that it would have simplified matters had he simply picked Oswald up at that point, since it appears he was meeting him in Oak Cliff. That is not difficult to answer, for the very reason his car was observed in North Beckley by Mrs Roberts. Had he been seen picking Oswald up where he was known, a great deal relating to the conspiracy would have been exposed.

At Oak Cliff, Oswald was not known, and for a police officer to be seen questioning an individual only to drive off with him would be relatively commonplace, hardly worthy of a mention. It is my firm belief that Tippit had been engaged by ex-CIA agent Roscoe White to ferry Oswald to Red Bird airfield. Officer Tippit may have left his car to approach Oswald for one of two reasons: he may simply have been clever enough to disguise the pick-up as an arrest; or else he may have been tuned in to the APB describing Oswald and decided he was not getting into aiding and abetting the president's killer. Roscoe White, or whoever was monitoring the pick-up, decided it was the latter and that Tippit, because he knew too much, had to be eliminated.

Before I attached any significance to Officer Tippit's role in what was going on, I took my ruler and placed it on a map of Dallas, with one end at the Texas School Book Depository. Accommodating North Beckley and the Oak Cliff the ruler led in a straight line for Red Bird airfield. At Red Bird airfield there was waiting by the perimeter fence a small aircraft, revving up for quite a while, the noise of which was irritating those who lived nearby. It would seem obvious that the plane was standing by ready for take-off.

I have to say at this point that had Lee Harvey Oswald been told he was being taken to catch a small plane to Cuba he would, I believe, have willingly accepted that this was in respect of his new CIA assignment, in readiness for which, he believed, he had been 'sheep-dipped' in New Orleans. Taking the overall view, however, and after considering long and deep the consequences of Oswald reaching that small plane and being piloted to Cuba, I realise what the appearance would have been in the context of his role as patsy. It would have confirmed in everyone's mind that he really had killed the president and it would have promoted the belief that the Cuban communists had sent him. The consequences of such a created scenario would have been a war with Cuba, for which the CIA had been spoiling since Castro had come to power. Whether such a war could have been contained without accelerating into a full-scale world war is not known, but there would have been an enormous risk involved. I find it difficult to comprehend that any human being would lend himself to such a risk. The CIA would not have President Kennedy and his troublesome brother to contend with any more, however, nor the threat of extinction, clearly on the cards. Also, it goes without saying, the military-industrial complex would have had more business on their plates than they could have handled. Unbelievable? I would like to think so.

One of the small insights into the background for this scenario comes from three sources. One was the work of Professor Popkin, who researched the sightings of 'the Oswald who never was'. For some time before the assassination, 'Oswald' was seen in a number of different circumstances in which he attracted attention and generally disgraced himself or made a nuisance of himself. This led to the Warren Commission investigating the instances quoted to them, and they found that it certainly was not Lee Harvey Oswald who was seen on those occasions. They did not, however, persevere to find out what the purpose of the bogus Oswald was, or who was responsible for the subterfuge. We accept the commission blackened his character and made him a more likely villain, but there was much more to be revealed had they dug a little deeper.

It would seem the appearances of the man purporting to be Oswald were never intended to be investigated and they certainly would not have been if Oswald had boarded that small plane, regardless of whether he actually reached Cuba or not. It would have been declared a political assassination and Oswald would have been labelled traitor as well as murderer of the president. That he never made it to his plane left a trail that would have been useful if explored. The Warren investigators were not interested in such exploration. In fact, they were diametrically opposed to it.

The introduction of a link to Cuba provided another insight supporting what might explain the mysterious visit paid by the two Latin Americans with an American referred to as Leon to Sylvia Odio, which we described in Chapter 22. Whatever this did or did not achieve, it certainly introduced the idea of Cuban involvement in the assassination and virtually threw in her face that the man who would carry it out was the American ex-Marine, Leon. Sylvia Odio retrospectively identified 'Leon' as Lee Harvey Oswald when she saw his picture on television, credited with being the president's killer. It stands up that had he 'escaped' to Cuba, people would no longer have been looking to make sense out of the visitation to her house.

Finally, the most telling aspect of validity relating to what has been described above relates to Vietnam. Vietnam might be said to have been a festering sore at the time of the assassination. Originally designated as 'observers', hundreds of non-combat US personnel had, over a period, been dispatched there by President Eisenhower. In spite of the fact that President Kennedy was being advised by Eisenhower when he first took office and added to the number of 'observers', it was not long before he went on record expressing his intention of seeking a peaceful solution to the Vietnam problem. Roger Hilsman, a key foreign policy official, reported that Kennedy had said to him:

> 'The Bay of Pigs has taught me a number of things. One is not to trust generals or the CIA, and the second is that if the American people do not want to use American troops to remove a Communist regime 90 miles away from our coast [Cuba], how can I ask them to use troops to remove a Communist regime 9,000 miles away?'

President Kennedy decided to pull all US personnel – including CIA agents – out of Vietnam, and at a meeting of top brass in Honolulu had already ordered the first thousand men back home. (In fact, they arrived back in the United States before Christmas 1963.) On the Sunday following the assassination, however, and before the murdered president was even buried, President Johnson called most of those who had met in Honolulu to a meeting in Washington, where, effectively, he reversed Kennedy's decision. The outcome was the escalating war in Vietnam where 50,000 young Americans were killed, as well as millions of Vietnamese.

It generated business for the military-industrial complex, however, worth in excess of $200 billion. It is worth reflecting that while such a sum today is incredibly huge, 50 years ago it was mind-bogglingly astronomical.

I suggest that the validity of patterns of evidence as a research tool has been established.

35

RED BIRD AIRFIELD

RED BIRD AIRFIELD WAS BELIEVED TO HOLD SECRETS relating to the assassination from the very first day. Researcher Mary Ferrell told me that, having been glued to her television set during that day, she recalled a curious event which stuck in her memory. In such a continuous, open-ended assignment as the television coverage that day, any odd item of news, regardless of apparent significance, was mentioned on the local channel. Everything was welcome to the reporters hungry for news titbits. One such item was a complaint received by the police of the noise of an aircraft located near to the perimeter fence at Red Bird airfield which was constantly revving its engine. The occupants of houses close by found it unbearable and so complained to the police.

The police department duly dispatched an officer to investigate and they found it was a small aircraft ready for take-off. The FBI was informed and an agent went to look into the matter. In the climate of suspicion which followed the assassination of the president, the engine was stopped and the plane was simply locked away in a hangar pending further investigation. Following this: nothing. No information has ever materialised to explain why the plane was there, and why, at that particular time, the engine was running. It is fair to assume that it was running in order to effect a quick take-off.

On the Wednesday before the assassination, Wayne January had a visitation from two scruffy individuals who, it appears, were CIA agents, though Wayne did not know this at the time. He was a partner in a charter company for small planes, the Royal

Aircraft Company. The duo arrived in an elderly – 1947 – black car and parked it close to the office block, right outside his office window. They left a passenger in the car while they came inside to talk business. The business related to the chartering of a small aircraft to fly them to Yucatán on a vacation. During a whole series of questions, unusual questions in relation to the hiring of a small aircraft, January weighed the two up. His thoughts ran in two directions: for one thing, they didn't look as if they could afford such a trip, which would be costly, and he feared it might be related to drug smuggling. The other was that if he was piloting this plane, could he be sure he would live to make the return journey? For these reasons, he declined the charter, which irritated the two enquirers.

117. Red Bird airfield. (Matthew Smith Collection)

He accompanied them as they left the building because he wanted a look at the old car they had come in. His interest lay in the coincidence that he had the same model, which he used for carrying his tools around in. As he looked, he saw the waiting passenger clearly. He was someone he recognised a few days later when he saw him on television: it was Lee Harvey Oswald. It should be recalled that the Wednesday morning before the assassination took place Oswald had breakfasted late, at 10 a.m. This fitted with his arrangement to be taken to see the small plane which would be waiting to take him out of Dallas to begin his 'new CIA mission', for which he believed he had been 'sheep-dipped' in New Orleans.

The tailpiece to Wayne January's sighting of Oswald at Red Bird airfield came some time later. He told the FBI what had happened and that he had seen Lee Harvey Oswald, and they wrote up a report on what he told them. Wayne was not sent a copy of that report. He first saw it after I located it in Harold Weisberg's massive file of documents obtained under the Freedom of Information Act. Incredibly, the report, accurate in all other respects, placed the visit of the two seeking to hire a plane and Wayne January's sighting of Oswald in the previous July! January's first reaction when he read it was: 'But how would I have been able to identify someone on television that I had seen only once months before?' More FBI tampering, but, in spite of being so unbelievable, it achieved severing the link of CIA personnel with Lee Harvey Oswald and the booking of a small plane and, of course, complicity in the assassination.

* * *

Wayne January was probably greatly relieved that the plane revving up by the perimeter fence was not one of his. The company's fleet was normally made up of small planes such as Cessnas and Pipers. The exception to this had been when the government had given them a contract to provide aircraft for research into radar which they were conducting out of Red Bird. For this, they purchased a small fleet of medium-sized aircraft, big for Red Bird airfield and big for them. When the contract ended, they sold off the medium-sized aircraft, for which there was no demand at Red Bird. All except for one plane: a Douglas DC-3, which normally had about 25 seats. They had taken the seats out in order to accommodate the radar test equipment and they expected to put them all back when they eventually sold the DC-3.

118. Wayne January interviewed by the author. (© JoAnne Connaughton)

The sale of the Douglas DC-3 came on the Monday of the beginning of the week in which the president was killed. January described the man who came to complete the sale. He was a military type but dressed in casuals. He was told later that he was an Air Force colonel knowledgeable on DC-3s. He had brought with him a younger man, who was to pilot the plane out of Red Bird. This younger man, smart, muscular, was to work with Wayne January to achieve a 'make ready' for the sale and the flight from the airfield. Wayne apologised and said he could not begin the work until the Wednesday because he had a day off the coming Tuesday, which was his birthday.

The work related to checking out the plane from stem to stern. Selling a used plane is not like selling a used car, which might break down at the first corner after the sale. The work included replacing the seats, and the whole operation was quite time-consuming. The buyer's pilot, Wayne January thought, was just a bit peculiar in that he would never join him in eating at the airfield restaurant. The result was that Wayne brought sandwiches back to the aircraft, where they ate them together. He learned a great deal from the friendly relationship he obtained in doing this. To begin with, the younger man told him his expertise with

Douglas DC-3s stemmed from the fact he was Cuban born and had served as a pilot in Castro's air force, attaining high rank. He had, however, been recruited into the CIA and had been involved in the Bay of Pigs debacle.

His openness suggested that he believed Wayne January was a CIA agent. This was, no doubt, because of his being involved in the government's radar programme, which had resulted in his name appearing in a CIA agent's handbook as someone reliable to deal with. He talked freely with January as the work progressed. On the Thursday, which was 21 November, he sat with Wayne January and sombrely told him, 'Tomorrow they are going to kill your president.' Wayne was dumbfounded! How do you respond to someone making an announcement like that? In his mind, he was rehearsing the consequences of his repeating this to the authorities. His reaction was that they would think him crazy, and they do not allow crazy men to fly aeroplanes. Flustered, he said he found it hard to believe. He asked who would want to kill the president. The reply was that the CIA agent survivors of the Bay of Pigs hated the Kennedys, whom they blamed for their failure in the action. 'You will see,' said the Cuban pilot, who also said that they particularly wanted to get Robert Kennedy, at the president's side throughout the time of the Bay of Pigs invasion, and, he added, any other Kennedy 'who gets into that way', indicating towards the presidency.

The work was not progressing as it might have done, no doubt because of Wayne having taken the Tuesday off. They decided they would have to work Friday morning to complete everything required. The plane was ready for take-off after lunch. But it was then that the news reached Wayne January that the president had been shot. He was beside himself. At least he knew the man he had been talking to had not been involved in the shooting, but nothing else. He left for the day to sit by his television set; during the afternoon, the Douglas DC-3 took off. There is little doubt that Wayne January had, unwittingly, provided the means of exit for the entire team of assassins.

When he had had time to think, his instincts were to report

what he knew, but he hesitated. By then, a pattern was emerging of the sudden deaths of people who had knowledge of or who were in some way connected with the assassination. He began fearing for his life and the lives of his family, so he said nothing, until, after 30 years had elapsed, he chose me to hear his story. He said it had weighed on him for all those years and he was glad to get rid of the burden.

119. Wayne January. (© JoAnne Connaughton)

I told him I would like to publish what he had told me and that I would not reveal his name to preserve his security. I explained that this, however, introduced problems which could only be overcome if he was prepared to meet with a senior researcher who would guarantee the same degree of privacy and protection and retold his story. He agreed to this and I arranged for a meeting between him and Mary Ferrell. Mary met with him and they talked. Afterwards, she told me that she had sought information from Wayne January at the very beginning of her research but he would not respond. She assured me he was most reliable and 'as sound as a dollar'. I could have confidence in all he told me. I was, of course, most grateful for her reassurances, not because I had any doubts about what he had told me, but because it allowed me to tell the story to the world without compromising his security and that of his family. He became, therefore, 'Hank Gordon', a resident of Phoenix, Arizona, who carried out the work on the DC-3 for the Red Bird company. I staunchly adhered to the promise of anonymity until, sadly, he died a few years ago, after which I spoke to his wife and she kindly permitted me to reveal his real name.

It will come as no surprise that Wayne and I had become good friends. It would be true to say that this, however, was not because of my work investigating the assassination. It was because we found common ground in that we were both Christians. That answers the question of why he selected me to confide in.

Wayne January told me quite a lot about the Douglas DC-3 aeroplane. For instance, he told me the number of the plane and the date of the transaction with the new buyers. The number of the plane was N-17888. The transaction was registered with the Aircraft Owners and Pilots Association and, on my behalf, it was to their offices Wayne went to enquire about the buyers. He gave them the number and they checked and said it related to a Cessna aircraft. He told them that this could not be so, but they said that it would be costly to open up the archive material to check. He paid the fee and was rewarded with the confirmation that the number N-17888 was indeed originally allotted to a Douglas DC-3 and that it had later been transferred to the Cessna.

I spoke to L. Fletcher Prouty on this subject, taking advantage of his superior knowledge of Air Force matters. 'How often,' I asked him, 'was the number of an aircraft changed?' He replied, 'Never, except by the CIA.'

Wayne January discovered for me that the purchaser of the DC-3 was listed as the Houston Air Center. I engaged the services of a former CIA agent working out of Houston to make enquiries and he reported that the Houston Air Center was a front for the CIA. Finally, I obtained the names of the two individuals who ran the company and who were legally responsible for the purchase but decided there was no point in taking the investigation further. There is a time to be prudent: a time to stop poking the hornet's nest. I had completed the circle.

I had long maintained that those behind the assassination were the Bay of Pigs CIA agent survivors. Now I had confirmation. Whoever actually pulled the triggers, it would appear that the CIA agent survivors were the organisers and in command. In this case, it would be likely that they made the choice of marksmen and the entire team of assassins. In this, I had also learned how the entire hit squad had escaped, and this represented progress in taking me that bit further to finding out who actually killed the president. Before resting on my laurels, however, I realised that there was much more to it than I was aware of at that point.

36

WHO KILLED KENNEDY?

SOME THINGS WE CAN SAY AS A MATTER OF certainty. Regardless of what the United States government asserts, and in spite of the two most voluminous books ever published on the subject in defence of its position, it is quite apparent that there was a conspiracy to kill President Kennedy. That is, unless there really are 'magic bullets' that change direction and cause mayhem in doing so, and, of course, unless there are rifles from which the bullets turn corners.

There is much more to it, however. Highly reliable sources have produced overwhelming evidence indicating a number of people in collusion to get rid of John F. Kennedy as President of the United States. It mattered nothing to them that those to whom the government was responsible – the people of America – liked the man they had elected and more and more of them were anxious for him to continue as their president. His achievements were belittled by those we identify as his enemies. His great strides towards reconciling black and white were ignored, as were his recognition of the needs of the farming industry and the practical support he introduced, and, perhaps most of all, his pursuit of peace, the fact that he signed with Soviet Russia the first nuclear test ban treaty and that he resisted those who would have taken the country to war during his time in office. These were not always popular things to strive for among the people with whom he had to work and rub shoulders, but they were enormously popular with the American people. The freshness of his approach breathed new life into government, but, unhappily, it appears that it signed his death warrant among those who wished for the status quo to remain intact and individuals who cared nothing for what he had achieved but who saw his policies hacking at the roots of their personal well-being, which, they felt, was being threatened.

I must stress that this chapter, though I acknowledge the many who have contributed to it one way or another, may not represent the conclusions of every researcher. Consider this my personal contribution, rightly or wrongly drawing upon what evidence we have over the past 50 years jointly produced.

First of all, I see the steely cold hand of CIA involvement, and I shall later enlarge on this to share what I know on this aspect of things. Though the CIA was, perhaps, the foremost beneficiary of the murder of President Kennedy, 'benefits' were not, however, exclusively theirs. Following the Bay of Pigs debacle, those agents who were there and survived had a venomous hatred for the Kennedys, who, they maintained, had been the main cause of the failed attempt to invade Cuba. It may be a gross oversimplification, but, as I see it, the situation had become as follows: while it was not the government's policy to invade Cuba, neither was it the president's. It *was* the CIA's policy and the CIA was, particularly at that period in time, making too many independent decisions, regardless of government policy. So much so that they had become an invisible 'other' government. But then CIA policy on Cuba and elsewhere was highly agreeable to the military-industrial complex.

At one time, I believed that the instigators of the conspiracy to kill President Kennedy were exclusively the agent survivors of the Bay of Pigs. Now I perceive a force deeper into the CIA than anyone could have guessed: a supreme manipulator in the counter-intelligence department, no less. A manipulator who gave faces to those CIA agent survivors behind the carrying out of the assassination in order to provide a 'backstop' beyond which, if any investigation into the assassination ever got that far, no one would ever penetrate. In other words, a manipulator prepared to sacrifice a group of his own agents, if it became necessary, to prevent the real truth from being known.

The only researcher I know of who has written in depth about the forces 'deeper into the CIA' to which I have referred is John

Newman. The author of *JFK and Vietnam* and *Oswald and the CIA*, which he updated in 2008, and in which he masterly describes in detail what has brought him to believe that the CIA, as an organisation, were massively involved in the events which led to the assassination of President Kennedy. His new research, featured in the epilogue to his revised edition, concentrates on Oswald's mysterious visit to Mexico City. Ostensibly and apparently to comply with instructions from his CIA masters, he was applying for a visa to enter Cuba, from where he would proceed to the Soviet Union. Newman provides much more about the visit and takes us into the deeper implications of what was afoot.

120. John Newman (© Dan Wolff)

In attempting to present an abbreviated and simplified account of events in Mexico, may I say that my sketched account here must fall short of adequately acquainting the reader with the work of John Newman. When a visit was paid to the Cuban embassy to seek a visa, it likely was not Lee Harvey Oswald paying the visit but someone representing – or, more likely, misrepresenting – him. The Oswald impersonator appeared to be in action on so many occasions it is hard to know what role the real Oswald played in the proceedings, if any at all. Whoever it was spoke to Silvia Duran, a consular official, who took down details. Referred to the Russian embassy, since he was declaring an intention to go there from Cuba, 'Oswald' was asked a lot of questions by Ms Duran's counterpart at that embassy. Some time later, when that counterpart was asked about the interview, he commented on the applicant's poor command of the Russian language. There was no doubt it was not Lee Harvey Oswald he had been speaking to: Oswald spoke impeccable Russian.

Lee Harvey Oswald was clearly completely in the hands of the CIA while he was in Mexico. On analysis, and as briefly as I can express it, the first intention of the agents involved was to establish distinct and unchallengeable evidence of his association with Cuba and a continuing association with Russia as part of the CIA preparation for him being cast in the role of the patsy when the president would be killed a few weeks later.

Through copper-bottomed evidence of links which he describes in detail, John Newman traced what might be called the chain of command for the Mexico City operation to the highest authorities in the CIA. He traced it, in fact, to the office of James Jesus Angleton, no less, who was head of counter-intelligence. Newman also established that files on Oswald going back to his days in the Marines were controlled by Angleton, who manipulated them for his own purposes. If these clumsy paragraphs attempting to encapsulate the main drift of Newman's work achieve nothing more than to inspire my readers to examine his findings in detail for themselves, I will be satisfied that I have taken them to a vital development in the search for the truth. In other words, the whole matter is of greater complexity than I indicate here.

121. James Jesus Angleton, CIA head of counter-intelligence.

For those who wonder about the outcome of Oswald's applications for visas to enter Cuba and, eventually, Russia, he simply did not get either. In spite of Oswald's 'credentials' giving details of his pro-Cuban activities and his past time in Soviet Russia, the consul would not budge on the absence of Soviet documentation assuring his forward journey to Russia. The Russians, not being difficult, told 'Oswald' they were hamstrung because the procedure involved staff at the Washington embassy, whom they knew would not respond for some months. There was no chance of a piece of paper being stamped for him to present to the Cuban consul. In his negotiations, however, and vitally important to what the CIA was attempting, 'Oswald' eventually came to speak to Comrade Kostikov, who was believed by the CIA to be part of the sabotage and assassination team of the KGB. This represented a massive coup on the part of the conspirators. They would have achieved linking Oswald directly with 'the man who mattered' to their plans for endorsing him as the assassin of the president, with more than a broad hint in the direction of the Russians being knowledgeable about what he was doing.

While persisting in his attempt to obtain a visa to enter Cuba, Oswald was asked to provide a recent photograph for his application. He did so and why this did not blow the whole CIA manipulation out of the water is a mystery in itself. Mind you, just to complicate matters as far as they can go, it has to be said that Ms Duran herself is thought to have been in the pay of the CIA, and events following this episode were inclined to support this. Add to this a story put about that she was Oswald's mistress while he was in Mexico City, a claim at first confirmed but later denied by Ms Duran, and a full range of dirty tricks is exposed.

What was not in John Newman's epilogue was the fact that after the Mexico City affair the CIA requested Ms Duran's arrest by the Mexican authorities. An extract from the CIA cable ran as follows:

With full regard for Mexican interests, request you ensure her arrest is kept absolutely secret, that no information from her is published or leaked, that all such info is cabled to us, and the fact of her arrest and her statements are not spread to leftist or disloyal circles in the Mexican Government.

Ms Duran was in custody for several days and was only released **after she stated that the man whose application she had been dealing with in the Cuban embassy was Lee Harvey Oswald**. Because she had so much to say following her release, however, a further request was forthcoming from the CIA for her re-arrest, for which they asked the Mexican authorities to assume responsibility. Under no circumstances was Ms Duran to know the CIA was behind her re-arrest. Afterwards, she was not so forthcoming in what she said, although she reasserted her identification of Oswald. This did not last, however. Much later, she was questioned by researcher Anthony Summers, to whom she admitted that the man she saw in Mexico City was not the man she saw on television following the president's assassination.

* * *

When the Warren Investigation was established, its chief objective was to defuse the tinderbox tension resulting from the fact that Russia and Cuba were, in the minds of the public, the leading suspects for having killed John F. Kennedy. It should be noted that since there was no real hint of involvement on the part of either Cuba or Russia, it was the hotheads in high places – the Pentagon, for instance, and many other influential organisations by which the public could be influenced – who were the principal targets of what the Warren Commission was doing. In other words, the danger was from within. Of course, if any evidence, I repeat, *evidence*, of communist involvement had been established, it might have been a different story, and it was this possibility that had, it appears, persuaded Earl Warren to chair the commission.

What the CIA planned to do was to provide evidence of the involvement of the communists in the activities of the returned 'defector' Lee Harvey Oswald. Taken further than they achieved, this might easily have led to war with Russia and their ally Cuba, possibly developing into the nuclear war which the people of America, and indeed the world, feared. The alternative to these intentions may have been more along the lines of deflecting any possible suspicion from themselves and other participating parties.

Other than 'removing' the President of the United States, one is left wondering, however, what exactly their further intentions were. It is hardly credible that in planning to kill the president whom they hated they risked a nuclear war just to provoke further hatred of the communists. When it is observed, however, how quickly the vultures – in the form of the military-industrial complex – dived in after Kennedy was killed, anything can be believed, including sheer greed.

Another 'situation' which had been awaiting Kennedy when he arrived in the White House had been US involvement in Vietnam. At that point, there was no participation by the US in hostilities. It was somewhat more than merely sending 'observers' to monitor the situation, the 'observers' being military personnel. However, they had no brief in respect of involvement in a full-scale war, and Kennedy did not extend their brief. As we have previously said, there is evidence that he had decided to withdraw from Vietnam altogether. One piece of evidence relates to a meeting which took place two days before the assassination. It was a meeting in Honolulu between Dean Rusk, Robert McNamara, McGeorge Bundy, Admiral Harry Felt and Henry Cabot Lodge, who was the US Ambassador to Vietnam, to discuss a letter from the president which contained his decision to withdraw 1,000 personnel from Vietnam. This was seen as an indication that he planned, bit by bit, to bring everybody home, perhaps without the need for a big political decision being required. Indeed, the first 1,000 men did actually return home shortly before the Christmas following the assassination.

Literally two days after Kennedy died, however, and even before he was buried, President Lyndon B. Johnson convened a meeting in Washington involving most of those who had translated Kennedy's instructions into action in Honolulu. Their brief was a reversal of Kennedy's instructions which amounted to an about-turn. This was the consequence of National Security Action Memorandum 273, which overturned Kennedy's NSAM 263 and which ordered increased activity in Vietnam, the consequences of which President Johnson used to obtain congressional backing for a drastic escalation of the war there. The draft of NSAM 273 was dated 21 November, the day before Kennedy was killed, and the anticipation is both astounding and telling. Kennedy never authorised it and never saw it. President Johnson signed it the day after JFK was buried. More on this later.

THE WHITE HOUSE
WASHINGTON

~~TOP SECRET~~ - EYES ONLY   October 11, 1963

NATIONAL SECURITY ACTION MEMORANDUM NO. 263

TO: Secretary of State
           Secretary of Defense
           Chairman of the Joint Chiefs of Staff

SUBJECT: South Vietnam

At a meeting on October 5, 1963, the President considered the recommendations contained in the report of Secretary McNamara and General Taylor on their mission to South Vietnam.

The President approved the military recommendations contained in Section I B (1-3) of the report, but directed that no formal announcement be made of the implementation of plans to withdraw 1,000 U.S. military personnel by the end of 1963.

After discussion of the remaining recommendations of the report, the President approved an instruction to Ambassador Lodge which is set forth in State Department telegram No. 534 to Saigon.

McGeorge Bundy

Copy furnished:
   Director of Central Intelligence
   Administrator, Agency for International Development

                              cc:
                              Mr. Bundy ✓
                              Mr. Forrestal
                              Mr. Johnson
           ~~TOP SECRET — EYES ONLY~~ NSC Files

Committee Print of Pentagon Papers
BY H52   7/13/77

122. President Kennedy's National Security Action Memorandum 263, pulling personnel out of Vietnam and signalling complete withdrawal.

THE WHITE HOUSE
WASHINGTON

~~TOP SECRET~~   November 26, 1963

NATIONAL SECURITY ACTION MEMORANDUM NO. 273

TO: The Secretary of State
         The Secretary of Defense
         The Director of Central Intelligence
         The Administrator, AID
         The Director, USIA

The President has reviewed the discussions of South Vietnam which
occurred in Honolulu, and has discussed the matter further with
Ambassador Lodge. He directs that the following guidance be issued
to all concerned:

   1. It remains the central object of the United States in South
Vietnam to assist the people and Government of that country to win
their contest against the externally directed and supported Communist
conspiracy. The test of all U. S. decisions and actions in this area
should be the effectiveness of their contribution to this purpose.

   2. The objectives of the United States with respect to the withdrawal
of U. S. military personnel remain as stated in the White House statement of October 2, 1963.

   3. It is a major interest of the United States Government that the
present provisional government of South Vietnam should be assisted
in consolidating itself and in holding and developing increased public
support. All U. S. officers should conduct themselves with this
objective in view.

   4. The President expects that all senior officers of the Government
will move energetically to insure the full unity of support for established
U. S. policy in South Vietnam. Both in Washington and in the field, it
is essential that the Government be unified. It is of particular importance
that express or implied criticism of officers of other branches be
scrupulously avoided in all contacts with the Vietnamese Government
and with the press. More specifically, the President approves the
following lines of action developed in the discussions of the Honolulu
meeting of November 20. The offices of the Government to which
central responsibility is assigned are indicated in each case.

                          TOP SECRET   (page 1 of 3 pages)

123. President Johnson's NSAM 273, effectively reversing Kennedy's 263. Johnson's memorandum was drafted on 21 November 1963, the day *before* the assassination, and unseen by Kennedy.

The Pentagon generals, therefore, were soon released to conduct a full-scale war in Vietnam and the armaments people, the plane makers, the makers of tanks, guns and other weaponry, and not forgetting the oilmen supplying what was necessary to get the whole thing moving, had a field day. The multinational oil companies had prominently lobbied in 1963 for the US to intervene in Vietnam. We have earlier drawn attention to the fact that **it was estimated that the Vietnamese war generated in**

excess of $200 billion in business for these people. The perspective of this is worth considering: as time has gone on, we have frequently faced news reports of costs reaching into billions, but in the 1960s this was not the case. Billions, at that time, represented an incredible sum.

The steel people, the armaments manufacturers, the oilmen and the lot, like the generals in the Pentagon, had no doubt finished wringing their hands because Kennedy followed a policy of non-intervention and finding peaceful solutions to the problems in which America was involved. The 50,000 American boys who were killed in that war and those left grieving at home were not consulted on the issue.

* * *

The above-mentioned actions of Lyndon B. Johnson, in which he apparently anticipated the demise of President Kennedy, raise questions about his role in the assassination. I have to acknowledge that a distinct group of thoughtful researchers find it hard to believe that the vice-president was not involved in the conspiracy to kill President Kennedy. His unseemly haste in reversing the action of Kennedy relating to the development of war in Vietnam plus other pertinent pieces of knowledge which have come to light during our 50 years of investigation indicate that there is more to consider in this connection.

124. Madeleine Brown, present at Murchison's party.
(Courtesy Madeleine Brown)

I have known for some time of the story that Johnson was made aware that the president was to be killed on his visit to Dallas the night before it happened. That story emanated from his mistress, Madeleine Brown, who was present at the party held at the home of Clint Murchison, billionaire oil magnate who, additionally, had investments in other businesses. Among his guests were a number of very influential people, including Richard Nixon, in Dallas on legal business that day, and J. Edgar Hoover. They were joined by Johnson, who was attached to the presidential entourage, which was spending the night in Fort Worth. He made the brief journey to be at the party, which apparently came as a surprise to the other guests. The room fell silent as he entered, it was reported. When Nixon, Hoover and others went into conclave away from the remaining party guests, Johnson joined them. Since then, there has been a lot of wriggling on the part of those notables. Unsurprisingly, it appears that they are desperate to produce evidence that they were somewhere else at the time. Madeleine Brown's account of things rings true, however. She spoke of Johnson's reaction, presumably to what had taken place at the secret meeting. Best described as having 'smoke coming out of his ears', he passed her the whispered information that 'after tomorrow those damn Kennedys will not be poking fun at me any more'. In the version Madeleine told me – and recorded for me – the only change to that was that what he said came in an early morning phone call from Fort Worth. No change whatever to the statement excepting 'after today' as opposed to 'after tomorrow'. This, however, by itself does not evidence that he was part of the conspiracy as such.

125. Clint Murchison.

126. Richard Nixon.

127. J. Edgar Hoover with Lyndon B. Johnson.

It did indicate the he was an accessory to the assassination 'before the fact', however, his silence constituting high treason. It also meant that all the others in conclave were equally guilty of complicity and high treason, including Nixon and Hoover. A degree of corroboration that Johnson knew what was afoot may obtain to claims that he tried, unsuccessfully, at the very last minute before the cars left Love Field, to make a change in the motorcade seating arrangements in order to place Senator Yarborough, instead of Governor Connally, in the seat in front of President Kennedy. This would also link with reports that when the gunfire broke out in Dealey Plaza, when others in the motorcade were asking, 'Who's letting off the firecrackers?', Johnson dived immediately to the floor of the car in which he was travelling.

Another puzzling thing which occurred after the assassination related to the incredible speed at which he insisted on being sworn in as the new president. It will be recalled that this took place in Air Force One at Love Field, a justice of the peace being hastily obtained. The body of the dead president was to be flown to Washington in that aircraft, on the instructions of special agents, fairly obviously acting on the orders of 'a superior' (who may have been Johnson). **Under no circumstances was the body to be left, as the law demanded, in Texas for autopsy.**

128. Lyndon Johnson is sworn in with unseemly haste on Air Force One.

When I first heard the story of the speedy swearing-in, I credited Johnson with being cognizant of a need to demonstrate to the world that someone was immediately in charge again. I found I had to change my mind on this. I got to examining what might be described as Johnson's circumstances at that time, and indeed especially on that day. The vice-president was in deep trouble, to say the very least. It all had to do with corruption and sleaze. On the very day of the assassination, the *Dallas Times Herald* ran no fewer than three stories calculated to tell Johnson what time of day it was. They related to charges of influence-peddling and suspicion of irregular financial manipulation against Bobby Baker, who was closely associated with Lyndon Johnson, indeed something of a protégé. It was only a question of time before it broke right over Johnson's head, and that alone might have been sufficient to submerge him in the deepest mire from which there would be no recovery for a politician.

But that was not all Johnson was engulfed in. There was his involvement with (literally) his neighbour, Billie Sol Estes. The shady Sol Estes had held government contracts for the storage of grain and federal cotton allotments which had been scrutinised for malpractices. Henry Marshall, the agricultural agent assigned to investigate, was found murdered in a Texas ditch, having been shot five times. Unbelievably, the death was declared a suicide, no autopsy being conducted on the body. When the stench of this eventually reached Washington, the body was exhumed and an autopsy was ordered. Marshall had suffered a blow to the head and carbon monoxide poisoning before being shot to death. This was now a case of murder. This took place following the time of the assassination, however, and, Johnson having become president, federal charges were dropped.

Billie Sol Estes received a 15-year sentence for fraud, and later, for reasons of which I am unaware, he was granted immunity from prosecution and called before a grand jury investigating the murder of Henry Marshall. Estes implicated Lyndon Johnson in the murder to prevent his association with himself, Estes, from being exposed. Johnson was by this time dead and Estes was not the most reliable of witnesses, but since there was no risk to him of prosecution, it struck an odd chord for such a claim to be levelled against a neighbour who had also been a close friend. It was not the only death linked to Sol Estes, however.

129. Lyndon Johnson with Bobby Baker. Baker was surrounded by scandal and the bubble was about to burst.

Returning to Johnson's association with Bobby Baker, shortly before the time of the assassination, on 8 November *Life* magazine had run a story headlined 'The Bobby Baker Bombshell', which showed a picture of Baker with Lyndon Johnson, and on the day the president was shot they ran another story: 'Scandal Grows and Grows in Washington'. To add to Johnson's discomfort, the *Dallas Morning News* ran the headline 'Nixon Predicts JFK May Drop Johnson'. It was the eleventh hour in respect of Johnson's political survival. Had the assassination occurred later, it is extremely doubtful that Lyndon B. Johnson would ever have been sworn in as president. Bobby Baker was indicted on seven charges of income-tax evasion, larceny and conspiracy in 1966. He was tried in 1967. It seems to me that the importance Johnson placed on his being sworn in related to a race against time and to the possibility that at any moment the political ground might open and swallow him up.

* * *

Madeleine Brown told me of some her conversations with Johnson after he became president. She told me she asked him about the Warren documents sealed away until 2039. His response was, **'Remember Box 13? There'll be no information there to hang LBJ, that's for sure.'** The scandal of Box 13 related to his election to the Senate. The counting of votes indicated peril for Johnson. He was cornered and it all came down to the contents of votes cast in Box 13. The result announced was 765 for Johnson and 60 for his opponent. A recount produced the revised result of 965 for Johnson and 60 for his opponent, which put Johnson in the Senate. Oddly, there were many more votes counted from the box than the 600 ballot papers provided. Johnson tenaciously defended the last published count, obstructing attempts to have an investigation carried out. He fought in state court and federal court and even succeeded in capping a re-examination of all votes cast in South Texas, which included Box 13. Madeleine Brown knew what he was saying.

Suspicion also fell on Johnson in regard to the fact that he made sure others were not going to conduct an investigation into the assassination and he alone would be in control. This was not his original plan. He wanted the inquiry into the murder to be conducted by the FBI and the Justice Department, but others elsewhere – in the Senate, for instance – had different intentions for the investigation and, on advice given, Johnson ordered a Presidential Commission, which superseded – outranked – the other bodies and so spiked their guns. The move did not please Hoover, of course, who forecast it would turn out to be 'a three-ringed circus'. But Johnson was clearly determined to be in charge and, indeed, to watch developments carefully. It is recalled that as early as the time Oswald was being questioned at Dallas police headquarters the officer questioning him, Captain Will Fritz, received a personal telephone call from the new president instructing him to stop investigating on the grounds that he 'had his man'.

It did not go unnoticed, either, that Earl Warren was quoted as saying that, when Johnson was pressuring Warren to accept chairmanship of his projected commission, 'The president stated that rumours of the most exaggerated kind were circulating in this country and overseas. Some rumours went as far as attributing the assassination to a faction within the government wishing the presidency assumed by President Johnson.'

I am not known as a researcher who sees conspiracy around every corner, but I believe that events relating to Lyndon B. Johnson demand a much closer look, and it has taken me a long time to reach this conclusion. Questions not so far mentioned here begin to creep out, like why were the other guests at the Murchison party the night before the assassination so staggered by the appearance of Johnson that a hush fell on the gathering? Who was so shocked? Could it have been that the others knew about the plan to murder President Kennedy the next day, and were they expressing amazement that the principal beneficiary was sailing rather close to the wind in attending the gathering? Perhaps this indicates that Johnson was already 'in the loop'. It is plain that he knew the party was scheduled and where it was to be held, but perhaps he had not been invited 'in the circumstances', thereby causing amazement when he turned up. There is also a hint of a possible explanation regarding the puzzling fact of his emerging from the meeting looking distinctly 'frazzled' and upset. Had someone dared to tell him, the president-to-be, how risky, and indeed stupid, it was to attend that particular party that particular night?

It must be said that, including the party, there is nothing in what has been said which provides evidence that Johnson was part of the conspiracy. As we have previously said, however, if he was told what was planned the night before the assassination, it would make him guilty of being an accessory before the fact and, in this specific case, treason.

* * *

How far have we come in identifying who was behind the assassination and how confident are we about our findings? I am reminded of a biblical quotation: 'By their fruits shall ye know them.' President Kennedy had gone on record saying that he intended to totally dismantle the CIA, and it was believed that this would be a prominent feature of his second term in office. Linked to this was a belief that he would also get rid of corrupt FBI boss J. Edgar Hoover. There is no doubt that the CIA and the FBI were quite alert to forthcoming prospects in a second term. Of course, Kennedy might not have been re-elected, but all indications were that his popularity had increased significantly, and if they had waited to find out the result of the election it could have proved too late. The president, therefore, had to go before there was any chance of re-election for a second term, and the front-runner in planning his removal was the CIA. The support of Hoover, and through him the FBI, would never be in doubt.

Then it appeared quite clear that President Johnson could not wait for Kennedy to be buried before preparing the ground for developing Vietnam into a full-scale bloody war which would satisfy military aspirations and line the pockets of the industrialists in the complex. The oilmen, as part of the complex, would be delighted, and the United States would assume a world role in which its military-industrial prowess would be observed and acknowledged, as history has regretfully proved. When the new president was asked by Madeleine Brown who was behind the assassination, she told me he said: 'It was the oilmen with the CIA.' 'Oilmen' in this context should be interpreted as 'military-industrialists'.

And what now? Short of naming names and bringing survivors to justice, what more can we do? Can we ever name names? True to form, we can depend on the CIA lying its head off. Those in the military will likely fall back on 'I was only carrying out orders', and those who have made fortunes from warfare will claim they were only serving their country when it needed their product.

This is not to say that every person on the CIA, FBI and military-industrial payrolls will remain silent, however. Yes, names could well be forthcoming, names of those alive as well as those now dead. But the future is uncertain. It is time to call a spade a spade. Those behind the conspiracy to murder President John F. Kennedy have been well insulated by a deep, deep political mire of treason, padded by lies and deceit. We all know that. We also have seen that the policy of finding peaceful ways of resolving international problems adopted by Kennedy was ruthlessly swept aside. We learn from what we observe.

It has been speculated that documents which would have immediately identified the traitors were destroyed by the CIA and the FBI soon after the assassination, and the suggestion is that they have been replaced by substitute documents which, when released, will carry all the signs of authenticity with the intention of fooling the historians. Is this enough to put us all off trying any further? That would suit the conspirators down to the ground. Dedicated researchers are not deterred by speculation of this kind.

The attempted destruction of documents attracts honest individuals who secrete them away until it safe to produce them. Those witnessing such destruction also have to satisfy conscience and integrity. While there are honest men and women in the world there is always the chance that the deviousness of the conspirators will be defeated. And there is an old saying: 'There's more than one way of skinning a rabbit.'

An important quote to remember: Earl Warren, when he considered his work completed, made the following statement to reporters: **'You may never get the truth in your lifetime, and I mean that seriously.'** Almost certainly, he felt confident in saying this in view of the documents he had had locked away until 2039. Did that really say it all, however? Warren had no idea how much individual researchers would uncover in the 50 years which followed his statement, *without* the aid of the government, and in spite of the FBI, CIA and Secret Service.

The small army of individuals from all walks of life – academics, professionals, specialists of one kind or another, and all the others simply determined to help – are as dedicated as ever. Their tenacity does them credit; the results of their labours thoroughly justify their efforts: they have come a long, long way, even if it is not all over yet. What they have achieved has helped to restore the faith of many people. Their quest for the truth places them at the head of the massive army of those throughout the world who are not prepared to accept that evil won on 22 November 1963.

If any rallying call is still required, it is here. Jim Garrison, the six-footer who was called 'the Jolly Green Giant', was in sombre mood when he wrote:

130. DA Jim Garrison. (© Peggy Stewart)

The question now is whether we have the courage to come face to face with ourselves and admit that something is wrong, whether we have the will to insist on an end to deception and concealment with regard to the execution of John F. Kennedy – or whether we let the official fairy tale be told and retold until the truth itself fades into a vagrant rumour and finally dies forever.

If we will not fight for the truth now – when our President has been shot down in the streets and his murderers remain untouched by justice – it is not likely that we will ever have another chance.

131. Commemorative postage stamp.

BIBLIOGRAPHY

Benson, Michael. *Who's Who in the JFK Assassination*. Citadel Press, New York, 1998.

Bishop, Jim. *The Day Kennedy Was Shot*. Funk & Wagnalls, New York, 1968.

Blair, Joan and Clay Jr. *The Search for JFK*. Berkley Pub. Corp., New York, 1976.

Blumenthal, Sid (ed.). *Government by Gunplay*. Signet, New York, 1976.

Brennan, Howard L., with J. Edward Cherryholmes. *Eyewitness to History*. Texan Press, Waco, Texas, 1987.

Buchanan, Thomas G. *Who Killed Kennedy?* Secker & Warburg, London, 1964.

Crenshaw, Charles A., MD. *JFK: Conspiracy of Silence*. Penguin Books USA Inc., New York, 1992.

DiEugenio, James. *Destiny Betrayed*. Sheridan Square Press, New York, 1992.

Douglass, James W. *JFK and the Unspeakable*. Touchstone Books, New York, 2005.

Epstein, Edward Jay. *Legend: The Secret World of Lee Harvey Oswald*. Hutchinson & Co., London, 1978.

Fonzi, Gaeton. *The Last Investigation*. Award Books, New York, 1993, rev. 2008.

Fox, Sylvan. *The Unanswered Questions About President Kennedy's Assassination*. Award Books, New York, 1965.

Galanor, Stewart. *Cover-Up*. Kestrel Books, New York, 1998.

Garrison, Jim. *Heritage of Stone*. Berkley Medallion Books, New York, 1975.

Garrison, Jim. *On the Trail of the Assassins*. Sheridan Square Press, New York, 1988.

Gatti, Arthur. *The Kennedy Curse*. Regnery, Chicago, 1976.

Giancana, Sam and Chuck. *Double Cross*. Warner Books, New York, 1992.

Gibson, Donald. *Battling Wall Street*. Sheridan Square Press, New York, 1994.

Gibson, Donald. *The Kennedy Assassination Cover-Up*. Nova Science Publications Inc., New York, 2000.

Groden, Robert J. *The Killing of a President*. Viking Penguin, New York, 1994.

Groden, Robert J. *The Search for Lee Harvey Oswald*. Bloomsbury, New York, 1995.

Groden, Robert J., and Harrison E. Livingstone. *High Treason*. The Conservatory Press, Baltimore, Maryland, 1989.

Hancock, Larry, with Debra Conway. *Someone Would Have Talked*. JFK Lancer Productions, Dallas, 2010.

Hepburn, James. *Farewell America*. Frontiers Publishing Co., Vaduz, Liechtenstein, 1968.

Hoffman, Ed, and Ron Friedrich. *Eye Witness*. JFK Lancer Productions, Grand Prairie, Texas, 1997.

Hosty, James P. Jr. *Assignment: Oswald*. Arcade Publishing Inc., New York, 1996.

Joesten, Joachim. *Oswald: Assassin or Fall Guy?* Iconoclassic Books, New York, 1964, later revised.

Keith, Jim (ed.). *The Gemstone File*. IllumiNet Press, Atlanta, Georgia, 1992.

La Fontaine, Ray and Mary. *Oswald Talked*. Pelican Publishing Co. Inc., Gretna, Louisiana, 1996.

Lane, Mark. *Rush to Judgment*. Thunder's Mouth Press, New York, 1966, rev. 1992.

Lane, Mark. *Plausible Denial*. Thunder's Mouth Press, New York, 1991.

Lasky, Victor. *JFK: The Man and the Myth*. Macmillan, New York, 1963.

Law, William Matson. *In the Eye of History*. JFK Lancer Productions, Dallas, 2004, rev. 2013.

Lifton, David S. *Best Evidence*. Macmillan, New York, 1980.

Manchester, William. *Death of a President*. Michael Joseph Ltd, London, 1967.

Manchester, William. *One Brief Shining Moment*. Little, Brown & Co., New York, 1983.

Marrs, Jim. *Crossfire*. Carroll & Graf, New York, 1989.

Marrs, Jim. *Rule by Secrecy*. HarperCollins, New York, 2000.

Marvin, Richard. *The Kennedy Curse*. Belmont, New York (no pub. date given).

McClellan, Barr. *Blood, Money and Power*. Hannover House, New York, 2003.

Meagher, Sylvia. *Accessories After the Fact*. Bobbs-Merrill Inc., New York, 1967.

Morrow, Robert D. *First Hand Knowledge: How I Participated in the CIA–Mafia Murder of President Kennedy*. SPI Books, New York, 1992.

Newman, John. *Oswald and the CIA*. Carroll & Graf, New York, 1995.

North, Mark. *Act of Treason*. Carroll & Graf, New York, 1991.

Popkin, Professor Richard H. *The Second Oswald*. Avon, New York, 1966; Boson Books, Altadena, California, re-released 2008.

Posner, Gerald. *Case Closed*. Random House, New York, 1993.

Prouty, L. Fletcher. *The Secret Team*. Institute for Historical Review, Costa Mesa, California, 1973, 1992.

Russell, Dick. *The Man Who Knew Too Much*. Carroll & Graf, New York, 1992.

Scheim, David E. *Contract on America: The Mafia Murder of President John F. Kennedy*. Shapolsky Publishers Inc., New York, 1988. Published in the UK as *The Mafia Killed President Kennedy*. W.H. Allen, London, 1988.

Shaw, J. Gary, with Larry Ray Harris. *Cover-Up*. Thomas Publications Inc., Austin, Texas, 1976, 1992.

Sorensen, Theodore C. *Kennedy*. Harper & Row, New York, 1965.

Summers, Anthony. *The Kennedy Conspiracy*. McGraw-Hill Book Co., New York, 1980; rev. Warner Books, New York, 1992.

Thompson, Josiah. *Six Seconds in Dallas*. Berkley Medallion Books, New York, 1967.

Twyman, Noel. *Bloody Treason*. Laurel Publishing, Rancho Santa Fe, California, 1997.

Weberman, Alan J., and Michael Canfield. *Coup d'État in America*. Quick American Archives, San Francisco, California, 1975.

Wecht, Cyril, MD, JD. *Cause of Death*. Penguin, New York, 1993.

Weisberg, Harold. *Post Mortem*. Harold Weisberg, publisher, Frederick, Maryland, 1969.

Weisberg, Harold. *Case Open*. Carroll & Graf, New York, 1996. Also *Whitewash*, *Whitewash II*, *Whitewash III*, *Whitewash IV*, *Photographic Whitewash* and *Oswald in New Orleans*. Publishers various, publication dates various.

Wrone, David R. *The Zapruder Film*. University Press of Kansas, 2003.

Zirbel, Craig I. *The Texas Connection: The Assassination of John F. Kennedy*. TCC Publishers, Scottsdale, Arizona, 1991.

NAME INDEX

Italics indicate an illustration of or relating to the subject matter